THAT DESERVES A
WOW

THAT DESERVES A
WOW

Untold Stories of Legends and Champions,

Their Wins and Heartbreaks

Chris Myers

with Travis Thrasher

wm

WILLIAM MORROW

An Imprint of HarperCollins*Publishers*

Page 299 represents a continuation of the copyright page.

HarperCollins books may be purchased for educational, business, or sales promotional use. For information, please email the Special Markets Department at SPsales@ harpercollins.com.

FIRST EDITION

Designed by Kyle O'Brien

Library of Congress Cataloging-in-Publication Data

Names: Myers, Chris, 1959- author. | Thrasher, Travis, 1971- author.
Title: That deserves a wow : untold stories of legends and champions, their
    wins and heartbreaks / Chris Myers With Travis Thrasher.
Description: First edition. | New York, NY : William Morrow, an imprint of
    HarperCollins Publishers, [2024]
Identifiers: LCCN 2024024213 | ISBN 9780063345881 (hardcover) | ISBN
    9780063345904 (ebook)
Subjects: LCSH: Myers, Chris, 1959- | Sportscasters—United
    States—Biography. | Fox Sports (Television program)
Classification: LCC GV742.42.M94 A3 2024
LC record available at https://lccn.loc.gov/2024024213

ISBN 978-0-06-334588-1

24 25 26 27 28 LBC 5 4 3 2 1

This book is dedicated to all the good people I worked with and worked for

Talent alone won't make you a success. Neither will being in the right place at the right time, unless you are ready. The most important question is: "Are you ready?"[1]

—Johnny Carson

Contents

CONTENTS

Foreword

This book, *That Deserves a Wow* (*TDAW*), is much better than I expected. There now—that's enough of a foreword. Concise, encouraging, while speaking directly to the hearts and minds of readers all over the world of the surprising power of this read.

But how about more powder puffs of blown smoke? Well, then I'd probably lose the right to say "concise." What kind of author wouldn't want my words to be brief and allow his true literary brilliance to pop through the clouds? With my luck, probably this guy. So perhaps he needs me to carry on a bit.

Let's see. . . . This book is written by a sportscaster, an eyewitness for the masses drawn to the game and sporting events that have become our most common shared experience, excepting clouds in the sky, and grace from above.

What, or better who, is a sportscaster? A blazer, tie, and immobile hair paired with an authoritative voice that rings the cathedral bells of sports truth. Clad in these vestments they enter the inner sanctums of the side-line and the locker room to ask the great questions for us:

How are you feeling right now?

How is your life lived, and how did it come about?

What is the purpose of your life?

Do you wish to be a role model or are you simply a being who has directed his will at the one goal he dreamt to achieve?

Chris Myers is our guy who has the tools, skills, wit, and his own delighted amazement at the persons and events in front of us, in addition to the most immobile hair in the business.

I could hear it in his words covering the Westminster Kennel Club Dog Show, his voice cresting over a roaring crowd, "The miniature poodle, coming up big when it matters the most!"

TDAW.

—Bill Murray

THAT DESERVES A
WOW

Prologue

People often tell me that I've got the best job any guy could ever want, and I agree with them. There is nothing like standing on the field while the Super Bowl is taking place right in front of you. Or listening to coaches and players in a dugout during a World Series. Or feeling the rush of race cars approaching 200 miles an hour at the Daytona 500. We all fall in love with sports during our childhood, but it is a rare thing to build a career around being a kid at heart.

Every sports fan is waiting for those special moments—the walk-off home run, the game-tying touchdown to send it to overtime, the knockout punch. But as a kid, I was fascinated to hear the athletes talking afterward about those moments. I loved listening to them. A part of me always wondered what made certain athletes so great and why they did what they did in certain situations. Where did they come from? How did they get to this point in their career? Some kids grew up wanting to be superstar athletes, but I wanted to be the guy talking to and interviewing them.

This genuine appreciation and curiosity about their skill set has led to a lifetime of interacting with the most talented athletes in the history of sports. I have been able to ask the questions that people have wanted to ask themselves. And I've been paid to do it!

One of the best parts of my job has been the variety I've had. I've always been interested in lots of different things, and I've had the chance to do many of them. Some broadcasters only do play-by-play; others will only focus on one particular sport. I've been in all kinds of roles in all different sports. I've reported the sports news of the day behind a desk, and I've also been a sideline reporter watching it happen in real time. I've interviewed players in the sanctuary of a studio and have also run after them on a field. I've been the pregame/postgame host and I've done play-by-play. But here's the thing . . .

This book isn't just about me.

It's the story of a journey through six decades of sports. A journey that starts with a kid who found his way through childhood by dreaming of becoming a broadcaster on the radio talking about sports. This dream brought him face-to-face with the greatest athletes of all time. It took him to the Masters and the Super Bowl and the World Series and so many other major games. But it also brought him to witness other incredible events—an earthquake at the World Series, a bombing at the Olympics, the death of a NASCAR driver at the Daytona 500, and the O. J. Simpson double-murder trial.

This book is about those moments and many more. I happened to be the one person right in the middle of it all, and I'm privileged to tell you about it.

Everybody has a story. For those exceptional few who get to play in professional sports of any kind—those athletes put under the bright lights and the cameras and the public eye—people have so many questions. We all want to get to know these star competitors. We want to see what makes them tick. What makes them triumph. What they do when they lose. And I've been able to ask those questions. I've asked them for myself out of curiosity. I've asked them for my network. I've asked them for my colleagues and for fellow athletes. But most of all, I've asked them for the audience. For the viewers. For you.

Everybody has a story, and this is mine. This book isn't the life of Chris Myers; it's the life experiences he has seen along the way. It's about the greatest athletes in the greatest games. It's about winning and losing. It's about life and death. But most of all, it's about finding meaning in some of sports' greatest moments.

ONE

Swinging on a Star

Most of us in our high school years are trying to find our way. I found mine at age sixteen shortly after humanities class.

"Hey, Chris. We need you to go over to the Fontainebleau Hotel tomorrow afternoon to interview Muhammad Ali. Get your tape recorder ready."

My boss at WKAT radio in Miami knew he didn't need to ask me twice. Sonny Hirsch was the sports director at the station and hosted *Sportsline*. For years he did the play-by-play for Miami football, basketball, and baseball games. He had a folksy, friendly style, and eventually he would become a legend calling the football national championships and baseball national titles won by the Miami Hurricanes. His two-hour show came on every weekday evening. Since he wasn't always able to get out of the studio to do interviews, Sonny sometimes asked me to go talk to an athlete or a coach.

"I can go right after school," I told him. "I'll get some quotes."

Sonny gave me a wide smile. "Show the other guys who's boss."

I'd been working at WKAT in Miami for over a year, starting as a board operator, until Sonny gave me my first big break. He allowed me to host a college football scoreboard show. Even though the job only paid $25 a day, I loved it. Being on the radio was something I had always dreamt about. After hosting my own call-in sports talk show, I took over for Sonny as sports director when I was nineteen. My very first interview was with Miami Dolphins linebacker Bob Matheson. Even though I was extremely nervous, Matheson was kind and answered my questions the same way he would have done with any sports reporter. I was becoming more confident with each interview.

"Get Ali to say something about George Foreman," Sonny said. "He always has something to say about George."

Sonny was an old-school sports guy—sarcastic, knowledgeable, opinionated. He showed tough love while educating me about the business. He also gave me opportunities people rarely got, especially one like this. Of course, I didn't realize how incredible an opportunity this would be. I knew about Muhammad Ali; he was a boxer with a big personality. I knew he could fight and loved to do interviews. But I didn't understand that I was about to interview the greatest boxer ever to fight, and in one of the most important periods in his life.

It was early May 1975, and Ali was training for a bout against Ron Lyle on May 16. This fight stood almost dead center between two historic matches. Six months earlier, Ali had knocked out George Foreman in the eighth round in the famous "Rumble in the Jungle" fight held in Kinshasa, Zaire. Later that year, on October 1, Ali would compete against Joe Frazier in the Philippines, a fight that would be known as the "Thrilla in

Manila." Ali would knock out Frazier in the 14th. If Ali ever needed proof of his greatness, these two fights would do it.

Ali was in Miami Beach, training at 5th Street Gym on Washington Avenue. Many world champions had trained at this famous gym. Chris and Angelo Dundee, respectively known as the "Wizard of Oz" and the "Prince of Oz," ran the gym. The mystique of 5th Street Gym attracted all sorts of celebrities over the years. Ali had spent many hours there in the '60s.

The next day after I got out of class, I drove over to the Fontainebleau in Miami Beach where Ali would be giving his press conference. It was a famous hotel that had attracted many famous people over the years. When it was built in 1954, it was considered the most luxurious hotel in Miami. Scenes from the James Bond movie *Goldfinger* and the Jerry Lewis movie *The Bellboy* had been filmed there, it's where Frank Sinatra and Elvis Presley performed, and John F. Kennedy and Marilyn Monroe separately had slept in their rooms. The hotel had lost a lot of its luster by the mid-'70s, but it was still sprawling in size.

When I arrived, I avoided the valet parking and spent a few minutes finding a lot where I could park myself. I was driving my first car, a used and beat-up Ford Falcon. It only had an AM radio with a plastic radio dial that was cracked. I was so embarrassed at how it looked that I taped a piece of cardboard over it. After I parked, it took me a while to find the ballroom where Ali was surrounded by reporters and making them laugh.

This was a scene out of a black-and-white movie from the '50s, like the classic Paul Newman boxing film *Somebody Up There Likes Me*. The reporters in the room gave off an old-school feel; some chewed on cigars, while other wore hats with their suits. They smelled like cigarettes, and sweat dotted their foreheads. They were experienced writers, some with national publications, and others affiliated with boxing. As I worked my way around the reporters, I can only imagine what they must have thought of me. *What's this long-haired kid doing here? Who let him in the room?* But I was representing WKAT with a big microphone attached to my tape recorder.

I couldn't help being a little nervous. Would I even get the opportunity to ask Ali a question? All I had to do was put the microphone out and get comments from him. But I thought, *I'm here for this and it's Ali. I'm going to ask him something if there's a chance.*

I'd never stood amidst reporters before, nervously waiting for my turn to shout out a question. I had to be careful not to interrupt anybody, and to be sure Ali had finished answering the prior question. And more than anything in the world, I didn't want to ask something stupid, especially since I wasn't as well versed in boxing as I was in other sports. That might make me the target of his humor.

After a dozen questions from other reporters, I finally threw out the one I'd prepared. "Would you say your fight with George Foreman was your toughest fight ever?" I asked.

Ali's eyes went big, surprised.

"You're not as dumb as you look, kid," he said in a friendly and teasing tone. "That was a great match, but I'd say my toughest fight was against Sonny Liston back in '64. Before you were even born."

I wasn't about to tell him I was born in 1959. His comment made all the reporters laugh, including me. I was grateful he had responded. Knowing he had our full attention, Ali continued:

"One thing I always say: Don't be a fool—stay in school."

In this moment, with a group of reporters who ate and breathed and lived sports day and night, I witnessed what greatness truly looked like outside the ring. Here, in a press conference, it wasn't about Ali's speed and footwork, nor his toughness to withstand fierce blows from formidable opponents. Here I watched a warrior commanding a room, not with his punches but rather with his words. His quips and soundbites. He was entertaining and quick-witted. He played off people and never ran from a question. He was never stumped by a reporter. The banter captivated all of us.

This was my first brush with greatness. Seeing Muhammad Ali in person sharing bits of himself, some humorous and others inspiring, made him even more fascinating to me. I wanted to continue to ask him questions so I could understand him further. Not the fighter but the individual.

As I left the Fontainebleau with my first big interview recorded and ready to go, I didn't fully appreciate the magnitude of this moment. It had been exciting to be in the room with adults talking about sports and competition and life. But I hadn't stood there in awe and I hadn't been intimidated by the larger-than-life athlete in front of me. This was like looking at the vast Atlantic Ocean for the first time and feeling right at home.

• • •

THE DAY AFTER MY ALI INTERVIEW, AS I WALKED INTO OUR HIGH school, I felt a sense of pride and accomplishment about the interview. I didn't brag about it, however, because I didn't know how I'd done. People would soon start to realize what I was doing—that I was working for sports radio and doing interviews. This explained why I was so busy, and why I missed out on things like going to the prom. Instead of dancing with my prom date, I was interviewing Roger Staubach. Back in grade school, however, nobody would have ever imagined I'd be speaking to sports legends.

The spark first came in second grade when my classmates were talking about the recent World Series and I had no idea what they were talking about. We didn't watch much baseball in our house, so I wasn't in the loop on players and teams and rules.

How many games are in a World Series? Five? Ten? Where are the Tigers and Cardinals from? Are all baseball teams named after animals?

When someone said, "MVP," I didn't even know what that meant.

"What's an 'MVP'?" I asked my classmates.

They laughed and couldn't believe I didn't know the abbreviation of Most Valuable Player. I felt a bit stupid and realized I was totally out of the loop, so I decided that day to start learning more about sports. I began studying sports fanatically—I started collecting cards and listened to any radio sports talk show I could. Back then, there weren't a thousand different ways to watch and listen to sports, so you had to be creative.

I had never been a great athlete. I was always that sixth guy on the basketball team, the backup quarterback, the utility infielder. But just because I didn't have a lot of great abilities didn't mean I didn't have a lot of interest in athletics. It grew from that second-grade experience. This interest made me start listening to sports radio, dialing in to the station in Miami Beach. It began an unlikely journey from listening to WKAT to actually getting a job with them.

By the time I reached my teenage years, sports had become an obsession for me. Not playing sports, but watching games and listening to others discuss them. I would sit in my bedroom with the door closed listening to *Sportsline* on my portable radio. The black plastic box crackled whenever I turned it on. Many nights I ignored my homework while Sonny talked about subjects like the Miami Dolphins and the NFL. If I was lucky, I would get on the air when I called in.

Our three-bedroom, two-bathroom, and one-TV house in North Miami was small for two parents and five children. I shared a room with my two brothers, while our two sisters shared another. We only had two phones in the house—one on the wall in the kitchen, the other in my parents' room—so I would have to sneak down to the only possible place I wouldn't be overheard calling in to the radio station. Many times Dad was working while Mom was cleaning up after dinner and my siblings were in the family room watching television. It might take a few minutes before I got through, but I was a regular caller, so they knew me well.

"We have Chris from Miami calling in," Sonny said. "What's on your mind this evening?"

"How're you doing, Sonny?" I said, trying not to sound like my age. "I was calling about my Los Angeles Dodgers and our trade with the Chicago Cubs."

Sportsline had a national flavor, with people calling from all over the country, especially from New York and Boston. I was among the regular callers, alongside Hannah of Brooklyn, a Dodger fan like me; Greg from Baltimore, who was a big Orioles fan; and Scott, a diehard Cubs fan.

"The Dodgers traded Geoff Zahn and Eddie Solomon to the Chicago Cubs for Burt Hooton," I said into the phone receiver. "I think it was a good trade. Hooton's a good pitcher and we need one."

For a few moments Sonny and I spoke about the Dodgers and about baseball in general. When I was finished, I hung up, then dialed the radio station again, hoping for another conversation. You were only allowed one call a night, but "Chris from Miami" wasn't calling them back. Thankfully I got back on the show ten minutes later.

"Yeah, this is Duke from North Miami," I said as I disguised my voice, speaking in a deeper tone with a John Wayne–type delivery. "I agree with Chris from Miami that the Dodgers-Cubs trade was a great one."

Duke was much older and wiser than Chris, the resonance of his voice articulating facts and figures on baseball. Nobody at WKAT radio knew that Duke and Chris were the same person. They also didn't know I was a ripe fifteen years old.

For over a year, Chris and Duke called in to *Sportsline* to chat with Sonny. Nobody had figured out that I was only a sophomore going to Chaminade High School in Hollywood, Florida. Until an invitation to the station changed everything.

• • •

MAYBE I HAVE AN AIR CONDITIONER TO THANK FOR MY CAREER. Growing up, we didn't have central air, so on one of my birthdays I asked for an air conditioner for the room I shared with my two brothers. My dad worked two jobs and didn't have a lot of money, but he was able to buy us a portable window unit. I slept directly below it in one bed while my brothers shared the bunk bed. Since I wanted the temperature to be colder than my brothers did, I would take the plastic tracks for my Hot Wheels toy cars and stick them in the AC vents, then aim them directly at me.

After a while of sleeping like this, I began to wake up with a bit of a post-nasal drip, and it affected my voice a bit. Around fifth and sixth grade, my voice became noticeably different. I would go to school sounding a bit like John Wayne, but I fought through it since I wasn't sick or anything. I was never given an official clinical diagnosis that this was how I developed a lower register for my voice, but I grew used to pushing my voice out in a certain direction and talking that way.

By middle school, my voice was so deep that some of my friends asked me to call in to school and impersonate their parents so they could skip class. In return, they'd help me with my homework or give me a ride home. I'm not proud of this now, but I did take a few of them up on it. I left messages on the school answering machine, saying things like, "Hello, this is Freddie's father. No need to call me back. He's feeling under the weather today but he'll be fine tomorrow."

Freddie's father sounded a bit like Jimmy Stewart.

"Hi, this is Patty's dad. She is going to be coming in late to school today. She has a dentist's appointment."

Patty's dad remarkably sounded a lot like Johnny Cash.

I could have gotten in a lot of trouble, but my school never questioned the authority of the deep voice spoken from a sixth-grade student. Neither did the people at the radio station. Nobody ever had any idea how young I might be. They eventually learned when I showed up at their studio one day.

• • •

"WE'RE GOING TO HAVE FAN NIGHT HERE ON *SPORTSLINE* NEXT WEEK, so we're inviting some of our regular callers to come down to the studio so we can put you on."

The voice on the other end of the phone was John Harper, the producer of the show. He said he wanted to host a roundtable with the regulars to talk about sports live in the studio. I listened with a combination of excitement and fear as he listed the familiar names I had come to know and love. Hannah from Brooklyn and Greg from Baltimore, Chris from Miami, and of course, Duke from North Miami.

"Yeah, sure, that would be a lot of fun," Chris from Miami told him in his very mature voice.

What the heck was I gonna do?

The first problem wasn't my age or the fact that I had no twin brother named Duke. I didn't have my driver's license, so I had no idea how I'd get down to the studio in Miami in the first place. We lived in North Miami, a thirty-minute drive to get downtown to the radio station. So I went to my father and explained the situation to him.

For Eugene T. Myers, sports were more of a luxury. As I said, my dad worked two jobs. He understood tough times, having grown up in the Depression and then later served in the Navy during World War II. He was only a teenager when he stormed the beach at Normandy on D-Day. He taught us the values he grew up with: work hard, get good grades, stay up on current events, and make something of yourself. Paying attention to baseball, football, or other sports wasn't a priority to my dad. Even though he never said this, it was as if sports were only for the elite. *You're not there, yet,* he seemed to be telling me. *Work hard and one day you'll have a chance to do the things I wasn't able to do.*

Dad and Mom and the rest of our family knew about my dream of becoming a sports broadcaster one day. When I was in fourth grade and my father was at work, I'd sometimes sneak into my parents' bathroom where there was less traffic and practice announcing baseball games. I'd grab my dad's toothbrush and step into the shower to begin my imaginary play-by-play commentary on a Dodgers game.

"There's a long drive!" I'd shout out.

My family would hear me doing this, and sometimes even our guests would, too.

"Is Chris all right?" they would ask my mom.

"Yeah, he's fine. He's just calling a World Series in the shower."

The only problem with me doing this was that I'd drop my microphone (a.k.a. Dad's toothbrush) in the shower, where he'd find it the next morning. He got up very early in the morning for work, so he found himself on several occasions looking for his toothbrush and eventually discovering it by the bathtub drain.

"Chris, you gotta stop the announcing," he once told me. "Or at least let us get you an extra toothbrush."

Even if Dad didn't fully understand my dreams to get into the world of sports, he never discouraged me. So when the opportunity to get onto *Sportsline* came, I knew I had to explain my unique situation.

After explaining it all, I asked what I should do.

"Well, you're going to have to tell them the truth," Dad said. "You tell them you're a lying little brat and you were supposed to be doing your homework."

"Come on, Dad."

He seemed to be thinking for a moment. With his grayish hair and beard, he resembled a colonel or a general. By now he wore glasses, and he chewed on a toothpick as he considered what to do.

"You have to tell them you weren't being honest. That's the first thing you do. But I'll drive you down there."

The radio station was on Alton Road in Miami Beach inside a nondescript building with a small sign indicating it was WKAT. Criteria Studios, where the Bee Gees recorded some of their biggest hits in the '70s, was right around the corner. When I told the receptionist they were expecting me for the panel, she looked surprised and called someone to verify that I was telling the truth.

"There's this kid here that says he's supposed to be on the panel. Says he's 'Chris from Miami.'"

When I explained the situation to the guys at the station, they thought it was pretty cool that I had made it that far. They told me I couldn't be dishonest while I was on air, but they allowed me to be a part of the panel.

I couldn't get over how the station looked. It didn't resemble any kind of radio station I might have imagined. A long hallway took you to a large room that looked more like a den than a studio. Heavy curtains hung over the windows and there was a sort of fireplace mantel that might be in a haunted house. In the center of the room was a comfortable couch, and next to that was a big desk with a microphone. I think they wanted a more familial feel since they were a talk show.

After the panel, John Harper, the producer, came up to me and told me I did a good job. Then he surprised me with a job offer.

"You're a creative kid and seem to know a lot about what's going on. What do you think about working for us part-time once you get your license? On the weekends. You can run wire copy in."

"Sure, I'll do that."

The only other job I had was doing lawn work in my neighborhood.

So I can thank Duke from North Miami for getting me a job at WKAT radio after I turned sixteen and got my license. Duke would have to retire from the broadcasting world. Chris from Miami, however, was just getting started.

• • •

I GREW UP ALWAYS WONDERING WHAT MADE ATHLETES GREAT AND why they did what they did in certain situations. I was curious about where they came from, the cities they were born in and where they went to school. That's just part of my personality. By the time I was working for the radio station, I didn't want to be an athlete. I wanted to be the guy talking about and interviewing them.

Not long after the Ali interview, I was able to interview Don Shula. I already had a connection with him in that I went to school with his son, Dave. After the radio station liked what they heard with my interview with Ali, they asked me to visit a Dolphins practice and get some quotes from the coach. To me, this was a bigger deal than interviewing Ali.

The National Football League was my first connection to sports as a child. My older brother, Dan, helped introduce football to me. I was in second grade and watching a John Wayne movie when Dan came in the family room to watch an NFL game. With only one television in our house, he needed to find a way to convince me to turn on the game.

"Just watch it for a few minutes and give it a chance," Dan told me.

"I don't know . . ." I said.

"Look—you pick one team and I'll pick the other. We'll see who wins."

I liked this idea of competition. So when he turned the channel, I saw the Miami Dolphins playing the Los Angeles Rams in L.A. When I saw the horns on the ram, I knew that was my team. Even though I didn't understand everything that was happening, I enjoyed watching the game. Especially since my team won.

Soon the game engulfed me. I more than rooted for my team; I *became* them, living and dying emotionally with each win and loss. It was an escape from homework and the noise of a turbulent world. It was hours of an investment in excitement and unpredictability. It was a thrill ride.

After my first interview with Miami Dolphins linebacker Bob Matheson, I had thought to myself, *This isn't that difficult*. But this was Don Shula, the winningest coach in football at the time. The Miami Dolphins dominated the league, winning back-to-back Super Bowls and going undefeated in the '72 season. With his chiseled jaw and broad shoulders, Shula resembled a mythic figure like Vince Lombardi or Knute Rockne. Before interviewing him, I watched him on the practice field with large running backs and defensive linemen, getting in their faces and challenging them to be better and to work on certain things. He wasn't just yelling at them; everything with Shula had a purpose. I could tell he was highly principled and deliberate with everything he did, and that included interviews.

I observed Coach Shula at practices and watched him on television and read articles about him, and to me he was like a king of football reigning over his soldiers. One simple frown from him could intimidate anybody. Maybe that was my image of him or the image he wanted to project. He was a tough and intimidating guy to interview, someone who was always very firm and spoke with conviction. When I caught him coming off the field after a practice and asked if he had time for some questions, he told me he had time for one or two. As I went through my interview and got to my third question, he just looked at me and then looked down at his watch. This was his subtle way of saying, *Look, kid, I got things to do*. If you missed that signal, then he'd just walk away at your fourth question. That showed how disciplined a coach Shula was. I remember thinking, *Boy, this guy's not messing around*. I'd even seen him walk away from questions that he deemed to be ignorant.

I continued to do a lot of work for WKAT behind the scenes, helping gather clips and quotes and sports info. One Saturday when a host couldn't get to the station, they asked me to step in. The boss told me not to lie about my age on the air, but at the same time I shouldn't tell everybody. They knew I sounded older and that I could roll with somebody when they called—they had heard me doing this already for the past year. So I got that chance, and that developed into having my own program on the weekends. This also led to me filling in for Sonny Hirsch himself during the weekdays when he wasn't there.

I grew interested in the art of interviewing, too. Just like sports, I had always been interested in talk shows and hosts who asked questions. And I didn't actually realize that I had spent my entire life interviewing people. This included probing the young men my older sisters would sometimes bring over for dinner.

"So what year is your Mustang?" I once asked.

My sister's new boyfriend, who was sitting next to her at the dinner table, gave me a curious look. They had met in high school and this was the first time any of us had met him.

"It's a '72," he said.

"When did you get your license?"

This time he just laughed. "This kid is grillin' me. What is he—a detective?"

Everybody laughed, even though to my family this was nothing new. There was a genuine curiosity on my part, especially whenever one of my older sisters showed up with a new guy, but I guess looking at it now, I was pushing them a bit. I was interviewing them more than my dad. But as a young person, I always found myself asking people questions. At family gatherings, I would always be asking an uncle or an aunt questions. Interviews were a natural part of my life.

I loved talk shows growing up. The classic ones. Mike Douglas in the afternoon. Merv Griffin. And Johnny Carson, of course. Carson to me was the standard because of his range and how he treated his interviews like it was a different kind of show. He wouldn't necessarily do comedy during his conversations. He always made the guest feel comfortable.

Once I got my weekend show and occasionally filled in for Sonny Hirsch during the week, I was able to interview more athletes. Sometimes they would be guys stopping in or calling in to the station. I remember the quarterback great Johnny Unitas once stopped in.

And Dolphins QB Bob Griese would swing by once in a while. Other athletes were in South Florida either with a visiting team or on vacation. I loved to find out which teams were on the road in Miami. Sometimes I would call a hotel and ask to talk with certain players.

All of this felt natural and normal for me. The more opportunities I got at the radio station, the more I enjoyed it. And I kept looking ahead, wondering what was next. Trying to figure out the next thing to get involved with. For me, it was obvious that getting into television made sense. So I began to pay a lot of attention to the local TV stations in Miami Beach. I might have still been a teenager, but I was very driven.

Thinking back on getting my first break in the radio business and being able to interview Muhammad Ali and Don Shula, I realize that I was able to start at the top. Most people have to build their way up to asking the greats questions. Maybe interview the hero on your high school basketball team first, then get the university quarterback, and next interview a professional athlete. But I started out with the best of the best. And while I hate the term "GOAT" and think it's way overused in sports, I believe that Ali and Shula were the greatest of all time in their areas. They would come to set the standard for my career. If I could interview them, I could interview anyone.

• • •

MY PARENTS WERE THE PEOPLE WHO INSPIRED AND INFLUENCED ME the most when I was growing up. I was closer to my mom, in part because my dad worked so much so I spent more time with her. She was one of the driving forces who instilled confidence in me and influenced my work ethic. Eleanor Myers was more outgoing than my dad, and she loved to entertain. She would invite her older sister and her friends over on a regular basis to play pinochle. Sometimes I would sit by the table and watch these women in their forties play. Other times I joined in myself. While I enjoyed getting to know how to play the game, what I loved the most was listening to their conversations. They would often ask me questions.

"So how's the girlfriend, Chris?"

"I don't have a girlfriend."

"Why not?"

"I'm ten—what do you want from me?"

My dad enjoyed being around people as well. Not only did he have a good sense of humor, but also of theater and entertainment. I feel those were things I inherited from him. Perhaps his greatest talent, however, was his singing voice. At family gatherings and weddings, he would be asked to sing songs. Even sometimes when we were out at a restaurant and somebody was playing a piano, my dad would ask if he could sing a song to accompany the music.

When Eugene T. Myers was younger, he won a Bing Crosby singalong contest. It was a big deal for him; they were going to fly him to New York and do stuff with that. One of his favorite Crosby songs was "Swinging on a Star." I can hear him now, singing "would you rather be a mule" and "would you rather be a fish." Frank Sinatra did a version of that song that I used to play for our kids.

My dad had a passion for singing and music, but he ended up joining the Navy and was dating my mom, so other things took priority. With Dad's father passing away at a young age, he and his brothers were taking care of their mom, too. All these things resulted in him taking a different path in his life. Music might have been one of his loves, but he had bigger responsibilities. Perhaps that was why he was so supportive of my own dreams of becoming a sports broadcaster. Maybe he looked at my own dreams and thought, *Here's a career that a kid can follow. I didn't get to chase after my dreams, but you can chase after yours.*

Dad never said this, yet sometimes I sensed it. His love of singing never faded, either. Later in his life, he would go to retirement centers and sing songs with others. He was like *The Music Man.*

Thanks to Mom and Dad, I was prepared for a career that relied on my talents and my passion. I'll always be grateful for that.

TWO

A Rising Star

"Nicklaus is gone, done. He just doesn't have the game anymore. It's rusted from lack of use. He's 46, and nobody that old wins the Masters."[1]

A week before the 1986 Masters Tournament, a golf writer for the *Atlanta Journal-Constitution* named Tom McCollister penned an article breaking down all the players who would be competing that year. His summary of Jack Nicklaus ended up becoming notorious. How could the winner of five previous green jackets possibly be an underdog?

Coming into this Masters, nobody was talking about Jack Nicklaus. The Golden Bear had already cemented his legacy in the 1960s and '70s while winning seventeen majors, the most by any player then and still today. But by 1986, his last major title had been the 1980 PGA Championship, and his last win had come in 1984. He wasn't playing as much due to back ailments. But Jack would receive some added motivation coming into this tournament thanks to McCollister's story.

When Nicklaus's friend John Montgomery read the article, he clipped it and taped it onto Jack's fridge door. Nicklaus would later admit that even though he kind of agreed with the statement, it also helped him get going. The results made sports history. And I was there in person to witness it.

My unlikely journey to Augusta National when I was twenty-seven years old came courtesy of WWL TV in New Orleans. I had moved to the Big Easy in 1982 after they hired me to be their sports anchor. I would remain at the CBS affiliate for six years. My responsibility at the Masters was to cover Hal Sutton, the Louisiana golfer and once heir apparent to the Bear. In fact, Nicklaus had once said he thought Sutton would win a lot of major championships after the twenty-five-year-old beat him at the 1983 PGA Championship. That would turn out to be Sutton's only major win, however. At this particular Masters, Sutton was no longer playing on the final day after having not made the cut. Thankfully, WWL let me stay and watch the rest of the tournament.

This was one of the reasons why I had agreed to leave my hometown and move halfway across the country. After working my way onto Miami radio, I had gone on to WCIX TV, a local independent, at the age of twenty while still doing radio. Then a year later I made a big step up to WTVJ, a CBS affiliate in Miami, where I was doing weekend sports. But my eye had always been on a bigger prize, which was to get to the network. Even though New Orleans was technically a smaller market than Miami, WWL was a CBS affiliate, and it was a powerhouse that dominated the market. That's why they had local reporters like me covering national events like this.

I'd seen the Masters on television and heard about the history of Augusta National, but it felt overwhelming to see the magnificent golf course live and in person. This was one of sports' greatest shrines, comparable to Yankee Stadium, Madison Square Garden, and the Rose Bowl. It seemed like I had gone back in time, too, where cheese sandwiches were served and leaves were raked and garbage was nowhere to be found. A lone gum wrapper would be scooped up immediately. There was a great order to how everybody moved in lines with muted conversation.

The grass was greener than green, everything pristine and spotless. There was an unmatched perfection everywhere I looked—the snow-white bunkers, the rolling hills, the perfect balance of trees and flowers. I felt like Dorothy in the Technicolor world of Oz.

With some referring to him as the Olden Bear, Nicklaus didn't make any headlines with his first two rounds of 74 and 71. Coming into the last day of play, he was four shots behind the leader, Greg Norman, fifteen years his junior. A host of other great players—many much younger—were ahead of him, such as Nick Price and Seve Ballesteros and Bernhard Langer. Nicklaus scared no one on this Sunday.

Some of the greatest moments in sports come when competitors defy our expectations. It can be when rookies take the stage for the first time, but it can also be when legends leave one last memory for their legacy. On the final ten holes at the Masters, Nicklaus shot the following: birdie-birdie-birdie-bogey-birdie-par-eagle-birdie-birdie-par.

When forty-six-year-old Jack Nicklaus made a 12-foot birdie shot on the 17th hole and moved into the lead in the final round of the Masters, the eruption of the crowd could have easily come from a football stadium or basketball arena. On this gorgeous April day in 1986, history was about to be made.

Watching Nicklaus earn his sixth green jacket made me become a true golf fan. I had played and covered some golf in my life, but this was the crowning moment, when I told myself, *I'm all in on this.* As Jack Nicklaus came walking down the 18th fairway with his son Jackie carrying his bag, I couldn't help getting the chills. It was one thing to interview a legend like Nicklaus, but watching him perform live and in person took things to a whole new level. This was about as good as it gets.

• • •

"achievement is largely the product of steadily raising one's level of aspiration and expectation." When I saw him win his last major in 1986, I already fully believed this. I had been carrying around aspirations and expectations since my childhood days in Miami. The crazy thing was I first started writing them down in lipstick. I can thank my older sister Diane (number two in the sibling order) for that.

When I began to imagine myself as a sportscaster, all my siblings had to put up with hearing either the radio announcers talking about sports or my own voice pretending to be them. One day, Diane came into my bedroom.

"You're pretty serious about this sports stuff, huh?"

"Yeah," I said.

"Okay. Take this lipstick."

I looked at the tube in her hand as if it was radioactive. I had no idea what she was talking about.

"This is to write on your mirror," Diane said as she wrote **GOALS** at the top of it. "That way you can see your goals every day. You're *forced* to see them daily. And it's easy to rub them off when you've accomplished them."

So I began to write down my goals. Early on I just had a couple. **GET ON THE RADIO. BE AN ANCHOR ON TV.** But as the years progressed, I would write more down. I also graduated from red lipstick on glass to black ink on paper, which made me look less like a serial killer. By the time I was living in New Orleans, I wrote my goals down on notecards and kept them in the drawer of the nightstand beside my bed. I tried to keep the number down to around ten so I could easily remember them. On any given morning or late night, I would pick up the stack and go through my goals.

Become an anchor in L.A.

Lose 15 pounds.

Have my own talk show.

Win an Emmy.

Buy a new car.

The goals ranged from personal to professional. Some were immediate and others were long-range. But all of them reinforced a common trait of mine. I once told Troy Aikman that this trait could be the title of my memoir: *Driven*. Aikman smiled and said, "Why am I not surprised?" Driven sums up how I've always approached my career. I never wanted to be obsessed, to fall into the rut of being a workaholic. But in those early days before getting married and starting a family, I could afford to have lofty and ambitious goals. Even coming to New Orleans in the first place was ambitious.

By the time I graduated high school, I had already achieved one of those goals I wrote in red lipstick on my bedroom mirror. I got on the radio, and that led to me eventually getting on television. Attending what was then Miami Dade Community College (now Miami Dade College) gave me some good hands-on experience with TV and radio equipment, but with working on the radio during the week and TV on the weekends, I had to put all my energy into those job opportunities. I ended up dropping out, always feeling like I would eventually go back. But the opportunities kept coming.

When WWL in New Orleans reached out to me, I was pleasantly surprised. Sure, the goals I had written down meant that I would be moving to different places in the country and to different stations. But having an offer made me think hard. I knew the guy at my station in Miami doing the weekday sports was going to be there for a while. The main sports anchor at WWL, however, was supposed to go on to CBS within a year or two, so they were interested in hiring me to become their Monday-through-Friday guy. Only twenty-one years old, with my contract coming up, I knew it was a great opportunity.

"What's it going to take?" the general manager for WWL asked me.

Deep down I wasn't exactly ready to move yet, and since I didn't have an agent at the time who could do the negotiating for me, I decided to just throw out an offer to them. I asked for double what I was making in Miami, an income not bad for a guy my age. All the while I expected a "No, thank you, maybe down the road, let's keep in touch." But after I gave them my offer, the general manager said, "Okay, let's do a three-year deal."

I couldn't believe it.

"That's very nice of you," I said, holding back my shock. "Can I think about it for twenty-four hours?"

The decision weighed on me. Opting for New Orleans meant leaving my family and my hometown. It wasn't like I was going off to college; I was moving to the Big Easy where I didn't know a soul. On the other hand, I could report on major events like the Masters, and really grow my career. Staying in Miami meant a nice raise and the status quo. I made the decision to devote myself to learning the craft. Instead of dividing my time between radio and television, I would be all in on TV. A goal I'd set for myself. One I saw written in lipstick daily every time I combed my hair.

• • •

THERE'S A HILARIOUS IRONY IN THE FACT THAT THE SPORTS TEAM THAT had the most impact on my personal and professional life happened to be the New Orleans Saints in the mid-'80s. When I arrived in Louisiana in 1982, the Saints were dubbed the "Ain'ts" because they had never had a winning year since the team began in 1966. These were the lovable losers who in 1980 had a 1-15 record and prompted local sportscaster

Buddy Diliberto to wear a paper bag over his head until they won, creating the baghead tradition in the NFL. I could have never imagined that the same organization would play a key role in both my getting married and my landing a job at ESPN.

The 1982 NFL season was notable for the players' strike that ended up reducing the sixteen-game schedule to only nine games. The Saints had hired Bum Phillips as their new head coach in 1981 after the disastrous one-win season the prior year. Phillips previously coached the Houston Oilers, who won 58 out of 93 games and made three consecutive playoffs. Expectations were high for the coach who wore his trademark cowboy hat and boots on the sidelines. Too high, as it turned out.

As a local reporter and TV announcer, I witnessed season after season of losses: 4-12 in '81; 4-5 in the abbreviated '82; 8-8 in '83; 7-9 in '84; and 5-11 in '85. Bum had brought in two Hall of Fame players from the Houston Oilers: quarterback Ken Stabler arrived with him in '81, while Bum traded the Saints' number one draft pick for running back Earl Campbell in '84. Both players were on the back end of their careers, big names who were barely hanging on. As time went by, I would ask Coach Phillips tough questions about the losses. One day he called me out during a meeting.

"You're always so critical," Bum told me.

This was a tough man. During World War II, he enlisted in the Marines and fought in the savage battles on the islands of the Pacific. His comment could have easily shut a reporter up. But I've always kept asking questions.

"I'm asking you the questions that fans are wondering about, Coach," I said. "I don't mean to be disrespectful, but I'm at the practices and I'm at the games. I'm not a coach, but I can see the problems this team has."

Bum, known for his notable quotes, gave me one on this day.

"Just because you walk through a hospital doesn't make you a doctor," the coach said.

I paused for a moment and nodded, then answered, "Well, yeah, but I don't have to be a doctor to know when somebody's sick."

Bum chuckled at my comment. "All right—you got me, kid."

Coach Phillips didn't last in New Orleans. In 1986, Jim Mora was hired as the head coach, coming from the USFL, where he'd led his team to three straight championships, winning two. Mora was a tough guy who brought a lot of his assistant coaches with him. He slowly built the Saints into a winning team that eventually went to the playoffs for the first time. Throughout his career, Mora never hesitated to speak his mind. Everybody remembers his infamous "Playoffs? Don't talk about—playoffs? You kidding me? Playoffs?" That quote would come years later when he was the coach of the Indianapolis Colts. But in New Orleans, I heard plenty of memorable statements from the passionate coach.

I got to know Mora by doing a weekly radio show with him. When the Saints weren't doing well, I still had to ask the coach the questions fans were wondering. No surprise that Mora could be a little difficult and cranky whenever I talked about the team's losses and struggles. It turned out his wife, Connie, had been listening to the show and had noticed his attitude toward me at times.

"Connie told me I need to tone it down," Mora said to me. "She said I'm being rude to you, that I need to be a little bit nicer. She said you have to ask me those questions, so I can't take it out on you for doing your job. So I'm going to try to ease up on you."

I admired Coach Mora for even bringing that up, as well as heeding his wife's advice.

There always has to be a balance between a journalist and the coaches and athletes he covers. For me, I've always preferred to get to know the individual I'm interviewing. In some cases, I've actually become friends with the person. That has never prevented me from asking the tough questions. With someone like Bum Phillips, I never had the opportunity to get to know him very well, but with Coach Mora it was different.

On one occasion before the winning 1987 season, I attended what turned out to be a very important dinner with Jim Mora. For several years I had been dating Susan, a woman I met shortly after moving to New Orleans when she was doing volunteer work in the press box during halftime for a game I was covering. Susan and I were invited to have dinner one night with Jim and Connie at Commander's Palace, a New Orleans landmark in the Garden District that had been around since 1893. Our table was in the garden room of the restaurant.

I knew Mora was an intense coach on the sidelines, but he could also be intense simply enjoying a night off at a fine-dining establishment. Mora had a Jimmy Stewart kind of delivery in the way he talked, the difference being he was more of an edgy George Bailey from *It's a Wonderful Life* after Uncle Billy loses the funds at the building & loan. Susan ordered a signature dish from Commander's Palace, the bread pudding soufflé that's so special they recommend you order it twenty minutes in advance. We were in the middle of a conversation when Mora noticed her dessert plate and blurted out like a coach ordering a blitz, "Are you going to finish that?"

We were a little taken aback. Susan said she loved the bread pudding, but she was full and only able to eat half of it.

"It looks delicious," he added. She offered it to him and we all chuckled as Mora relaxed and ate the rest of the dessert.

During the same meal, Mora also couldn't help but speak his mind when it came to my relationship with Susan.

"You guys have been going out for a while, right?" the coach asked us.

"Yeah, for a few years," I said.

"So you're sitting there with the number one draft pick," Mora said about Susan. "When are you guys gonna get married?"

I'd already been thinking about this, so I decided to make a bet with Coach Mora. Albeit a safe bet.

"You guys make the playoffs and we'll get married," I told him.

History was on my side since the Saints had never made the playoffs. They hadn't even had a winning record. Sure enough, they made the playoffs that year. And, sure enough, Jim Mora sent a registered letter to Susan:

To Chris and Susan,

    This letter is official documentation of the bet we made that Chris would marry Susan when the Saints made the playoffs.

                        Sincerely,

                        Jim Mora

We laughed over the letter that Mora had signed. So I guess you can say that Jim Mora and the Saints helped give me the extra motivation I needed. Susan and I married in 1989. Both of us will always have a soft spot for the Saints organization.

· · ·

ONE LATE EVENING AFTER GETTING OFF WORK AT WWL TV, I WAS driving from the studio in the French Quarter toward my place in the suburbs. When I stopped at a traffic light, I noticed a young teenage boy near a shopping area bus stop. Even with the limited lighting I could tell this kid was being bullied by three teenagers who were bigger and definitely older than him. So I pulled over to the side of the road and rolled down my window.

"Hey, what's going on here?" I yelled out.

The younger kid looked pale and scared, while the teenagers gave me annoyed looks.

"Are you okay?" I asked the younger kid.

His weak voice told me these guys were bothering him.

"Why don't you get lost?" one of the bullies told me.

I wasn't going anywhere. "Not until you let the kid go."

They grabbed the kid and started hitting him. I quickly climbed out of the car, then I yelled at them, "Don't make me get my gun!"

Instantly the bullies scattered, leaving the younger kid by himself.

Of course, I didn't have a gun, but in the moment I felt like that was the quickest way to break this up without getting into a brawl. I had also been careful to make sure they didn't have a gun on them . . . at least one that I could see.

"Do you need me to call your parents?" I asked the kid.

"No, I'm okay. I'm going home."

Two weeks later, I was back in the studio when my producer told me I had a personal call.

"It's from a state trooper," he said.

I wondered what I'd done wrong, so I took the call, curious to know what was going on. The man on the phone was not only a state trooper but was also the father of the young boy who had been bullied a couple of weeks earlier. His son had told him what happened, and later on he saw me on television and tracked me down.

"I just want to tell you thanks for helping my son not get beaten up," the man said. "He shouldn't have been out so late on a school night."

I told the state trooper I appreciated him finding me to show his gratitude. Before he got off the phone, he added, "By the way, it's not safe to say you have a gun when you don't have one," he cautioned. "This time you got lucky."

He was right, I knew. When the guys at the office heard about this story, they started to joke around with me.

"Here he comes, Walker Texas Ranger."

"Don't mess with Myers—he's the enforcer."

• • •

MAYBE I'VE ALWAYS HAD A THING FOR UNDERDOGS, WANTING TO stick up for them or at least speak out for them. Perhaps it was meant to be that I was in New Orleans with the greatest NFL underdogs of their time. My fascination has always been to see what drives underdogs to win, despite loss after loss. What happens when they finally get their due? It gets down to the thing I've loved ever since I began to listen to sports radio—the human element of competition.

Two of my earliest pieces that ended up catching the attention of ESPN focused on this human element, on underdogs finally finding success. One was a story I did on the LSU baseball team in 1986. The Louisiana State University Tigers were making their first appearance in the College World Series in Omaha, Nebraska. My piece showed what the players did on their day off, and I injected a little bit of my humor into it. When they went to the zoo, we had them all looking completely bored. They also went to the Gerald R. Ford Birthsite and Gardens, where I did my best impersonation of President Ford falling down the stairs. I was no Chevy Chase.

The other piece was a story called "They Never Played the Game." It profiled the New Orleans Saints coaching staff who had finally turned the team into playoff contenders. A few of them had dabbled in playing football in high school and college, but none of the coaches had ever played at the NFL level. All of them had only been average in college; none of these guys were superstars or even stars. They were just guys who loved football and tried to play it. They were a likable bunch who finally found some success for the Saints.

Life is full of "what-ifs." Sometimes I wonder what might have happened if someone at ESPN hadn't caught one of those pieces and decided to keep an eye on me. I never could have imagined when I was having fun putting those reports together that they would serve as a job audition of sorts.

One career possibility that came my way in New Orleans was when the CBS station in New York called to say they were interested in hiring me to do their weekend shows. I went for the interview and it went well. They even drove me around looking at houses in area neighborhoods. But ultimately it didn't work out and they ended up hiring somebody else. At the time, I was disappointed, even crushed. I thought to myself, *That was my big break, my big chance, and it brushed by me and was gone.* But soon after that, ESPN called to say they wanted to hire me to be their first-ever full-time West Coast reporter.

• • •

"WHAT IF WE HAD A SHOW THAT GAVE US MORE TIME TO TALK ABOUT football?"

My question was a bit ludicrous. Everybody realized how popular football was becoming, but the New Orleans Saints were a losing team. The only franchise that had never had a winning record. But there wasn't enough time to cover all of the interesting stories about the team—to talk to the players and to those devoted fans who stuck with them despite their losses. I went to the salespeople at the channel and they found a sponsor for our show. Some people thought we were crazy, but they gave me an opportunity to get something started. I labeled the show *4th Down on Four* and it stuck.

It helped that the Saints finally had that winning season. On November 29, 1987, a victory over the Pittsburgh Steelers finally confirmed this as I reported on their history at the start of *4th Down on Four* while highlights and lowlights played on the screen. I talked about Archie Manning, and Dick Nolan, and Bum Phillips, the years of struggle and embarrassment, and ended with: "Then finally a new owner, a new coach, a new attitude. And tonight, one word that describes the New Orleans Saints . . ."

Winners.

The Saints were winners for the first time in twenty-one years. It was definitely great timing for our new show. When *4th Down on Four* started, most of the coverage centered on the Saints and the NFL. Occasionally I reported on college or high school sports, but I wanted to keep most of the focus around the Saints. Over the years the show has evolved into covering more sports. To date it is still on the air.

Whenever I did a program, whether it was reporting sports for the evening news or hosting *4th Down on Four,* I always reviewed the segments afterward to see how I did, a habit I developed in my radio days. I would evaluate my performance and give myself a grade. I was very hard on myself. My team at the local television station in New Orleans always teased me about it.

"Relax, Chris. You got the job."

That didn't stop me. Where were the gaps? Did I have the right inflection in my voice? What were the things I could and couldn't control? If things didn't go as planned, how did I react to them? This was all part of the learning process. And things rarely went as planned. That was one of the first things I discovered in sports broadcasting, something that has followed me to the highest level of sports. Things go wrong—it's all how you respond and handle them on the air. The audience doesn't need to know when things go wrong. Sometimes it's obvious, while other times you might let them know. But it's all part of the job.

Those days of grading myself with a B-minus or a C or a rare A are long gone, but I still always try to evaluate how I've done. Back then I tried to have an honest opinion of myself. Sometimes I was a little rigid as an announcer. Sometimes I wanted to show more of myself and my personality. But the news and the stories were always the thing. It was never about me. You can always add a little flair to the reports; that's why sports was fun. You couldn't throw in jokes when you were reporting news that dealt with tragedies and natural disasters. (Though I never could have imagined back then that one day I would be put in those very situations in my career.)

• • •

TWO YEARS AFTER WALKING OVER THE SACRED GRASS AT AUGUSTA National, I stepped through a sea of wide-brimmed hats and feathers at Churchill Downs. I had come to the Kentucky Derby to cover another unlikely underdog, a horse named Risen Star. His story was classic feel-good Hollywood fare.

Two New Orleanians paid $300,000 for the horse,[2] the son of Secretariat, the legendary Triple Crown champion. Louie Roussel III was a successful horse trainer and a devout man of faith; Ronnie Lamarque owned a local car dealership and loved being in the limelight.

At the start of the Kentucky Derby, Risen Star hung back early to avoid being stampeded by all the horses swinging to the inside. By the far turn, he showed his speed and charged hard down the lane, but he had been too far back and only managed to finish third.

Nearly two weeks later, Risen Star won the Preakness Stakes with a burst of speed, and a Louisiana star was truly born. While I was covering this story, Ronnie Lamarque began to make a name for himself, notably in making up song lyrics about his horse. After his victory in the Preakness, Lamarque changed the lyrics from "When you wish upon a star" to "When you wish for a Risen Star." Another time he entertained a crowd with a song that went, "He's going to win the race, just like his grand ol' dad, who scored by 31 lengths."[3]

The story only became more heartwarming when the local nuns of the Little Sisters of the Poor suddenly came into the picture. Sister Mary Vincent had approached Roussel and asked for a donation for their building fund program. After thinking about it for a week, Roussel told the sister that if she and the sisters prayed for Risen Star to win, he would give them some of the winnings.

At the Belmont Stakes on June 11, 1988, prayers were answered in a mighty way as Risen Star blew past the competition and won by nearly 15 lengths. The horse resembled his father, Secretariat. At the time, Risen Star scored the second-fastest time in the Belmont behind Secretariat's record-breaking pace. It was an incredible comeback.

While reporting on Risen Star, I did a feature on another fascinating story, this one of the human kind. So many years later, it has still stuck with me.

A guy at the Fair Grounds, the local New Orleans horse track, Allen "Black Cat" Lacombe, was a character straight out of a James Cagney gangster movie. He wore a white shirt, black tie, sports jacket, bowler hat, and big plastic-framed glasses. His dress shoes were black and beat-up. Hunched over and at first appearing kind of grumpy, Black Cat was really a friendly guy as you got to know him. He wandered around the racetrack all the time, betting on the horses and talking to everybody. He knew everything about the history of this track and loved to tell stories about racing through the years. Lacombe was someone I leaned on in my reporting on horse racing, whether it put him on camera or not.

Allen Lacombe had been a boxing promoter and at one time ended up teaching a course at Tulane University on handicapping. In 1948 he had run for the state legislature in New Orleans but lost. Twelve years later, he ended up running for governor but lost as well, using the tagline "If it's good enough for you, it's good enough for me."[4]

The story on Black Cat focused on him always being around the Fair Grounds. After the horse races were done and the people had left the track and the horses had gone back to their stables, Lacombe would still be there walking around those empty stands. One evening with the sun starting to fade away, I spotted him walking by himself, looking for white paper cups that he could stomp on and flatten out. I wasn't sure why he was doing this; it looked like a kid having fun and amusing himself. The cups looked like snow in the stands.

I pointed it out to my cameraman. "Can you get a really good shot of that?" I asked.

Lacombe never even knew we were filming him. And that's how we ended the piece. People told us they loved the feature even though Lacombe laughed and wondered what the big deal was. He probably would have laughed, too, if he knew that one day they'd have a race named after him.

"Cat" Lacombe was a real rare bird, the sort of guy you might see in a movie about Secretariat. Or one about his son, Risen Star. He seemed like a symbol of a time and a place gone by. A simple guy who appeared content with where he was in life. Something those of us who are so driven often struggle with.

At the time I couldn't relate to this sort of contentedness. Even though I had gone to a new place and achieved many of those things I had written on my notecards, I still had my eye on a bigger prize. I still had that stack of notecards right beside my bed listing the things I still dreamt of doing.

I loved my time in New Orleans, but deep down I knew I still had other places to go.

THREE

Don't Let Them Rattle You

San Francisco looked like a war zone the night of the 1989 Loma Prieta earthquake. Chris Berman and I rode in a car led by a police escort, making our way through the eerie darkness from Candlestick Park to the Westin St. Francis hotel where the ESPN crew was staying. We stared out at a city in panic and confusion, sirens echoing in the distance as we passed people on the streets looking for direction. The radio played a local news channel giving updates about the number of lives lost, damage inflicted, and road closures.

It was late at night on October 17, 1989, and Chris and I were drained and exhausted, and looking forward to getting back to our rooms, though I wasn't sure our racing minds would allow us to sleep. Game 3 of the World Series between the Oakland Athletics and San Francisco Giants had just begun when the earthquake arrived. Now, hours later, after covering the scene at Candlestick Park live on the air, questions filled our minds. There were the pressing questions about the surrounding Bay Area and the people in it, and the more mundane questions, such as when Game 3 would take place and where it would be held.

When we arrived at the hotel, we entered a lobby lit by candles. People had the antennas on their radios covered with tinfoil for better reception. Since our rooms were on the tenth floor, Chris and I had to carry candles up the stairs to reach our rooms. Walking up ten stories in pitch black was quite the experience. As always, Berman kept the mood light.

"The good news is the toilets will work," he said. "At least for now."

Inside my room, I peered out the window to see the fires in the city below. One solitary inferno blazed in the Marina District by the water. Apart from the flashing lights of police cars, fire trucks, and emergency vehicles, the city was pitch black, the way it might be in a disaster movie. I couldn't turn on the television to hear the update on the size of the earthquake and how many casualties there had been. We had reported that Berkeley scientists were saying it to be a 6.5 to 6.7 at the epicenter, but we didn't know for sure. With no electricity, I was left alone in my room full of questions and concern.

· · ·

THE FIRST EARTHQUAKE I EVER EXPERIENCED CAME A YEAR EARLIER, shortly after I moved from New Orleans to Los Angeles in 1988. I had joined ESPN as their West Coast reporter, and was living in Marina del Rey. I enjoyed being back around a beach; I had missed the ocean and the waters that I had grown up with in Florida. While at home one day, I felt the floor shaking beneath me, then looked up and noticed the pictures on the wall rattling. Items on the shelf were moving. I thought I was dreaming. The earthquake was minor and didn't last long, but the memory stayed with me long after.

The following year, in October 1989, I was covering the World Series in San Francisco. ESPN was there doing pregame and postgame interviews and reports. This was a unique series, dubbed the "Battle of the Bay," because it featured teams from the same metropolitan area. The San Francisco Giants and Oakland Athletics played each other on opposite sides of the San Francisco Bay. The A's were heavy favorites with their star players like Mark McGwire and Jose Canseco and with Tony La Russa managing.

After Oakland won the first two games, Game 3 was to take place on a beautiful warm day at the Giants' Candlestick Park. This was also the home of the 49ers, a worn-down stadium built on the sturdy bedrock of Bayview Hill in a picturesque spot with excellent views of the sunset. With a World Series between two really good teams, not to mention city rivals, the vibe was exciting, especially for me since this was my first official World Series to cover.

Twenty minutes before the game was scheduled to begin, I was in the Candlestick Park auxiliary press box with the two headliners of ESPN, Bob Ley and Chris Berman. If there was ever a Mount Rushmore of ESPN, the first two faces would be these guys. At the time, they were the pillars of the network. Ley was more of the nuts-and-bolts news guy, while Berman was the fun highlights guy. Their different personalities made them a great team. They were good guys, welcoming this young reporter from local TV getting his first chance on the up-and-coming sports network. We had just gotten off the air with *SportsCenter* as coverage of the game shifted to Al Michaels on ABC.

As we sat in the outside booth in the upper level of the park, fired up with the game set to go, a rumble came out of nowhere. It sounded like a small plane crashing into the back of the stadium. For fifteen seconds, the ground shook, and the field appeared to be rolling in waves of green. Ripples went through the stands. Those seconds felt much longer to the thousands of us in the stadium.

Bob Ley looked rattled and asked us if this was "the big one." He would later admit that he was genuinely scared. Ley knew that this was a major story we had to get on. Berman gave more of a "Hey, that was wild" sort of response, laughing and looking more amused than alarmed.

The stadium had been built into bedrock, so the earthquake felt especially powerful. We had heard that Candlestick Park had recently undergone seismic retrofitting, and while that clearly had a positive effect, we still had no idea about the magnitude of the earthquake or if anybody had been injured. For a few moments, the entire crowd appeared stunned, wondering what just happened. There was some nervous hooting and hollering, but when the lights went out and they saw players and field personnel begin to scramble, fans realized something was not right.

Everything for us shifted from viewing the ballgame to getting out of the ballpark. Chris, Bob, and I rushed down to our satellite production trucks parked in the stadium parking lots. The crowd around us had started to exit, but I didn't feel any panic from them. There was a rush of concern to get to the ground. When we reached our trucks, we huddled outside to lay out a reporting game plan once we knew we could broadcast from there. One member of our team was future Baseball Hall of Fame coach Joe Torre, whom ESPN had brought on as a postseason guest analyst while he was between managing jobs. There were lots of questions that needed to be answered.

"Do you want us on the air?"

"What's the size of the earthquake?"

"Is everybody okay at the stadium?"

"Is there any visible damage?"

We had heard that ABC had been knocked off the air, but they got back on and used some of our footage to show viewers what was happening. Since ESPN was the only entity that had a generator, our satellite dishes helped keep ABC's broadcast on the air. We were all trying to get as much information as we could get, but the phone service was in and out and not very reliable.

For the next four hours, ESPN provided live reports from the stadium. We first tried to talk to a couple of players or managers to get their reactions. Right away it was clear the players were scattering to make sure their families were okay. For many of them, the game was now an afterthought. Players helped their wives out of the stands and onto the field, and they held the hands of their startled children. The field soon became occupied by first responders. Meanwhile, fans watched and waited to hear news reports. The ESPN *SportsCenter* remote crew that was there to do pregame and postgame coverage also waited and remained ready to roll if that was a possibility. But with every passing moment and every incoming detail, that possibility seemed doubtful.

The reactions of the players and their families on the field filled me with fear. Even though in the park nothing felt terribly wrong—there was no visible major damage and nobody was hurt—seeing the concern and at times panic on their faces made this very real.

Since ESPN had the only truck parked on that side of the stadium, authorities decided to set up the police compound in our lot. This meant we had direct access to police and to information related to the earthquake. We all knew this had become a much bigger event than just a World Series that we had to stay on top of. This is where your journalism background kicks in: you're there to broadcast the whole story and what's happening in real time.

With footage from the ABC station in the area, we were finally able to see the damage from the earthquake. Bob Ley shared his thoughts with the audience as he saw the devastation on the Bay Bridge firsthand on the monitors.

"And there it is—oh, my Lord," Bob said. "There's a very dramatic picture. And that was at rush hour. And there are no rescue vessels or vehicles in sight. And I don't know how many thousands of vehicles a day travel that bridge."

Since I had gone through an earthquake, Bob brought me on live to discuss that and to share what I was hearing. I was no earthquake expert, but I could describe the differences between the two.

"When you're in a house or an apartment in Los Angeles, it feels—the way to describe it—like you're in a shoebox and someone is shaking it. This was different. We were at the highest section of Candlestick Park, a reserved press section—"

At that point Bob interrupted to say that he'd been told the earthquake was a 6.5.

We saw footage of fires breaking out across the city and I relayed the details I had learned so far, of smoke across the bay, the swaying and rolling of the stadium, and the slow realization among the fans of what was happening.

The magnitude of the Loma Prieta earthquake would ultimately be confirmed to be 6.9. It was the most damaging to hit the city since the notorious 1906 San Francisco earthquake. Along with the collapse of a span of the top deck of the Bay Bridge, the upper deck on the Cypress Freeway also gave way, crushing the vehicles below on the lower level and killing forty-two people. There would be sixty-three deaths in total and at least thirty-seven hundred injured as the area suffered $6 billion in damage.

My wife was among many of those who watched our broadcast. She was at her job when the earthquake happened, so right away she panicked wondering what had happened to me. There had been no way for me to get word to her before we went on the air. When she saw me reporting live on television with Chris Berman, she knew I was okay.

"He looks a little bit rattled," she told her coworkers. "His hair is messed up, but I think he's okay."

We shared every piece of information we received from the authorities in terms of damage done and loss of life or injury. Once we knew everybody was okay in the park, we all wondered when the game would continue. Was it going to be safe enough to play in this stadium again? Our cameras showed whatever examples they could, like the back part of Candlestick Park where you could see a concrete structure had come apart. People were out by then as we spoke about the potential risks that had thankfully been avoided. One particular seat a camera zoomed in on had been split right down the center.

Our focus went on the players and coaches from the two teams. How were they doing? How were their families? What were the guidelines if they didn't play? Would this be a draw? How were they handling the situation? What was going through their minds? Sports wasn't the most important thing in the big picture, yet since we were an all-sports channel covering the World Series, we would provide those answers for our viewers, too. This meant moving through the crowd trying to find members of the Giants and A's teams to interview.

I saw Tony La Russa by the team buses guiding his wife and daughter through the crowd, looks of concern on all of their faces. As they stopped and the A's manager scanned the crowd looking for others, I asked him a question.

"One second—let me make sure my family's safe," he told me as he walked by to find someone else.

Mark McGwire stopped to give me a few thoughts.

"When you're out in the open, it doesn't feel like it's that bad. I didn't think it was that bad. But it turns out to be a devastating earthquake."

He appeared to get teary-eyed as he spoke.

"The concern's now for all the people on the bridge," McGwire said. "You know—who knows?"

Before leaving the stadium, Tony La Russa came back around so I could interview him. He summed up the situation to me.

"This is a game," La Russa told me. "You have two teams trying to win a game and be a champion. It doesn't compare to life."

• • •

TONY LA RUSSA WAS RIGHT. AT THE MOMENT, WHILE THE WORLD watched to see what was happening in San Francisco, this wasn't a game anymore. People's lives were being affected, so the reporter inside of me felt obligated to continue to get facts and details to everybody. None of us inside the stadium knew if relatives and friends at home were impacted. This is when the human element came into play.

Just like I had been doing since I first interviewed Muhammad Ali, I approached each interview from the standpoint that this was a human being who was experiencing some type of emotion at the moment. It might be winning or losing a big game, and it might be looking ahead or reflecting back on a career. But this was something new. This was dealing with raw emotions during a frightening time. I had enough experience by then to know that I was still doing a job, so I needed to get this story out to people. Stay cool and calm so I could keep reporting. As a journalist, you have to control your emotions in the moment so you can process what's happening and tell other people about it.

It's a trait I first noticed in myself in fourth grade. My mom and I had gone to the store one day, and as we were getting out of our car, I heard a guy close by yelling and cursing. I looked around and spotted a muscular guy in a tank top yelling at an older woman. The man was in his twenties and appeared to be screaming at the lady for taking his parking spot. Another man who looked to be in his sixties or seventies rushed onto the scene and began to tell the young man to ease up and stop yelling.

"It's only a parking spot," the older man said.

The younger man suddenly hauled off and punched the older gentlemen in the face, sending him to the ground. It was jolting to see up close.

Seemingly pleased with what he did, the younger guy walked off to his car and climbed in without appearing to be in a rush to leave.

"Mom—we have to do something," I said. "We have to tell somebody."

I suggested that we write down the attacker's license plate number We found a pen and something to write on, and before he drove off, I jotted down the plate number. Later, when we got home, my mom called up the police to report the incident. It turned out that the man who got slugged was a retired FBI agent, and he decided to press charges against his assailant. The punch had broken his jaw. After the attacker was found and arrested, I was notified to come to court to testify against him. For a fourth grader, this was a big deal.

After I told my classmates about everything, I became a big shot at school. Forget sports—I was going to court to testify. Everything about the experience felt surreal, yet I remained calm throughout. I didn't refuse to enter the courthouse, nor did I begin to shake as I walked into the courtroom. I was a bit nervous as they swore me in, though. The judge looked out for me before anybody asked me questions.

"Don't let them rattle you, kid," he said.

On the stand in the hot seat, I recounted what happened in a steady manner. That was why I was there. I knew my job that day: to report on the incident. There was an argument, the older guy walked up to try to help out the woman, and the younger guy knocked him down. When the defense attorney began to interrogate me, he got a little tough. He asked where I was standing the moment the older guy got hit. Where was the younger man's arm? Were they arguing? Did the older man strike out first? I answered every question with no problem.

Mom was proud of me not only for taking the initiative to write down the plate number but also for being a great witness. The attacker got off relatively lightly since he lied and said that the retired FBI agent had supposedly reached for a gun and that's why he punched him. It was disheartening to see the verdict, but at the same time it was exciting to have been part of the judicial process.

After the case was over, the FBI agent came over to our house and gave me a book that he signed to me. It was a history of the FBI that featured some really cool pictures. At least it was cool for a fourth grader.

"Hey, Chris. If you ever think about getting involved in law enforcement or anything like that, we'd love to have you, kid."

When I look back at it now, I wasn't doing it for recognition, but to do *something*. I didn't think about myself in the situation. I wasn't thinking about my safety or my ego. All I was thinking was that I had a job to do in that moment, so I did it.

That same mentality remained with me during a situation like the San Francisco earthquake. It would also be there in future moments when sports became the backdrop for something much bigger.

• • •

THE MORNING AFTER THE EARTHQUAKE, AS A SMOLDERING CITY awoke amidst rubble and carnage, baseball commissioner Fay Vincent gave a press conference at the Westin St. Francis hotel. It was a surreal atmosphere as candles were brought in for the event. All of us had been up most of the night without electricity. With a glowing candelabra on a table nearby, Vincent gave an announcement that didn't surprise anybody.

"We've made the decision not to play tonight. That's the only decision we made."

Commissioner Vincent put things in the proper perspective.

"It's a difficult time for San Francisco and indeed for the whole Bay Area," he said. "And the great tragedy is that it coincides with our modest little sporting event here."

Reports stated that there were no injuries to players or their immediate families, and there wasn't significant damage to either baseball stadium. Vincent did not speculate on where the games might be held next and said the priority would be to play them in the Bay Area, but only after consideration of the mood of the community. He didn't want to take police and other government officials from other duties that were a higher priority than a baseball game.

For the entire week after the Loma Prieta earthquake, I stayed in San Francisco to provide ESPN with daily reports on if and when the series would continue, how the teams were coping, and on the recovery of the city. Baseball commissioner Fay Vincent was very helpful. I respected his process on deciding when to call off the game. He had taken a slow and steady approach of wanting to know all the facts before making a decision. Some people instantly wanted to cancel the series, but Vincent knew what the World Series meant not only to baseball fans but also to these cities. They weren't going to rush the decision, but they also weren't going to drag things out. Game 3 was eventually played on October 27, ten days after the earthquake. In the end, the Oakland A's swept the San Francisco Giants in four games to win the World Series.

There was no traditional ticker-tape parade held for the A's out of respect for what had happened. A's pitcher Dave Stewart, the World Series MVP with two wins, summed up the feeling about not holding the celebration. "In respect to the lives that were taken, the destruction that had happened, all of the craziness and disarray and the rebuilding of the area, I felt that was the right thing to do to not have a parade and to not have a championship celebration. We got the trophy."[1]

FOUR

Life and Death

"A life is not important except in the impact it has on other lives."[1]

One of Jackie Robinson's greatest quotes is etched onto his headstone. It's a reminder that every professional and prominent athlete is more than just a competitor. They are more than their victories and numbers and accolades. A life well lived is one that serves and helps others.

In the summer of 1989, ESPN assigned me to cover the All-Star game in Anaheim. On the way to the game, our boss, John Walsh, who'd joined ESPN a year before I did, alerted me to some interesting information on one of the players.

Tim Burke, the Expos pitcher who was scheduled to pitch in the All-Star game, had recently received approval to adopt a child. Burke was Montreal's top relief pitcher in a year when the Expos were in a pennant race and contending for a playoff spot. He and his wife, Christine, had been married for seven years. Two years into their marriage, tests revealed that Tim couldn't father any children.[2] After adopting a Korean girl they named Stephanie in 1987, the Burkes decided to adopt another child. This one was a boy from Guatemala.

When I spoke to Tim, he said that he was planning to leave that night on a late flight out of Los Angeles in order to get to the adoption center in Guatemala to sign the necessary papers. After I mentioned this to John, he suggested I tag along with Tim to report on the trip. All I had to do was ask the pitcher. I didn't want to intrude on something so personal, but it was a great story on many levels, and it was entirely his call.

"I hate to be rude, but would you mind if I came along to report on this?" I asked Tim.

He told me that was fine. "But I'm not sure how this is all going to turn out."

The Burkes had found the child after looking through a book from Holt International Children's Services. He was a boy named Juan Jose who had been abandoned at birth and suffered from hypothyroidism, a condition that hindered his growth. Four days before the Burkes were planning to go to Central America, they discovered that Tim had made the All-Star team. No longer having a few days off for the All-Star break, Burke felt torn. Christine told her husband he needed to go, that it was a once-in-a-lifetime opportunity.[3] And they would figure out a way to do both things.

For the first time in his five-year major league career, Tim Burke pitched in the All-Star game on July 11. He threw two scoreless innings. He made it clear that if the game went into extra innings he would have to bow out in order to make his midnight flight to Guatemala.

We assembled a crew to travel with Burke: myself, along with our cameraman, Rick Tullis, and our producer, John Hamlin. We didn't know what to expect, but we planned to document each step Burke made along the way. It was wild to see him pitching and then leaving the All-Star game while it was still being played.

"There is such excitement just being a part of an All-Star game," Tim told us. "But come midnight tonight, I'll be on a flight going down to Guatemala to see a son that I've never seen before."

We took an old Pan Am jet to Guatemala City. The airport was not that big at the time, so it resembled a scene out of *Raiders of the Lost Ark* with its weeds and cracks covering the runway. A blast of thick heat greeted us. Our team ended up being detained at customs since we had left so quickly that we hadn't gotten the proper clearance to haul our equipment into the country. Someone eventually arrived at the airport and explained why we were there, so they let us through.

We filmed Burke right before he left for the orphanage. I asked him if he was feeling anxious or nervous.

"Yeah, I'm nervous," he said. "Scared. Not knowing what to expect. Kind of the fear of the unknown. But I'm ready to go see our son. And it's going to take a little while, I'm sure, for him to warm up to it."

His wife, Christine, had arrived two days earlier, so she had taken care of all the necessary paperwork to pick up their son. Tim carried with him a photograph of the boy.

As we drove through small villages surrounded by jungle, we noticed lizards and large iguanas in plain sight. I wondered if our vehicles were going to give out in the middle of the wilderness. There wasn't much to eat and I was starving, so I kept an eye out for a McDonald's or anything familiar. Someone offered us iguana with peanut butter, but I decided to pass. The closer we came to the orphanage, the louder the animals seemed to sound in the jungle.

We caught the emotional moment when the Burkes first saw their child and held him. I couldn't help tearing up watching this new family forming right before my eyes. Susan and I weren't parents just yet, but we had talked about having children in the future. Both of us wanted to be more settled since we were both working and I was traveling quite a bit. But we knew the importance of family, especially since we both came from sizable ones, me from a family of five kids and Susan from a family of ten children.

Watching the Burkes leave the orphanage with their son is an image I will never forget.

"When I got to the orphanage, we were still on—we were kind of still on his territory and he was still attached to the workers there," Burke told us. "And instantly when we left and it was just us, I started feeling that, that fatherly feeling, and I really got choked up."

They named their son Ryan Walter after Tim's good friend who played for the Montreal Canadiens. For the rest of the day, the Burkes toured Guatemala with Ryan, feeling it was important to get to know the country that their son had been born in. Underneath a blue sky in a foreign land, Tim summed up how surreal all of this felt.

"I was just thinking—I mean, I'm in Anaheim Stadium in the middle of an All-Star game less than twenty-four hours ago. And here I am in the middle of Central America. It doesn't make sense."

It didn't make sense to us either. We knew you couldn't make this stuff up.

The following morning, the happy trio boarded a plane bound for the States. Family was Tim's first priority, clearly, but it was also critical for him to get back home so he could be there for the Expos' next game. They arrived on Thursday evening, just in time for Burke to be rushed to the ballpark for a game. He wasn't simply tired; he felt numb from the trip. Yet the first-place Montreal Expos were playing the Cincinnati Reds at their Riverfront Stadium, so he needed to get back to work. He arrived at the game to be congratulated by his teammates.

For a while, the Expos trailed the Reds 3–0, but the Expos rallied for a 6–3 lead heading into the ninth inning. That's when Expos manager Buck

Rogers called on his best closer to finish the game. Sure enough, Burke got the first two batters out and struck out the final batter to end the game.

An emotional and elated Burke gave us his feelings afterward.

"Unbelievable," the exhausted pitcher said. "I don't even have words to describe this with all the things that have been going on this last week. I've been on the go nonstop. Just amazing emotion."

It was an incredible way to complete the day. In the piece we quickly put together and aired on ESPN a few days later, I tried to capture the poignancy of it all.

"Still an All-Star pitcher and husband but now a father with a son, Burke notched another save on this date to help his team stay on top in the pennant race. But there's no doubt, his best outing came a day earlier in Guatemala. Chris Myers, ESPN."

The Tim Burke piece not only moved hearts with its emotional storyline, but also ended up winning ESPN their first reporting and *SportsCenter* Emmy award. I never could have imagined that only nine months later, I would be reporting about another moment bigger than sports. This one, however, was the opposite of the Burke story. This one dealt with sorrow and grief.

· · ·

ON MARCH 4, 1990, MY WIFE, SUSAN, AND I WERE IN A THEATER WATCHing Tom Cruise in *Born on the Fourth of July* when my pager went off. We were on a double date with Susan's sister and her boyfriend. This was 1990, so the only way to reach me was through my pager. Right away I knew this was work-related, so I left my seat to call the ESPN assignment desk. Mike Matters, a coordinating producer, filled me in on the news.

"Hank Gathers just collapsed on the court during the tournament," Mike told me. "We don't know for sure, but this may be life-threatening and we want to try to go live, so we're sending a crew over to the hospital he was brought to. Can you run over to meet them? We'll have a satellite set up."

For a moment I stood there with the pay phone pressed against my ear, stunned. Hank Gathers was the best college basketball player in the country. A senior at Loyola Marymount University, he led the nation in both scoring and rebounding during his junior year. He was projected to be the number one draft pick for the NBA. The Loyola Marymount Lions were playing a West Coast Conference tournament game at their home court, so Gathers had been rushed to nearby Daniel Freeman Marina Hospital in Marina del Rey.

I hadn't been around Gathers that much since we didn't cover a lot of college basketball, but I knew he was the headline star player for the underdog Lions. Coach Paul Westhead had come up with a creative run-and-gun, back-and-forth style of play where players were constantly firing off shots and going for rebounds and then getting back on defense. Gathers had taken the college basketball world by storm as the rising star for the Lions. Not only was he very talented and popular, but I knew he had a future in communications. He had interned at one of the local Los Angeles stations, so he was already looking ahead and working to develop other talents.

Mike gave me the details he had on the situation. After dunking the ball, Gathers collapsed around midcourt with 13:34 left in the first half. He tried to get up, but dropped again and briefly went into convulsions before losing consciousness. A few minutes later he was lifted onto a stretcher and brought out of the silent arena.

Three months earlier during a December 9 game, Gathers had fainted on the court and afterward was diagnosed with an abnormal heartbeat. He ended up missing several games while tests were done on him. He had been cleared to play and all signs showed that he was fine and healthy.

As fate had it, my sister-in-law's date was studying to be a brain surgeon, so I asked him if he could drive me to the hospital so I could ask him some medical questions on the way. There was no time for me to go home and change clothes for the interview; the family would be at the Daniel Freeman Marina Hospital, so I had to get there as quickly as possible. During the car ride, I asked the future brain surgeon basic questions that would help me in any interviews I would do: background on heart rates and preexisting conditions and how a healthy young man only twenty-three years old could just collapse like this. Was this a seizure? That's what we all thought at first, but none of us knew.

When we arrived at the hospital, I ran into the Associated Press writer Joe Resnick, whom I'd met covering other stories. Resnick was a seasoned, well-respected reporter who was always prepared and showed up at every major L.A. sports event. He was friendly and thorough and one of the best in the business. I asked Resnick if I could borrow his suit jacket for a moment, explaining that I was about to go on live in about ten minutes. Thankfully, he took it off and let me use it for my report.

On camera, I explained what was happening around me and who was there, including family members and Coach Westhead. Back in the ESPN studio, Chris Fowler and Chris Berman talked about Gathers's career, all of us still waiting on any word. When the doctor and the family came back out to address the media, we could all tell what had happened by the shocked looks on their faces. Gathers was pronounced dead at Daniel Freeman at 6:55 p.m.

One moment I was in the midst of grieving family members and teammates who had just been told the news, and the next I was going live on ESPN in front of the hospital to share everything we knew and to ask the doctors the questions on everybody's mind. I needed to be sensitive—we weren't trying to blame anybody, and obviously time would sort out the details.

I first interviewed the athletic director of Loyola Marymount, Mr. Brian Quinn. I said, "The question that most will ask is, should Hank

Gathers have been playing basketball after that initial heart ailment in December, or that fainting spell?"

"A complete medical clearance was granted for him to participate in all athletic endeavors, so the answer certainly would be yes," Quinn said in a slow and somber tone. We would find out later that after missing two games, Gathers had been put on medication by cardiologist Vernon Hattori and cleared to play.

"The feelings right now with the family, with Paul Westhead—can you describe them?" I asked.

"Well, they're distraught, deeply saddened, as you would expect," Brian Quinn said. "Of course, the circumstances are very difficult to describe the pain they're feeling. But, you know, the family's together and I think they're a close family."

I then shifted the interview to Dr. Mason Weiss, a cardiologist. I wasn't putting him on trial but rather asking the questions that needed to be asked. That's what people wanted to hear. They all knew about the heart ailment that had been discovered earlier. So why he was playing now? Was this the correct move? Was he on medication, and could the medication have contributed to his death?

Many of my questions were ones that Dr. Weiss couldn't answer since he didn't have all the details, but he was thorough in describing Gathers's medical condition while not speculating about anything more. My curious nature came into play again, wanting to know more about the process for viewers at home to hear.

"Can you in simple terms again, Doctor, describe when he was pronounced dead, exactly what took place for the layman out there who doesn't understand the heart and all the intricacies of how it works?"

"I think basically he collapsed at the game," Dr. Weiss said, going into detail about what happened with Gathers, how his breathing deteriorated and how they found no vitals compatible with life. "From that point onward, full resuscitative measures were undertaken on the court, in the ambulance, in the emergency room by the initial emergency room physician and subsequently myself. All told probably an hour and a half of all resuscitative measures without any evidence documented of any cardiac rhythm or blood pressure or anything else. Even under those prolonged circumstances, there's still a chance that he could come back. And that's why things were continued for that duration of time. But unfortunately, all to no avail."

In the days that followed, the Loyola Marymount campus had a dark cloud hanging over it. I remained at the college to report on this tragedy.

"Basketball was good to Hank Gathers; life was unfair," I said in my piece on *SportsCenter*. "The day after his tragic death, the court was empty. The campus saddened. The flag at half-mast. Loyola's alumni gym looked more like a chapel."

The president of LMU, Father James Loughran, summed up the situation. "This is a great tragedy. There's no explanation for it that I know of. Our whole campus is grieving."

The teammates who played with Gathers and witnessed his greatness now struggled with the reality of losing their leader.

"Before the game, in the locker room, Hank said, 'I feel as strong as ever,'" Jeff Fryer, an LMU guard, said. "We just don't understand how a man that strong could leave us so quickly."

Coach Westhead shared this about Gathers: "He was our guide, as a player and as a person. He was the leader of our team. He was the fiber of what we are."

The Tuesday after Gathers's death, a memorial mass was held for all to mourn his passing. In the nearly forty-eight hours that had passed, the deep-felt sorrow for Gathers remained unchanged. The university suspended all classes Tuesday, and the memorial service was moved from the school's chapel to Gersten Pavilion to accommodate the thousands who came to pay their respects. People lined Loyola Boulevard. On the same floor where he took his last breath, a multitude gathered for the mass in his honor. It was eerie to see a gym overflowing with students and faculty remain so silent. Music played and tears flowed as his casket was carried in by his teammates.

Sitting in the audience, I tried to take it all in so I could report on this. But for the moment, I wasn't focused on an athlete or a sport. I was overtaken with grief by the loss of a young, strong man who died so suddenly. Everyone, including myself, had trouble fighting back the tears. This tragedy shook us, reminding us of our own mortality. As a thirty-year-old, I had thoughts I'd never contemplated before.

Young people aren't supposed to die. It's unfair.

The truth is that it happens on a regular basis, but until it affects you or hits close to home, it's easy not to think about mortality at such a young age. There are no rules there; it can happen at any age to anybody, and that's a depressing and scary thought. We all know we're going to go at some point, but for a kid in college?

Who knows where his life would have taken him?

In his message at the service, Reverend Thomas Higgins said that Gathers was an impact player, someone who impacted not only the court but also the university, the city, and the country.

"Maybe God needed a power forward in heaven," Reverend Higgins said.

Coach Westhead reminded us why we had come to know and love this young man: "Hank represents the little kid in all of us because to Hank Gathers, basketball was play, and we all want to play."

Covering this heartwrenching story was very emotional. It made me think about what it would be like to lose one of my brothers. At the time, Susan and I didn't have children yet, and the only loss I had experienced in my life so far was my mother passing away from cancer at an early age. It made me grateful for the life I'd been given, and for each day that comes.

Meanwhile, Coach Westhead said that Loyola would continue in the NCAA tournament, that Gathers would have wanted it that way. Amazingly, the LMU Lions went on quite a run, playing games in honor of their fallen teammate and being the first team in their league to reach the Elite Eight since San Francisco in 1957. Each victory was both heartwrenching and emotional. They eventually lost to UNLV, but not before inspiring a country rooting for them.

• • •

THE HISTORY OF SPORTS IS FULL OF MANY CLASSIC "WHAT-IFS."

What if the Red Sox had never sold Babe Ruth to the Yankees?

What if Drew Bledsoe had never been injured?

What if Michael Jordan had continued to play baseball?

What if Wayne Gretzky wasn't traded?

Among those imagined scenarios comes one often asked:

What if Hank Gathers never died?

For the short time Gathers had, he made an impression on those around him and those watching him, one that's still felt today. I can't help but think of a statement that Kobe Bryant made in 2017.

"You are responsible for how people remember you," Kobe said. "If you do it right, your game will live on in others . . . So leave everything on the court. Leave the game better than you found it. And when it comes time for you to leave, leave a legend."[4]

FIVE

Licensed to Kill Gophers

Laughter is the shortest distance between two people."[1] This quote from Victor Borge, the old-school comedian my dad was a fan of, has helped me live my life and do my job. It's also probably one of the reasons why I'm friends with Bill Murray. Along with our love for sports, we share a love for comedy. Our unlikely friendship began back in those early days at ESPN.

In 1994, the network hosted its second ESPY Awards at Madison Square Garden. ESPY is short for Excellence in Sports Performance Yearly, and one of the presenters and performers who planned to be on the cable network show was Bill Murray. By this time, Bill was already an iconic figure. The forty-three-year-old had starred on *Saturday Night Live* from 1977 to 1980 during the show's earliest seasons, doing sketches alongside Chevy Chase, Gilda Radner, John Belushi, and Dan Aykroyd.

His movies—some of the most quoted films of all time—were classics like *Stripes, Ghostbusters, Caddyshack, What About Bob?,* and *Groundhog Day*. The characters he played all had his unique take on them, whether they were an obsessive-compulsive neurotic or a narcissistic, self-centered weatherman.

John Walsh, the managing editor at ESPN who had told me to get on a plane to get Tim Burke's story, had once worked at *Rolling Stone* magazine and made a connection with Bill back in the day. He helped get the actor to tape a special segment for ESPN, and he wanted Dan Patrick and me to be a part of the sketch. It made perfect sense since the ESPY Awards weren't just a sporting event but a show that featured comedians and celebrity entertainers.

Dan and I took a car to New York City where we met with a roomful of writers working on the ESPYs show. Bill planned to join all of us. The comedy writers were a talented group, some of whom wrote for *Saturday Night Live* and late-night talk shows. But when the always-unpredictable Bill arrived, he had other plans.

"We really don't need you guys for this," Bill told the writers. "Chris and Dan write their own stuff for *SportsCenter*. I'll talk to them about the sports world and we'll come up with something funny."

The writers were understandably a little miffed. They had already written material for other parts of the show, but Bill didn't need their creative input. He had watched us enough to know what he was working with. He began riffing on the *SportsCenter* theme song, then rattled off sports facts and funny lines. He improvised by using one of his favorite catchphrases, which I had come up with:

"You, you're not good," he said.

At the time, I thought, *Bill Murray is quoting me?* He obviously watched and enjoyed *SportsCenter,* so it was a nice compliment. Even though a whole roomful of writers were disappointed not to be working with Bill, Dan and I were thrilled to be able to come up with some fun ideas for the ESPY Awards. The final piece had echoes of Bill's "Nick the Lounge Singer" character from *SNL,* where he sang and spoke to the *SportsCenter* theme song.

After the ESPY Awards, I ended up hanging out with Bill. He told me some of his brothers were in town and asked me to join them for a drink. Right away it felt like I was at home. Bill grew up in a Chicago suburb with eight siblings, so as someone with two brothers and two sisters, I felt that family connection with him. That night I met Brian Doyle-Murray, Bill's older brother, as well as younger brothers Joel and John Murray. They all felt like a bunch of sports fans in a showbiz family. Bill was the big star, Brian had written *Caddyshack* and was a busy actor in many films and sitcoms, including several with his brother, and Joel and John were both actors as well. This was the start of a friendship with Bill and his brothers. Before leaving, Bill said, "Hey—when I'm in New York, let's go to a game sometime."

Bill loves his sports, especially baseball. Before ever taking on a leading role in a film, he participated in a fun marketing stunt during the summer of 1978. When *Saturday Night Live* cast members were asked about something they had always wanted to do, Bill mentioned that it was playing professional baseball. So for one day, he joined the independent Grays Harbor Loggers team representing Aberdeen and Hoquiam, Washington.[2] He played in one game where he brought in a couple of runs and went 1 for 2 with a single.

In the *SNL* segment titled "What I Did Last Summer," Murray played himself as a comedian who decides to quit comedy.

"What the heck—I'm not going to give up until I drink from the silver cup," Murray says in a dramatic tone for the piece. "And for me, that means going out and playing ball."[3]

During an interview, Bill once told me that if he could have been any type of professional athlete, it without question would have been a baseball player, despite how much he has played and promoted golf over the years.

"Baseball's just—those guys are having much more fun than golfers," Bill told me. "Golfers aren't. They're all kind of—they're mental."

Over the years, Bill and I have had a lot of fun, whether it's been in a ballpark or on a golf course or simply hanging out. Befriending Bill was one of the many highlights of my time after I made the big decision in 1991 to move from L.A. to Connecticut, where ESPN's home office is located. I always say these were the golden years of ESPN, when the cable network took over and changed sports viewing. During those days in the '90s, there was no other way to get all the sports highlights on television. Before this there were newspapers and radio, but never twenty-four-hour coverage. ESPN was like CNN when they first cornered the twenty-four-hour TV news market.

Moving to the home offices of ESPN was a great choice for my career. But for a while after moving to Connecticut, I did question the decision, especially during those first two particularly brutal winters there.

• • •

ONE MORNING IN THE DEAD OF WINTER AFTER A SNOWSTORM, I SAT IN my iced-over green Ford Mustang convertible, shivering as I gave it gas but remained stuck in half a foot of snow. The tires spun trying to get up the long driveway that wound up from our house.

When we first saw this three-bedroom house the previous summer, Susan and I had fallen in love with it. It was located in Canton, a suburb not too far from the home office in Bristol. The house sat on a couple of acres of land and it felt like we were in the country. Trees surrounded us and the driveway was winding and private. In the summertime, our surroundings were picturesque. In the winter, however, I felt like we had moved to the North Pole or Alaska.

What am I doing here?

ESPN had first invited me to come out the previous summer to fill in at the *SportsCenter* desk for a week. I enjoyed my time there, and soon they offered me the job. That meant we would have to move. This was where the action was, and the best way to grow in the company. It was another huge opportunity that I knew I needed to take. At the time, I could see myself having a thirty-year career at ESPN. But it meant moving from the warm weather of California to what felt like the middle of nowhere outside Hartford, Connecticut.

"New York or Boston aren't far away," they told me.

The truth was, those big cities were long drives away, especially if you weren't from around there. Still, we lived only fifteen minutes away from the offices, which was a lot better than Los Angeles, where I'd spend hours in my car. The commute was a lot shorter. Except, of course, when I got snowed in.

Our first two winters in Connecticut were two of the harshest ones they had endured for quite a while. Before we came, people told me that there were four seasons, but soon I felt like there were only two up here: one season where there's snow, and another where there's no snow. Sure, trees looked pretty covered in white, and the Christmas sleigh rides were fun, and the driveway was exciting for the kids to sled down as they got older, but I had grown up in Florida. From there I had lived in New Orleans and California. Now I was questioning whether this was the right move for my sanity.

The sun had to come out sometime. My sun lamp just wasn't cutting it.

For example, the first Halloween we were there, I carved a pumpkin for the neighborhood kids, and I threw it out in the woods after the holiday. It turned out that the pumpkin didn't thaw out until July! Some days when it snowed I decided to wait to get our mail since I needed a dogsled to get up to the mailbox, but that meant it would be a week before I got the mail.

Something else nobody ever told me about: black ice. My ESPN colleagues liked to joke with me about the icy morning I arrived at work when the parking lot was iced over. I slid in with my convertible Mustang (which I should've left in California). As they all watched in the glass studio above me, I climbed out of my car and tried to walk, but I kept slipping on the black ice. I clung to nearby cars and carefully inched my way across the lot until I got inside the building.

Eventually I had to wave the white flag and trade in the Mustang for a four-wheel-drive Bronco.

Winter weather aside, I had joined a fun group and a cool work environment. Cohosts Chris Berman and Dan Patrick helped break me in on the desk at Bristol, and later I would help break in Mike Tirico and Linda Cohn, among others. Mike and I became the staples of the 2:00 a.m. EST *SportsCenter,* a show that would start to rerun every morning at 7:00 a.m. EST on a loop. This decision helped grow our audience.

ESPN in the '90s was like MTV in the '80s. When MTV came out, there was this newness to music videos. It was the place to go to watch them, and it didn't have any kind of competition. That's how ESPN was. You only had your local news. If you wanted highlights of other sporting events or expanded coverage, this was the one and only place to go. Yes, we took it seriously and approached it with the same sort of journalistic approach that bureaus and news outlets used, but it was also fun.

That's why I had gotten into broadcasting in the first place. Because my biggest heroes made it look like fun.

• • •

I HAVE ALWAYS LOVED COMEDIANS, FROM GEORGE CARLIN OR DON Rickles when I was younger to Chris Rock and Jerry Seinfeld. I especially love the ones who do impressions. That was one of the things I loved to do for my relatives when we all got together. At a talent night in our high school, I performed three different impressions as a newscaster. For the weatherman, I was Ted Knight's character on *The Mary Tyler Moore Show,* Ted Baxter, the smug buffoon. Jimmy Stewart did the sports and John Wayne gave the news. I even changed my outfits for each. For another bit, I performed the Abbott and Costello "Who's on First?" routine with a friend of mine who later became a sergeant in the police department. It was so much fun to do things like this, and it really helped me both in handling live situations and working with people.

When I lived in Florida, I performed some stand-up comedy in Fort Lauderdale at some local clubs, and after I moved to New Orleans, I worked at some comedy clubs once in a while when I had weekends off. My humor consisted of sports and growing up in a mixed neighborhood. I knew that being a comedian wasn't the life for me, but I still loved and always appreciated the art of making others laugh. And it gave me some experience dealing with hecklers, which can't hurt.

Growing up, I was a Johnny Carson fanatic. By the time I was in middle school, my parents would let me stay up late to watch *The Tonight Show Starring Johnny Carson*. And not just his opening monologue, but the interviews he did during the rest of the show. They knew I was fascinated to see Carson talking with the stars of the day and asking them personal questions. Whether he was interviewing a superstar like Frank Sinatra or a comedian like Don Rickles or a ten-year-old kid from Iowa, Carson had this remarkable way of making the person feel comfortable. The interviews never felt like interviews; they were conversations. This show wasn't a Q&A session, and it wasn't *60 Minutes*. Carson's conversations were exactly what I longed to do when I grew up.

I loved repeating parts of Johnny's opening monologue whenever we had family gatherings with cousins and other relatives. We'd be at dinner, and during a quiet moment I would rattle off something I saw on *The Tonight Show*.

"In downtown Miami it's so hot," I said, quoting one of Carson's most famous bits.

I can imagine some of my family thinking, *Why is this kid talking about the weather?* But someone always obliged me.

"All right. So how hot is it, Chris?"

"It's so hot that I saw a fire hydrant flagging down a dog."

Maybe this was me trying to fit in with the adults, or maybe it was my love of Johnny's corny sense of humor. I enjoyed his demeanor and the way he delivered his punch lines. I was fascinated with how he always spoke about life in Los Angeles—about the weather and the freeways and Malibu. This was the place I dreamt of moving to.

Carson's influence could be seen in the early '90s on ESPN. While doing the 2:00 a.m. Eastern/11:00 p.m. Pacific *SportsCenter* with Mike Tirico, we sometimes had a minute or two left to fill out the end of the show, so Tirico always had a sports fact ready to throw out to the audience.

"So, Chris, did you know that in fourteen years of playing in the NBA, Wilt Chamberlain never fouled out of a game?" Tirico asked.

I reacted by saying what came naturally to me.

"I did not know that."

For those of you who watched *The Tonight Show* on a regular basis, you'll recognize this as one of Carson's most famous catchphrases. I just said it without thinking, and at the time I didn't realize I was saying it in the way the comedian might. But after we did it a few times, our producer suggested that we repeat this segment every night.

"What do you think about calling the bit 'I Did Not Know That'?" our producer suggested.

"We can't do that," I said. "That's Johnny Carson's line."

"Okay, so how about we call it 'Did You Know?'"

That's what the segment became. And ESPN liked it enough to make it into a regular segment that was branded and sponsored.

A few years after we started the "Did You Know?" segment, I was living in Los Angeles while doing *Up Close* and was attending the Mercedes-Benz Cup held at the Los Angeles Tennis Center located on the UCLA campus. I wasn't working at the time but attending as a fan. Since I had my press pass, I was in a private area off to the side of the court, and I spotted Johnny Carson sitting there. He was a huge tennis fan, so it wasn't unusual to see him at the Cup.

I'm not often starstruck, but this was definitely one of those times. My idol was sitting thirty feet away from me. And even though I knew he was famous for his privacy, I couldn't let this opportunity go. If I didn't go over there and talk to him—at least try to talk to him—I'd regret it the rest of my life.

There was a chance that Carson might think I was being rude if I approached him, so I waited for a good moment. I wanted to make sure it wasn't between any significant game, or that he wasn't in the middle of a conversation or munching on something to eat. It turned out I watched Carson the entire time instead of the match. When there was finally a break in the action and Carson was just sitting there, I glided over toward him as if I had some purpose to be there. Of course, my purpose was to meet Carson. So I walked up and greeted him.

"Excuse me, Mr. Carson. I'm Chris Myers."

I explained who I was and he nodded.

"I know who you are," Carson said.

I did my best not to gush about how much I respected him and how much I enjoyed his work, but I had to admit I was a big fan.

"I just wanted you to know a fun fact," I mentioned to him. "Not sure if you watch *SportsCenter* or not, but there's a segment we do called 'Did You Know?' It actually came from me watching you when I was younger. I always told myself that if I ever had the chance, I'd tell you."

Carson paused for a moment.

"I did not know that," he said.

Without another word, he walked away.

• • •

THERE WERE LOTS OF CATCHPHRASES THAT WE CAME UP WITH ON THE show. Many times they were simply generated from us sitting around watching games, looking at highlights, waiting to go live on *SportsCenter*. We'd see these big moments in games and say, "Wow, what a catch," or something similar, and then one day I said on the air, "That deserves a wow." Realizing that you could use "wow" in many ways to describe something, I continued using that phrase and it caught on. There were other catchphrases that were attached to me as well.

"I kid because I care" was basically my way to get away with teasing somebody. A lot of old-school comedians would say, "We kid, we love," so that was my take on that. Then there was "You, you're not good," the line that Bill Murray loved and used in our segment for the ESPY Awards. This came from the same sort of humor that made *Caddyshack* so beloved. There's a scene when Chevy Chase's character tells Ted Knight's character in a deadpan delivery, "You're a tremendous slouch." This was my version, my way of adding some levity to the highlights. It was trendy until some players (Jose Canseco among them) became a little irritated by it. "You're saying I'm no good?" they asked me. I decided to dial it back.

Some phrases came out naturally while doing the highlights commentary. I searched for words to describe things in a different way, to mix it up a little. "A hoop and some harm" was the opposite of saying "no harm, no foul." Then there was the three-point shot. People called it a three-pointer or a trey. While broadcasting Larry Bird highlights on *SportsCenter*, I was describing him hitting shots from all over the court—first the corner, then from the side, then the top of the key. I had been shooting pool recently, so the thought came to describe these highlights this way: "Three ball corner pocket." "Three ball side pocket." "Three ball top of the key." "He ran the table." To avoid the repetition of using first down while calling NFL games, I used a "fresh set of downs" or "new set of downs." Those have become common phrases we hear today.

Not all viewers loved my catchphrases. Once after I had used "I kid because I care" several nights in a row, I was at my desk when I received a phone call from a guy who had somehow managed to get through to me.

"Hey, is this Chris Myers?"

"Yeah, this is Chris."

"You know—I watch a lot of you guys. All of you do a good job. But stop kidding! Stop caring!"

Then he hung up on me. I sat there, surprised.

Okay. Maybe I was overusing it a bit . . .

Billy Crystal gave me another catchphrase that I adopted for a wild celebration or a crazy brawl. I picked it up from his regular *Saturday Night Live* sketch titled "Fernando's Hideaway" where he imitated Argentine American actor and director Fernando Lamas. As Fernando, he interviewed a variety of celebrities on the show, like Ringo Starr and Hulk Hogan. His most famous line from the sketch was "You look mahhh-velous." Everyone around was using the expression. I ended up using another Fernando line, however:

"I was crazy going nuts—"

He would say this during skits that featured him interviewing George Steinbrenner and Howard Cosell. I began to use "crazy go nuts" many times for a wild celebration or crazy brawl. When I met Billy, I told him about it and he gave me full permission to use the expression. "Go for it," he told me.

Once when Billy was hosting the Oscars, he appeared on *Up Close* when I was host. He was not only a talented comedian but also a great sports fan, so it was a thrill for me and our crew to have a guest like him on. Comedians can be entertaining to interview.

"Can we hear from your Fernando Lamas character?" I asked him.

"What is this? I'm taking requests now?" Crystal joked before starting to talk to me in his Fernando accent.

He did his act, saying I was sitting there with my Jimmy Olsen reporter notes asking him questions, and he slowly built up to his most popular Fernando expression.

"And you . . . You look fantastic," he said, changing the last word.

"I thought you were going to say mahhhvelous."

"It never occurred to me," he quipped.

That became an expression around the studio with all the guys on the crew. I'd always tell them, "It never occurred to me!" That's how catch-phrases began.

• • •

THE CATCHPHRASES WERE ONE EXAMPLE OF THE CREATIVE FREEDOM we had at ESPN, whether you were the anchor for *SportsCenter* or the college kid who was running the shot sheets. We wrote our own mate-rial, and we had a full hourlong show to fill, so we'd brainstorm a lot of stuff on the fly. "Hey, in the show tonight, why don't we try this?" Let's freeze the tape on this guy or colorize something before going to black and white. Barry Sacks, a coordinating producer at ESPN and one of the pillars of the network, once told me when it came to our highlight shows, "There are no rules. You can try whatever you want."

In those early days, there weren't layers of people to get clearance to do something on *SportsCenter*. Of course, if it didn't work, we would hear about it, but most of the time our ideas were accepted and per-formed. We had the freedom to throw out ideas without the fear of them getting instantly shot down. Nobody was telling us to stay in our lanes; not back then. As time went on, however, that would change. For now, though, ESPN was a new and growing channel, so things weren't as established.

It was cool to work at *SportsCenter* in the '90s. These were people who lived for sports. You could wear the sweatshirt of your favorite team around the offices. Since we were working at weird hours and sometimes didn't have a lot going on, I organized a touch football game that included guys like Stuart Scott, Mike Tirico, and Rob Stone along with production assistants and personnel. I also started a game night where we played board games like Clue, Taboo, and Monopoly. It gave people something to do on those cold nights when you didn't want to be outside. This game night became such a tradition that we continued it during warmer months, and I eventually continued to do it when I moved back to the West Coast.

As I mentioned, Tirico and I were on *SportsCenter* at 2:00 a.m. EST, so I'd arrive at the studio around 4:00 or 5:00 p.m. It sometimes felt like we were living in Alaska since it would already be getting dark by then. Then I'd work until 3:30 or 4:00 in the morning, which worked perfectly after our sons were born. Since I only lived fifteen minutes away, I might be getting home just in time to take one of the boys if they were crying or needed to be fed.

Steve Bornstein, the president of ESPN at the time, made a critical decision when he suggested that the network show reruns of our broadcast every morning. We filmed different intros to the program to make it feel fresh. This way viewers on the East Coast could see the highlights first thing in the morning.

One of the really smart creative decisions we made was to do the highlights in present tense. I think ESPN was among the first networks to do this. Many of the highlights came to us just after they happened, so it made sense to show them as if we were calling them live rather than recapping. For example, while showing highlights of an L.A. Lakers game in '92, I followed A. C. Green down the court as if it was happening in front of me.

"Off the fast break, he slams it to give the Lakers the lead. Only 23 seconds to play. Larry Johnson drives on Green and lays it in. Ties the game at 93. Just five seconds left. Green misses. Rebounds. Sam Perkins throws up the left-hander and hits! Lakers win it on the Perkins shot."

Of course, who can forget those famous Chris Berman nicknames?

Moises "Skip to My" Alou. Joseph "Live and Let" Addai. Sammy "Say It Ain't" Sosa. Mike "You're in Good Hands With" Alstott. Bobby "Bad to the" Bonilla. Andre "Bad Moon" Rison. There were hundreds of them over the years. Two of my favorites were Bert "Be Home" Blyleven and Frank Tanana "Daiquiri."

Having a fun attitude and creative approach made it feel like we were watching along with the viewers at home. There was an energy and excitement with presenting it this way. Those two words really sum up the experience of working at ESPN during that era.

It's fun to think back on those early days—the golden years—of ESPN. I remember after I first arrived, I was at a press conference with Frank Robinson, who was the manager of the Baltimore Orioles at the time.

"Excuse me—do you have a minute for ESPN?" I asked in a crowded room full of media.

"ESPN? What's that, a Spanish channel?" Frank replied while everybody chuckled.

"Well, no—we've actually been around for a while," I said. "We're an all-sports network."

He gave me a wide grin. "Really? Well, I have to watch more of that. So what's your question?"

That was the way things were back in 1989. Even though ESPN had been around for a decade, it was still building up its presence. At the time, some people laughed at the very idea of an all-sports network. "Sports all day? What are they going to put on?"

Baseball commissioner Fay Vincent once made a statement about ESPN during a baseball meeting in the early '90s: "Where would ESPN be without baseball? There are only so many tractor pulls and billiard matches you can televise."

A short time later while I was doing baseball highlights on *Sports-Center,* there was a cutaway of Fay Vincent at the game.

"Oh, there's Commissioner Fay Vincent," I said. "I guess there weren't any tractor pulls or billiards for him to attend."

Most people thought it was funny, though some thought it was a shot at him. But this was an example of the loose, playful part of doing those late-night, early-morning highlights. Later when I spoke with Vincent, he was a good sport about it and we got a chuckle. Major League Baseball eventually would have a broadcast contract with ESPN to replace tractor pulls and billiards.

The isolation that Bristol, Connecticut, offered was indeed a drawback for some employees, but it really didn't matter since we were living a dream. Work felt like college even though we were all adults. There was a wonderful mixture of people who had graduated from Princeton and others who had come from a junior college. It felt like a campus full of sports fans. Yes, we were living a long way away from Boston or New York, but we all loved sports and we got to focus on it all day long at work. We were able to watch sports and write about it and tell people about it. This was heaven for all of us. We had hit the jackpot no matter how much we were getting paid. There was a collective feeling of *This is where we want to be.* I never thought I'd leave, to be honest.

These truly were some golden years while living in Connecticut. Both of our sons, Christopher and Alex, were born there. I worked with some amazing people like Linda Cohn and Mike Tirico, along with Chris Berman, Dan Patrick, Bob Ley, and Craig Kilborn. During this four-year stretch, I was able to still go out and do stories and interviews along with doing *SportsCenter.* All the while, I continued to pitch ESPN about creating a studio in Los Angeles. I still missed the West Coast.

• • •

"HEY, CHRIS. THE METS ARE PLAYING THE CUBS. YOU WANT TO GO TO the game?"

Bill Murray had meant what he said about catching a game some-time. I was still living in Connecticut the first time we went to a game together. We got seats behind home plate at the Mets' Shea Stadium.

"I'll pull up and meet you in the front," Bill told me.

He wanted to be low-key since he didn't want to cause a commotion and distract from the game. When he arrived, he pulled up in this seedy old van, and then he climbed out wearing a cap with flaps over the ears and an untucked beach shirt that made him look like a bad vacation guy. It was basically his hideout costume, the sort a man in government protection might wear to a game. We went in and sat down in our seats without anybody really noticing him. But Bill Murray the sports fanatic couldn't help making an appearance.

While the Cubs' Mark Grace stood in the batter's circle, Bill whistled and hollered "Pittsfield!"—the minor league team Grace had played for. Grace acknowledged from the field with a bow and a wave, causing some of the crowd to suddenly notice the actor. When Grace got up to hit, the home plate umpire made a call on Grace that got a reaction from Bill. Then a second called strike made Bill stand up and rip off his hat and shout out to the umpire that it was a ridiculous call. It had no effect on the umpire, but spectators now knew Bill Murray was in the stands, and we suddenly got swarmed. With so many people around us it was impossible to focus on the game, so Bill decided we needed to leave early.

When an actor ends up disrupting a Cubs-Mets game, you know he's quite an iconic figure. Of course, Bill never takes himself too seriously. Not only is he well known for being a sports fan, but he's also become notorious for surprising fans and doing funny things with them. I've been no exception.

Once while I was in New York working at the US Open Tennis Championships, Bill reached out to me.

"I heard you're in town. Want to come over to the house?"

Bill had a house up on the Hudson River. I told him I had a day off and would love to visit him, but I didn't have a car to get there.

"That's fine—I'll send a car for you and you can spend the day here," Bill said.

The car that arrived was a giant oversized white Lincoln stretch limousine. It was ridiculous. I couldn't help laughing as I climbed in and sat in the back of a vehicle that could fit fourteen people. As I pulled up to his house, Bill was in the driveway filming me with a video recorder. When I got out of the limo, Bill was doing a voice-over for the recording.

"Hey, ESPN," Murray said. "This is how Chris Myers spends your per diem money. Make sure you check the accuracy of all his receipts!"

"Bill—turn that off!"

It was a beautiful summer day as Bill showed me around his house. As we walked in his backyard, I took in the picturesque view of the Hudson River.

"Be careful and don't trip," Bill warned me. "I got these holes in my yard—these damn gophers. I can't get rid of them."

I laughed, assuming Murray was joking around with me and making a reference to *Caddyshack*. But when I looked at his expression, I could see he was being serious.

"Wait—are you messing with me?" I asked.

"No, they're for real. I've asked our lawn guy to do something about them."

Bill wasn't even thinking about one of his most famous movie characters: Carl Spackler, the assistant greenskeeper. I kept waiting for him to utter his line, "It's about time somebody teaches these varmints a little lesson about morality and about what it's like to be a decent, upstanding member of society!" But nope.

"I don't know what to do," Bill said. "I don't want them trapped and killed. There's got to be a way to keep them from tearing up the yard. It's getting dangerous out here. You can trip and stumble over them."

As I stood there with Murray looking over gopher holes in his back lawn, I couldn't help asking that age-old question: Does life imitate art, or does art imitate life?

• • •

THE FIRST TIME BILL CAME TO MY HOUSE WAS SHORTLY AFTER WE moved to California. We had been at a charity golf fundraiser at Sherwood Country Club, and Bill offered to drive me home on the way to his hotel. When I told him I would alert my wife that he was coming, he told me not to.

"Let's surprise whoever's home," he said.

When we reached my neighborhood, he said, "Don't tell me your address. I'm going to guess what kind of house you live in based on your personality."

Only someone like Bill Murray would ever do something like this. He slowly drove past the various houses, studying each one carefully.

"That one can't be yours. Looks like they haven't cut their grass in two weeks. I bet yours is cut regularly."

I chuckled while he continued to drive and look out the windshield.

"You look like a three-car-garage kind of guy," Bill said.

I grinned and nodded. We did have a three-car garage, even though the third stall was used only for storage.

"Let's see—are you a gray house guy or a blue house guy?"

Eventually after a few wrong choices we arrived at my house.

"Thanks for the ride," I said, thinking that was the end of it, but then Bill asked to come in and say hi.

I wasn't sure what sort of circus was awaiting us inside our home. Our boys were two and four years old at the time, so life could be pretty chaotic. I could only imagine what sort of mischief the star of *Ghostbusters* and *Caddyshack* might get into with our kids. When a very surprised

Susan greeted us at the door, I introduced them to each other. Then I invited Bill to come inside.

There was a den off to the side of the foyer that served as a playroom for the boys. It was a mess, especially since I hadn't informed Susan I was bringing a guest home. Toys were scattered all around the carpet. If you didn't step on the Lego pieces, you'd slip on the Matchbox cars, or trip over the coloring books and piles of crayons and markers.

The room looked like a hurricane had just gone through it. Bill couldn't resist making a joke.

"I love what you've done to the place," he said.

Susan was highly embarrassed at the time, though later she found the story funny.

Years later, I visited Bill's house in New York when he had younger kids, and I came upon a similar scene. After stepping inside I walked into an explosion of toys. Murray gave me a big grin.

"We call this the Myers Room."

SIX

A Jacket, Tie, and Bermuda Shorts

In the middle of recording a segment for *SportsCenter* as I'm talking over the boxing results, I hear a booming sound. A thunderous boom. The loud blast comes from behind my back in the nearby distance.

What the hell?

It's 1:25 a.m. on July 27, 1996, and I'm on the roof of the Chamber of Commerce building right above the Centennial Olympic Park. Thousands of people are still watching a free late-night concert in the park. For the past nine days, Atlanta has been hosting the Summer Olympics. I've been in Georgia hosting *Up Close* on location, doing a couple of interviews a day and then staying to tape a late *SportsCenter* wrap-up. Even though the booming sound jolts me, I continue talking. The first rule you're taught as a broadcaster is that whenever you're live, you keep talking regardless of what happens around you. If you're live, you finish your story. That's my job—that's what I do.

My first assumption as I finish my segment is that this must be fireworks or something similar. There's a party going on down below me, so I figure it has to be that. But when I stand up and see people scrambling, I realize something's wrong. This isn't part of the midnight concert fun.

"Hold on a second, guys," I tell my ESPN team. "There's something going on here."

Even though NBC has the rights to the Olympic Games and the live broadcast, ESPN has been doing our thing around the events. Our cameras are down there in the Olympic Park, so when I see people panicking to get out of the area, my reporter instincts kick in.

"People are yelling," I tell the crew. "All right—we should be ready to roll."

As I sit back down, I notice my bare legs. The Georgia heat is thick and sticky, so I'm wearing baggy Bermuda shorts along with my coat and tie. Nobody can see them hidden behind my desk. I begin reporting details live as they come.

"A number of ambulance and fire and rescue units have been called to the area," I share as I see them arriving down below.

Nothing in me wants to leave. This is one of those moments when we're here in the middle of it all and we have a job to do. We have to be reporting this. And soon enough we learn that a huge explosive had been detonated. My producer tells me that the ESPN truck on the ground shook with the blast. None of us know the magnitude of the blast or the exact location. Was there one bomb or multiple bombs? Will there be more?

We have to stay in the area to find out, even though they're clearing everyone out.

"Security is ushering people out of the park," I say on the air.

Soon security arrives on the roof to tell us to clear the building. As I talk to them in my yellow-and-black shorts, I decide to stretch the truth a bit.

"We're okay to be here," I say. "Another guy told us we could stay here and keep reporting."

Yeah, I'm lying, but only for a good reason. People need to know what's happening. This may save or affect the lives of people who are watching or coming to the Olympics.

I continue reporting the details as they come in. "We are getting a confirmed report that the explosion took place on a tower near the stage at the AT&T mobile village."

An hour after the security guy came and told us we needed to leave, he arrives back on the rooftop and doesn't look as hospitable.

"There was no other guy," he tells me in an annoyed tone. "You guys gotta get out of the building."

As we begin to head downstairs to the street below, I'm reminded that I'm still wearing those Bermuda shorts with my coat and tie. I didn't think anything of it since at that point I didn't know I was going to be on call live for the next eight hours overnight.

• • •

AS A KID, IT WAS EASIER TO IMAGINE MYSELF ENTERTAINING AN AUDI-ence like Johnny Carson rather than informing a television audience like Walter Cronkite. But it was only natural for me to pay attention to the news and to news broadcasters as well. It always impressed me how news anchors handled dramatic events in history, such as when a president was shot or a national tragedy occurred. Even though they were broadcasting live, they remained calm and professional. They had to choose their words carefully and control their emotions even though they didn't have any time to let the news begin to sink in. They did what people wanted them to do: deliver the information they had while remaining authentic. They had to tell the truth about the situation, even when it sometimes hurt to say it to the audience. That was their job.

For many years in Miami, the local news legend was Ralph Renick. He was Florida's version of Cronkite. As the first anchor for Miami's WTVJ, Channel 4, Renick was always credible and accurate. Like with Cronkite, you felt comfortable and safe when he delivered the news. Bernard Goldberg also caught my attention as an outstanding news reporter.

Radio is in my roots and will never leave me, but as I stepped into local television in Miami, I became somewhat of a television news geek. When traveling as a sports reporter, I watched every local market news or small-town TV station talent along with the regular network news. I began to pay close attention to how reporters covered live unfolding events like hurricanes and earthquakes and even wars. There was no way to rehearse for these things. I watched how quickly and clearly they framed things and used pictures to support what was happening. If they had no pictures, then I noted how they best described things. I saw that you had to be firm but warm and friendly, depending on the information you were delivering.

I had already been in situations such as Hank Gathers's death and the Loma Prieta earthquake, but still never imagined I would suddenly be covering a bombing in the middle of a US metropolis during one of the biggest sporting events in the world.

• • • •

THE CENTER OF ATLANTA IS IN A STATE OF CHAOS. FOR A CITY SO EXcited to be hosting the XXVI Olympiad, the scene after the bomb blast is surreal. The thousands of people watching the free concert at Centennial Olympic Park are stunned and confused and wandering the streets. After our ESPN crew has to evacuate the building, I grab a cameraman and begin reporting from the ground to get details and pictures. We need to find out what's going on.

These are still the days of operating with a mentality of *anything to get the facts,* of zeroing in and focusing solely on the story at hand. Who was injured? How many were injured? How secure are the athletes and the Olympic Village? There's an adrenaline rush to get the job done as accurately and immediately as possible. Since I have a cameraman by my side with remote ability, we'll stay long enough to get shots of everything that is going on. Someone from ESPN calls my family to let them know I'm okay.

White and red lights from ambulances and police cars and EMT vehicles flash all around us. Sirens and horns sound from every direction. We become surrounded by fire trucks and cops on motorcycles and military troops. Authorities are trying to direct traffic; police try to clear away barricades so ambulances can get in while also constructing a perimeter around the blast area to keep people out.

For a moment I stand and soak it all in, wondering who to talk to first. Thousands of spectators stand and sit and move around the fringes of the park, all looking nervous, some desperate to leave, everything in a state of complete gridlock. There are people on the ground, some bleeding, others weeping, with medical staff and firemen trying to assist. Police are hollering out orders. A triage is set up nearby.

The people I talk to share a similar story.

"The ground shook beneath us."

"I thought the blast was part of the musical act."

"We were dancing and then boom—it went off."

It's so amazing that the network is able to keep us on the air reporting. It's the beauty of ESPN at the time. While someone is back at the studio hosting and keeping updates on information, I am able to go to different locations to do reports and see if people have been injured and who might be getting put into an ambulance. Our guys back in Bristol, Connecticut, remain in my ear the whole time. Since we're there and are the only ones with a camera, we stay through the night. NBC is broadcasting the Olympics, but it takes them time to get cameras and people set up since it's two in the morning, so we are really the only ones on the air all night at different locations.

At first there is no official discovery of a bomb, but eyewitnesses verify the idea that there was an explosive device. We don't realize there are other bombs in the area. The first time I feel the true danger of the situation comes when I speak to a Georgia cop off camera.

"I was in the village when the bomb went off," he tells me. "A guy right in front of me is killed by shrapnel."

The big man shook his head and let out a deep sigh.

"I never thought I'd ever see a man die at the Olympics," he says.

I'm careful to report only the things I can confirm, so I don't share this on the air. As it turns out, a forty-four-year-old woman is killed by the bomb, while a cameraman for Turkish television ends up dying of a heart attack while running to safety after the bomb goes off. Maybe the cop assumed the man died in front of him instead of only being seriously injured. In these circumstances, communication is very difficult. We're not carrying cell phones and don't even know what the term "social media" means. So as I learn things, I have to run up and talk to police officers or National Guardsmen or medical people just to make sure the information I have is accurate.

There are still only pieces and fragments of details to comprehend. One person says the blast appeared to come from a garbage can. There is a lot of talk about one of the towers in the park. There are no confirmed fatalities, while reports say that between 150 and 200 people have been injured. Security supposedly told people to move a few minutes before the bomb went off.

I've always said I'm a suit kind of guy when I'm working, and I've joked that I even wear a jacket in the shower just in case a sports story breaks so

I'm ready. True to form, I am wearing a jacket and a tie. But, as I mentioned, I'm missing my pants. In my colorful Bermuda shorts, I wander around the streets that they've barricaded looking like a freeloader on vacation. When authorities see me, I have to convince them that I'm legitimate.

"No, really, guys—I'm with ESPN. I'm working here. The shorts are usually hidden behind my desk."

With nothing open, finding anything to eat or drink is impossible, not to mention finding a bathroom. Specific details about what happened remain hard to determine as well. The complete story unfolds over the course of not days but weeks and even months.

The hero of the night was thirty-three-year-old Richard Jewell, whose tragic story has been well recounted in articles, documentaries, and movies. At the time Jewell was an AT&T security guard, and while working that night he discovered an abandoned backpack tucked under a bench close to the tower in Centennial Olympic Park. He quickly alerted an agent with the Georgia Bureau of Investigation, who ended up calling for bomb technicians. Jewell and the agent helped evacuate between seventy-five and a hundred people from the area before a pipe bomb filled with nails and screws went off.[1]

Initially hailed as a hero, Richard Jewell became the target of investigation for the crime even though there was no evidence to support this. For three months the saga unfolded in the public eye, and even though in October Jewell was fully cleared of any responsibility, his name and his life were forever tarnished. The real bomber was arrested in 2003 and pled guilty in 2005 to a series of bombings, including the Olympic bombing.

• • •

THAT NIGHT, THE OLYMPIC GAMES ARE PUT ON PAUSE. THE WORK I'VE been doing slips into the background. For the time being, I'm not reporting on competition; I'm talking about life-and-death issues.

Earlier that day, I'd enjoyed interviewing Charles Barkley. He was once again playing for the US men's Olympic basketball team, the so-called second Dream Team that was following in the shoes of the 1992 team. While Barkley's team didn't have the big-name players the '92 team had, such as Magic Johnson, Michael Jordan, and Larry Bird, Barkley was still playing with greats like Karl Malone, Scottie Pippen, and David Robinson.

Barkley is one of many people I interview that week. Others are athletes like Michael Johnson and the great swimmer Janet Evans, as well as people connected to the Olympics and sports. I enjoy interviewing Tom Brokaw as he talks about being a big sports fan.

The Olympics will be a blur to me after this night. I'll barely be able to remember everything that happened, from Muhammad Ali lighting the Olympic cauldron despite showing the effects of Parkinson's disease to Michael Johnson breaking records and winning gold medals in the 200- and 400-meter dashes. The Dream Team will end up winning gold for a second straight Olympics, but another dream team will also win. The Magnificent Seven, the US women's gymnastics team, wins its first-ever gold medal in the team competition in dramatic fashion as Kerri Strug famously sticks the landing of her vault despite being injured.

I give all of the athletes at these games credit for continuing to compete and work hard at the Olympics despite the dark cloud that hangs over it after the bombing. I can't help thinking of the 1972 Munich Olympics when members of the Israeli team were held hostage by gunmen. Will this 1996 Atlanta Olympics forever be known as the one where the bomb went off?

• • •

IT'S EIGHT IN THE MORNING AND THE SUN HAS COME UP AND THINGS have calmed down when I stumble through my last report. I'm drained emotionally and physically. I'm also starving, and more than that, I need a shower. The summer heat and humidity in Georgia can be taxing. Producers finally tell me I'm clear to go back to the rental house where we've been staying. After I collapse in my bed, it suddenly hits me. The reality of what just took place at the world's most important sports gathering, the Olympic Games.

As I still hear the echoes of the bomb pounding inside my head, I can't help thinking about my father as a teenager in Normandy on D-Day.

He must've heard hundreds of bombs blasting all around him.

I went with my father to see the movie *Saving Private Ryan* in the theater in 1998. The first battle scene, where US soldiers stormed Omaha Beach, brought my dad to tears. I saw him wiping his eyes and looking away from the screen as the staggering twenty-minute scene unfolded, starting with the ramp lowering on the Higgins boat and the soldiers being ripped apart by German machine guns. The barrage that followed showed just how vulnerable our brave soldiers were on that beach.

My dad was only seventeen years old when he volunteered and enlisted in the Navy. Not being truthful about his age . . . sounds familiar. He had never really talked much about the war, or about the June 6, 1944, D-Day landings. After the movie, he shared some of his memories with me.

"I remember heavy clouds," he said. "The seas were rough. Our ship was getting bounced around. Some guys were getting sick and vomiting."

Eugene T. Myers worked at sea on an LST, a tank landing ship. Everybody called him "Deacon." On D-Day his ship was there to hit the beach and unload US troops and equipment.

"It was just like the movie. I saw so many guys die on the beach—falling in the water and drowning with all their gear on. The sound of bullets was piercing."

Dad said he was scared, but his ship had been in battle a few times before. He believed in the men and purpose they were fighting for.

Over the years, my father didn't talk too much about that day until later in life after attending crew and World War II reunions. He went back to Normandy for the fifty-year anniversary, telling me it was important to remember those who didn't make it back. He always spoke fondly of the crew and those he served with.

"Those were some of the most important years of my life," he told me. "I'm proud of what we were able to do—what our country was able to do—to end the war and stop Germany and Japan."

I think of my dad every time the national anthem is played at any sporting event I'm attending.

Now, overcome with emotion, I start to fall into a deep sleep. I'll end up sleeping for what feels like the next forty-eight hours. But before I drift off, I remember one last thing about my dad. A funny memory.

Dad never ate seafood after he came home from the war. Earlier, when training in the water for the D-Day landings, he had made a promise.

"If the fish don't eat me and I make it out of here, I won't ever eat them."

A sense of humor always comes in handy, even during the most difficult times.

When I finally wake up, the first person I call is my father.

SEVEN

Up Closer

Sports fans always have questions. Regardless of who's on the winning or losing side, the viewing public always wants to know details. How does it feel to win the championship? What's it like to lose in overtime? How did you become a professional athlete? How long do you think you'll keep competing? Is the fire still there? What lessons have you learned over the years? There are so many questions, but few get to ask them. I've been fortunate to be one of those few.

Everybody has a story to tell, and I like asking people about theirs. Part of me has always been curious; another part of me likes hearing what they have to say. This is why I love interviews. If folks are comfortable with you and trust you (even just a little), then they'll usually say a lot.

An opportunity to expand on my love for interviewing arrived in 1994 when Roy Firestone decided to step away from the *Up Close* interview show he had created to begin a new role hosting prime-time specials for ESPN. The network had bought the rights to the show and wanted to keep it going. I had filled in a few times for Roy over the years, so ESPN asked me if I was interested in taking over.

One very big and enticing fact: Roy was based in Los Angeles. ESPN knew that I was from the West Coast, and even though they preferred to have me doing *SportsCenter* in their headquarters, they also knew I'd been hoping to get back to California. The fact that this had been one of those goals I'd written on my early notecards over the years only made the move more thrilling.

Back in 1980 when I was still in Miami working as the sports anchor for Channel 4, I found myself in the studio one day watching Roy Firestone on *Up Close*. I leaned over to my producer.

"I want to do a show like that someday," I told him.

I had always admired Firestone. After starting in television, I sometimes called him to ask for advice. He was always gracious to give it.

So after I had been with ESPN for six years and lived in Connecticut for three years, an opportunity came and I jumped at it. Susan and I returned to the West Coast and never looked back.

• • •

LARRY KING ONCE GAVE ME THE BEST ADVICE ON INTERVIEWING. IT'S so basic and simple, yet at the same time it's critical.

"You have to listen," King told me. "When you ask a question, you have to listen to the answer. That's where your next best questions are going to come from. No matter what you have planned."

I ran into Larry King in 1980 while in the WTVJ studio in Miami. I was interviewing for the weekend sports anchor job, a role I later got. King had only been doing his show on radio for a couple of years. He sometimes did *The Larry King Show* at a diner named Wolfie's in Miami Beach not too far from WKAT, where I started in radio. I used to listen to him a lot before he went national; I enjoyed his interviews, many of which didn't involve sports. When we met, he had heard me doing sports broadcasting when I was first starting out.

"Hey, kid, you're going places," he told me.

When I asked him for some advice, he gave me the obvious starting point in journalism: know the five W's. The who, what, when, where, and why. But then he added a very insightful piece of information that stuck with me.

"Don't leave the audience out of your conversation," he told me.

He gave me an example of this. When he was going to have an author on his show to talk about their latest book, Larry King didn't read the book. He didn't want to act like he already knew it and leave the listeners out of the discussion. He would know what the book was about so he could ask questions, but he wanted to bring his audience into the conversation as much as possible.

King did his radio show until 1994, the same year I made my decision to start hosting *Up Close*. Of course, *Larry King Live* would continue to be broadcast on CNN until 2010.

Larry King mastered the art of having an interview consist of a conversational flow, of making the guest feel comfortable. He was so good at asking people meaningful questions. "Are you afraid of dying?" "What's your greatest regret?" And his guests always shared. I learned from him to always listen. I've never wanted to talk more than a guest, unless I needed to. Sometimes I would need to expand to give them time to set up. This meant I could come in with a certain question or angle. But I always made sure I was listening. And I've listened to a lot of people.

I don't remember the first person I interviewed on *Up Close* when I officially started as the host in January 1995. Considering how many interviews I did over the years, it's easy for my memory to be a bit blurry about them. We produced an average of five shows a week, and I ended up doing the show for four solid years. I worked at least fifty weeks a year, so I easily interviewed over a thousand different people for the show.

The one-on-one interviews lasted half an hour, and even though they were taped and aired on separate evenings, they were still essentially live because we never edited them. This was long before athletes had avenues where they could get out and freely talk about things. There was no social media, of course, and the online world was still fairly new to everybody. *Up Close* gave people a chance to finally get to know the amazing athletes that they watched and rooted for. Most of the time I would talk about a player's life—how did he become the athlete that he was? What were high points and low points in his career?.

More than anything, my goal was always to find the human element in sports. We love to watch great athletes and coaches, but I've always been interested in the person underneath the name. *Up Close* became an opportunity for viewers to get to know these individuals a little better. When I moved on to join Fox later in my career, I would emulate these interviews in *CMI: The Chris Myers Interview* show. The conversations were always unpredictable and enlightening. The following are a few of my favorite moments.

• • •

WE LOVE HEARING ATHLETES TALK ABOUT THEIR CHILDHOOD.

When Doc Rivers, the All-Star point guard who played in the NBA from 1983 to 1996, came on *Up Close,* I brought up a story I'd heard about him when he was a boy.

"When you were in fifth grade, you got called up to the blackboard. The teacher said, 'Write what you want to be when you grow up.'"

"'Write what you want to be when you grow up,'" Doc Rivers repeated with a nod. "I wrote, 'I want to be a pro basketball player.' The teacher grabbed the eraser and erased it from the board and told me to be realistic. She said, 'Write something else up on the board.' And I wrote it again. 'I want to be a pro basketball player.' She erased it again and told me she'd send me home from school if I didn't write something else up on the board. When I tell kids this story, I always tell them I have a father who was a police officer and a big man—carries a big gun. And I was thinking about all that walking up to the board. But I wrote, 'I want to be a pro basketball player' once again."

Very few who dream of becoming a professional athlete are able to see that dream come true. Fewer are able to have a successful career. Surprisingly enough, Don Shula never fulfilled those dreams.

We all equate Coach Don Shula with winning, but when he came on *Up Close* he told me the story about getting cut when he was playing in the NFL. Shula played with the Cleveland Browns and then the Baltimore Colts until the Colts waived him. He was absolutely crushed. Shula said he got in his car and drove around the stadium, almost running out of gas while wondering what he was going to do next. What was his life going to look like now?

After one season with the Washington Redskins, Shula retired from playing football. He was newly married and knew he didn't want to leave the game. Fortunately for him, the University of Virginia offered him an assistant's job even though he didn't have any coaching experience. We know the rest of the story.

Chris Evert, tennis Hall of Famer and winner of eighteen Grand Slam titles, grew up during a time when female athletes were perceived as hard and masculine. She explained that at the time she felt that "femininity" meant weakness.

"I was just a normal schoolgirl," Evert told me. "I had crushes on boys. I wore nail polish, jewelry, hair ribbons, ruffles on my bloomers, little balls on my sock. Yes, a really steely determination. But it was always important to me just to be a normal fifteen-, sixteen-, seventeen-year-old girl, you know? Because that's just who I was. So I felt a responsibility, if anything, to show that you could still be a girl, a woman, feminine and still be really determined and have a steely determination underneath and have backbone. And go for what you believed."

• • •

AS I ALREADY SAID, "GOAT" IS AN OVERUSED EXPRESSION IN SPORTS. The subject has come up many times in conversations, whether someone was talking about themselves or other athletes in their profession. I once asked Jerry Rice what he thought of the term.

"A lot of people would call me that and it just felt weird. You know, I can't call myself that. I'm still one of those guys that feel you have to work for everything. I wouldn't say I'm the greatest player of all time, but it's okay if the fans say that."

Tommy Lasorda gave me a great line once on the dangers of talking about being a great manager.

"Do you have to ask Richard Burton if he's a great actor?" Lasorda said.

So I asked Lasorda how he viewed himself after being inducted into the Baseball Hall of Fame.

"That's a little difficult for me to evaluate myself, because if I don't say anything, then someone says, 'Look at the guy being humble.' But if I say, 'I did this and I did this,' you're going to say, 'Look at this guy—what a braggart.'"

I once asked Wilt Chamberlain why it bothered him when people talked about Michael Jordan being the greatest basketball player of all time.

"We all have our opinions, and I don't think considering what he's doing, what he's done, and how the game is going, that he's better than Oscar Robertson, Jerry West, Bill Russell, a number of people."

Kareem Abdul-Jabbar didn't hesitate when asked the question.

"Oscar Robertson. At every level, he was the best ever. High school, college, and the pros. He's still got his NCAA record. He's in a class by himself."

Interviewing Rodney Peete, a quarterback who had played for both the Detroit Lions and the Dallas Cowboys, I had to ask the most obvious question.

"Emmitt Smith, Barry Sanders. You've handed off to both over your career. Pretty fortunate. If you were in a Super Bowl, Rodney, and you needed one of those guys, which one would you take to win the game?"

"I have been fortunate," he said, grinning.

"Don't sidestep this now," I said with a chuckle.

Rodney gave the best answer he could have given.

"I would take out the fullback and put them both in the backfield."

Some of the players I interviewed had just finished their career in professional sports, so I brought up the subject of the Hall of Fame. When I asked Dallas Cowboys quarterback Troy Aikman about what constituted a Hall of Fame player, he told me he wasn't exactly sure. He said if he was ever to get into the Hall of Fame, it would be because of his record and not individual numbers.

"My career was really defined by winning games," Aikman said. "There wasn't a lot of gaudy statistics. And I certainly was fine with that. [Winning] is why we play the game, and I'm very proud of that fact. I don't apologize for my lack of big numbers."

I asked him if he would rather have three Super Bowl titles and lower stats than a quarterback like Dan Marino who had lots of stats but no ring.

"Yeah. Those were great years, and I can't imagine having played this game and not have been given the opportunity to win a Super Bowl. And I was able to win three of them."

Many of those all-time greats never took credit themselves. Joe Montana was one of them.

"I was surrounded by a lot of great teammates. And when you have guys who are striving for the same thing that you are and at the same level you are, it makes accomplishing things a lot easier."

• • •

IT'S ALWAYS EASY TO TALK ABOUT AN ATHLETE'S OR A COACH'S SUC-cess, but it's another thing to bring up losses. But we all wonder about those who have been so close but have never won the "big" one.

Imagine you're a Hall of Fame quarterback who brought your team to four straight Super Bowls yet you never won one. You're hosting a golf tournament and a player from one of the opposing teams that beat yours in the big game shows up with his ring. That's just life and those things are going to happen. But for the Buffalo Bills' Jim Kelly, things like that still sting, as he told me.

"A kicker came to my golf tournament and he had his Super Bowl ring on when he played with the Giants," Kelly told me. "That sort of hurt a little bit because he was showing it around. He wasn't even wearing it. He's carrying it in his pocket. It makes it worse."

"A kicker, of all people," I joked.

An excellent kicker, too—two-time Super Bowl champion Matt Bahr, who won with the Pittsburgh Steelers and the New York Giants. Kelly smiled at my comment.

"Yeah, exactly, but yeah, it hurts," Kelly explained. "Everybody wants to win. Not everybody can. But when I'm done playing football, I'm not going to look back and say that it was a total disappointment that we didn't win one. Yeah, it was very disappointing. But I'm not going to say that it ruined my career or something I look back on and really feel very frustrated about. I still have a couple more years left. Hopefully we can get back. It's very difficult to do that, especially with free agency now, but I feel we still can."

At the time, Kelly was still playing in the NFL. He never did get back, but he also never let those losses define him.

Losing is part of the game.

January 22, 1989. Super Bowl XXIII in Joe Robbie Stadium in Miami. The San Francisco 49ers were favorites to beat the Cincinnati Bengals and win their third Super Bowl. Under the leadership of Coach Sam Wyche, the Bengals led the 49ers 16–13 with 3:10 left in the fourth quarter. San Francisco was starting its drive from the eight-yard line.

Only three minutes and ten seconds left for the 49ers to pull off a miracle. Of course, they had Joe Montana and Jerry Rice.

A decade after that game, I asked Sam Wyche about the finish.

"Thirty-four seconds away, Super Bowl XXIII. You're thirty-four seconds away from beating the 49ers and winning it all as a head coach with the Cincinnati Bengals. And then Joe Montana does it to you. When you think back, is that your toughest moment in football ever?"

"Well, I was so close to reaching the height, you know, being the best in your business and being the best at what you do among the best players in the world. The NFL has the best football in the world. And Joe Montana that day was too good for us. I just am happy that the game was decided on a good play rather than on a mistake, even though we had a chance there to almost intercept one just prior to the play. The game ended because Joe threw a perfect strike to John Taylor. A good coverage, but a better player offensively. And that's the way—if you got to lose, lose that way."

• • •

IT'S ALWAYS FASCINATING TO HEAR ATHLETES TALK ABOUT BECOMING a parent.

When Chris Evert came on *Up Close*, I asked her a question she hated to be asked. Evert retired from professional tennis in 1989 owning the highest winning percentage in pro tennis history. So I had to ask that annoying question.

"What else is Chris Evert doing with her life?"

"What did I do in my life since I retired?" she asked with a polite grin. "You know, people ask me that. Usually men who don't have children. I look at them and go, 'I have three children.' They go, 'Well, we know, but what are you doing with your life?' It's like, what do you mean, you idiot? I have three kids under five, and I'm a mom—a hands-on mom."

At the time Chris Evert had three boys ages one, three, and five.

"They're a handful," Evert said. "I mean, we have boys. I'm on my feet from seven in the morning until ten at night. Hockey and soccer and baseball, and I'm doing everything with them. I'm a better athlete now than when I was playing tennis!"

At the time I also had two boys under the age of five, so I could relate.

"I know it's a workout," I said, but I wasn't home with my boys all day. "How about the mental toughness, which was such a strength of yours when you were a player? Are you able to control your emotions with these three when they get out of control?"

"I thought I was patient. Playing on the red clay Roland Garros, you had to have patience. But until you have kids, it really does test your patience. Especially when you have three and one does something and the other's whining and the other one's grabbing your leg. It's an unbelievable challenge, but it's the most rewarding thing that's ever happened to me."

Kareem Abdul-Jabbar cited his UCLA basketball coach John Wooden as instrumental in learning how to parent.

"I would not have been anywhere near successful as a parent if I had not played for Coach Wooden. What he taught us had to do with basketball, but he challenged us and then let us fail finding our way, up to a certain point. Then he would put his thumb down and say, 'All right, now you gotta do it the right way.' And I learned something in that. Human nature is the same. So in dealing with my children, I had that example of a great teacher who knew how to do that. So if I've had any success as a parent, I have to give Coach Wooden credit."

Parenting can especially be challenging for those athletes whose children are following in their footsteps. Take Archie Manning, for example. The former New Orleans Saints quarterback and father of three boys opened up to me about how he felt while watching Peyton play his first NFL game.

"I'm a little disappointed in myself because I've been there before and I try to be calm," Archie said. "I've always prided myself and kind of go into a stadium or to a Little League game or whatever in a mindset that I'm going to sit there and I'm going to watch the game."

Archie said that he was fine leading up to the game, but once he sat in the stands he became extremely nervous for Peyton. More than he'd ever been before, even before Peyton's first start in college when he was a freshman at Tennessee. I asked if Archie felt more nervous than his own debut as a pro quarterback.

"I think more nervous, because when I looked out there—and I've been around pro football now playing or broadcasting for twenty-seven years—I think I know a little bit about the game. I could look out there and see how tough it was."

For someone who didn't go around bragging about his sons' accomplishments, Archie was candid with his pride and excitement for Peyton at the start of his career.

"I didn't groom Peyton to be a professional quarterback. He chose to participate in sports. His mother and I, his brothers—we just supported him, and we've just been there. I'm just trying to be his father."

Some athletes had a different take on parenthood. Dennis Rodman was one of them.

When I asked him what it's like being a father, he said, "Well, you gotta pay for them. Gotta keep working to pay for those damn bastards."

I laughed with him. "I'm sure they wouldn't want to hear their dad refer to them like that."

"I was just kidding. Come on."

"You kid 'cause you care."

"Yeah, I care about my kids," Rodman said.

• • •

THE '90S WERE THE ERA OF THE SUPERMODEL. KATHY IRELAND WAS one of them, and she became well known for her thirteen appearances in the annual *Sports Illustrated* Swimsuit Issue, gracing the cover three times. She was friendly, with a girl-next-door glow about her in person. As I introduced her, I lost my train of thought for a moment in the interview. I don't know why I said the following, but these words came out of my mouth.

"Well—you're married and so am I. What a coincidence."

She paused for a moment and looked at me, then began to laugh. I realized how awkward my statement sounded as I gathered my thoughts. We proceeded to have a fun conversation about sports and her modeling career and her future hopes of running her own business. Those hopes have certainly come to fruition.

I rode home from work that day thinking I have to try to be cooler the next time I'm around a supermodel.

• • •

SOME OF THE MOST CONTROVERSIAL ATHLETES ARE MISUNDERSTOOD. Take Barry Bonds. I knew his agent, so when Bonds left the Pirates to go to the Giants, I was able to break the story. Bonds was notorious over the years for disliking certain interviewers, but I was one of the few he tolerated. He struck me as someone who was actually shy, a guy who loved playing baseball but didn't like everything that came with it. It wasn't that he was antisocial, but being in the spotlight didn't drive him like some other guys. He told me that he felt the most free and comfortable riding his motorcycle along the coast.

Randy Moss told me that controversy had stuck with him over the years and that it was something he had to deal with. Away from the field, however, Moss said he was more laid-back than people would think or expect him to be.

"I try to live my life, normal day-to-day, just like the average human being," Moss told me. "I don't try to carry myself as a superstar until I hit the field."

Sometimes I asked players about their reputation. I once asked Alonzo Mourning if he would call himself an angry player. The NBA center who spent most of his sixteen-year career playing for the Miami Heat was known for being hot-tempered.

"I'm just an intense player," Mourning replied. "I think a great deal of people—they have misconceptions—"

"They've labeled you an angry player."

"Exactly. They have a lot of misconceptions about me. And that's unfair to me because that's my job. That's what I do. I mean, that's my work, right? So why form a conclusion on a person that you've seen on television just from perceptions of them? That I'm a mean person, I'm unapproachable. You know? But if you get to know me, the people that know me off the court, they understand me a whole lot differently and they know how I am. There's a difference between Alonzo the basketball player. This is my job. This is what I do. And Alonzo, the person you know, and I never let the two come together."

Such a great insight into the mind of a competitor, separating the warrior from the man.

When NFL linebacker turned actor Brian Bosworth came on, I asked him about his desire to punish people on the football field.

"You said you needed to hurt people," I said. "That without football you might as well be a corpse . . . So that anger that you had built up and also this passion for the game, you said it was difficult. How did you get through it?"

"Well, that was the only way that I could find a way to excel in my life. That's the one thing in my life I knew that I was good at. And I liked myself back then for that. I could take the anger that I had inside me and wherever it came from, I knew how to channel that anger."

I asked him about channeling that anger on a football field.

"Anytime that you can, you know, cold-cock someone on the football field, whether they're watching you or not, that makes you feel good," Bosworth told me. "At least it makes me feel good. To watch something, you know, come out of an orifice makes you feel good." I don't think I ever heard a player describe tackling quite that way. And when I thought later about the interview, I realized I didn't ever want to get a guy like that angry with me.

Sometimes controversy would follow a player into my studio. When I interviewed NFL wide receiver Andre Rison, he had been in the news after his girlfriend—Lisa "Left Eye" Lopes from the group TLC—set his mansion on fire and burned it down. Sometimes guests would pass by each other when I was taping back-to-back shows. When Rison saw San Francisco Giants slugger Kevin Mitchell, he told Mitchell that he and Lopes were planning to get married.

"Don't bring any matches to the reception," Mitchell casually joked.

For a moment Rison gave him a stare, then he laughed at the comment. I felt like a bad tour guide. *Let's move along. There's nothing to see here.*

• • •

UP CLOSE'S CASUAL STYLE OF INTERVIEWING FELT NATURAL TO ME. IT was something I had always wanted to do and the direction I had always hoped to go in. But it was also tougher than I thought. You never knew if someone was going to talk too much or not enough. The conversations were never scripted. I went into each of them with a topic to open with and then another to close with. But these were topics I wanted to cover; I never wrote out specific questions. This was why the show sometimes felt a little more conversational than a show like *60 Minutes*. I did not set out to grill anybody. It was more about being curious, something I never had to fake.

I once asked Derek Jeter if there were any questions that he didn't want me to ask him during our interview.

"You can ask anything you want," he replied.

"Okay—that's good," I said.

"I won't necessarily *answer* them," he said with a smile. "But you can ask them."

Touché, Jeter, but I've never hesitated asking people questions, even when they've sometimes been difficult questions. That's why one producer called me the "Velvet Hammer." One great example of this was during my interview with Wilt Chamberlain.

At the time we spoke, Wilt's autobiography, *A View from Above,* included a claim that caused a lot of controversy. He had said that if he were to count all the sexual encounters he had in his life, he would be "closing in on 20,000 women." I asked what sort of reaction he had received about that comment.

"In the last sentence of that chapter, I say that for all you men who think that having a thousand different women is really cool, I have found out that having one woman a thousand different times is really the way to go, but no one ever really picked up on that."

"How did you come up with that number, though?" I asked him.

"No, I came up with that number because I just tried to, like, guesstimate . . ."

"Are you close? Is it really that close?"

Wilt smiled. "Ah, well, you know—"

"Because I kept looking for pictures in the book," I said, trying to keep things light.

"You kept looking for pictures?" Wilt asked as he got my joke and began laughing.

My next question was more serious. "Are you sorry it came out that way?"

"I'm glad you asked that question," Wilt said. "I'm sorry it did because it took away from the book. But I'm more sorry because there's an apology owed by me to the women that I've known. They weren't meant to be put in a situation where it looks like they're just a number."

I asked him whether or not he was endorsing promiscuity and he said on the contrary, he wasn't advocating promiscuity but rather discussing how people should conduct themselves sexually. So once again, my curiosity couldn't resist asking him a follow-up.

"I don't want to pry, but have you cut back on the number?"

"Well, you know, I'm still a single man, and I'm still involved."

"Did you ever just want one, for it to be a monogamous—"

"Well, if you read my book, you'd see I'm saying to you that one is the way to go."

"But do you have to go through all those to figure that out?" I joked.

"Well—*I* had to," Chamberlain said as he laughed. "What you may have to do—"

"I have other problems," I deadpanned.

Chamberlain addressed the twenty thousand number one last time, stating that he wasn't promoting promiscuity.

"Just because I came up with the number, people started to act like it was something very bad. I haven't done anything bad. I didn't twist people's arms here. We're talking about mutual consent by adults."

"All right, and he is an adult," I said. "I kid because I care."

• • •

ONE OF THE THINGS I LEARNED EARLY IN MY CAREER WAS TO TREAT famous people like the average guy and the average guy like famous people. With these interviews, I needed to deal with the real person, even if it might be painful to bring up. I also had to treat them with respect, even if I had a job to do. I might not even ask a question but instead bring up an event.

"You lost your father at a young age, so you were angry and ran off and threw a baseball against the roof of the house," I might ask.

I wanted the guests to tell their story, then I'd react to what they shared.

"So you realized you had an arm to pitch, but playing baseball also helped you deal with the pain of losing your father?" I would respond.

It helped to have the producer or a staffer assisting with research. Sometimes during a break somebody might hand me a sheet taking note of a question or a subject we still needed to cover. "Don't forget to ask about this," they might write. But we never wanted to ruin the connection I had with the guest, even when we took breaks for commercials.

I rewatched all of my interviews, critiquing how I did. I was hard on myself, something I needed to do. *I should've asked that question. Why didn't I follow up that point?* But I always got a rush from a stirring conversation. Sometimes I had to steer it, but it's a kind of dance with another mind. And out of those conversations came some great anecdotes and one-liners.

When George Foreman came on, he talked about his children. The boxer has ten biological kids and two adopted daughters. Five of his kids are boys, and their names are all George. There's George Jr., George III, George IV, George V, and George VI.

"Why would you name all your sons George?" I asked him in disbelief.

"Well, that way if I forget one of their names, all I have to do is yell, 'George,' and they all come running. Then I can get the right one."

Foreman's interview was referenced on a different show. Ferdie Pacheco, a longtime boxing commentator and at one time the personal physician for Muhammad Ali, knew George Foreman well. As we were talking about safety in the sport of boxing, Foreman's name came up.

"For a guy who has on this program spoken in favor of headgear, should he still be talking about safety? Should he still be fighting?" I asked about Foreman.

"He may be the only one that needs headgear," Ferdie said as he began his entertaining critique. "I mean, he gets beaten sideways every time he fights—his head comes out sideways. Even the last guy beat him. I don't think George—listen—George was a great champion. Make no mistake about it. Had Ali not beaten him in Africa, George would have been legendary. He left to serve God, and that was a very useful and wonderful thing he did. He came back. That was not useful. That was not wonderful. He came back with a good excuse. He was going to go rebuild a church. Well, he didn't rebuild the church. And as far as I know, he's got enough money to rebuild a cathedral, a theme park, a parking lot."

"So he shouldn't—" I tried to interject to get off the George-Foreman–bashing wagon, but Ferdie continued.

"I believe that George has hit on a perfect character. The outside George. Big, fat, rotund, happy-go-lucky. And I love him. He's so great. He's a wonderful guy. But inside there is still the same old rotten George from Africa. Still the same old greedy guy saying, 'Give me some more money. I want some more.' Now, you know, whether George ever talks to me again or not doesn't make any difference, because he never talked to me before. And so afterwards doesn't make a difference. So I think he should get off and stay off."

So what do you really think of George, Ferdie?

• • •

I'VE ALWAYS FELT LIKE I CAN REASONABLY TALK TO ANYBODY ABOUT anything. Even if somebody was holding me up at gunpoint, I'd probably be able to make them talk about it. No matter what the situation or setting might be, and no matter what the story is behind my question, I believe I'm able to have a conversation. They might be angry or upset, and we might be on a crowded field or a busy street, but I still can get the job done. Maybe that's just an instinctive thing that I've been doing from an early age when I was observing interviewers on talk shows and grilling the boys my sisters dated.

The truth is, though, that people are unpredictable.

Late one night I received a call at the news desk. The assignment editor who took the call told me it was a guy saying he was Don King. At first we were both skeptical, but after confirming that the caller was indeed the famed boxing promoter, I picked up the phone.

"We did an interview a few years ago," King told me. "I just want you know that things aren't safe for me."

The voice sounded like him, but at the same time I received prank calls all the time. King hadn't been on *Up Close* yet, but I had interviewed him in the past.

"If something happens to me, I'm letting you know since you have a show everybody watches."

King sounded genuinely anxious.

"What do you mean if something happens to you?" I asked.

"There're people around my house. I'm not sure who they are, but I know I'm being watched."

"Did you call the police?" I asked, assuming I wasn't the first person he thought of when he feared for his life.

We eventually confirmed that King was worried about something to do with taxes. Nothing ever happened to him, and we never ended up putting that on the air.

I eventually interviewed King by satellite. While doing research for our conversation, I saw that he did almost four years of jail time for kicking a man to death in 1967. He would later be pardoned by the Ohio governor in 1983. King had also run a numbers racket in Cleveland, and over the years had been accused of stealing money and sued by many fighters. When I spoke to the always flamboyant King, I brought up these scandals, many of which had gone under the radar. I explained to him that I wanted to discuss allegations about his character so he could have a chance to clear the air.

"Chris Myers—all lies, all lies!" Don King said, speaking like a preacher as he shook his haystack of hair.

"Well, I have documents here," I said, starting to show them to the fight promoter. "I have a judge saying that—"

"Lies! All of them lies!"

Needless to say, it was a rocky interview, no pun intended. For months after this, I would be teased by our producers and the crew, who would always chant, "Lies! All lies!"

Another interesting conversation involved Mark Gastineau. Quarterbacks feared Gastineau. As a defensive end for the New York Jets from 1979 until his retirement in 1988, he ended up with over a hundred sacks in his career, including twenty in 1981 as part of the "New York Sack Exchange" defensive line. After the NFL, Gastineau began a five-year stint as a boxer and wrestler, and he had gained some celebrity status because he married actress Brigitte Nielsen. When we had him on *Up Close,* we planned to talk about his football career and his foray into boxing.

At the time, ESPN would fly some people in to do the show if they didn't live in the area. We taped *Up Close* in a studio on Hollywood and Vine, and guests would stay at the Beverly Hills Hotel nearby. When Gastineau came on, he started things off in a strange way. I wasn't sure if he was trying to be playful or if he was on any sort of substance or medication, but right before we were set to roll, he made a surprise request.

"Hey—I had my teeth redone by this company in Iowa," Gastineau said as he showed me by sliding out a dental bridge and holding it up. "I want to thank them and give them a little publicity."

"Well, we don't really do that sort of thing," I said.

"Oh really?" he asked.

Sitting across from me at the table, Gastineau dropped the bridge into my coffee mug. Then he grinned, showing his missing teeth.

"See? I don't look as good for your TV show. Maybe you can find a way to work this in now."

Oh boy, I thought. *It's gonna be a tough time today.*

Gastineau put the teeth back in his mouth and then our conversation turned to personal issues. He shared that he had been struggling ever since he and Brigitte Nielsen broke up.

"I'm sorry to hear that," I said.

"You know—we both had each other's name tattooed on our asses. I can show the audience."

"No, that's okay."

Gastineau stood up, but I was able to convince him to keep his pants on.

A few moments later while we were taping, he said, "I don't think you like me very much."

"No, no, it's not that I don't like you. I'm just trying to keep things focused on your career."

Instead of fake teeth and butt tattoos.

At another point, the defensive end looked at me and said, "You know I can beat you up, right?"

I laughed and assured him that I knew that. What I didn't know was whether Gastineau was teasing or being serious.

Eventually the conversation turned into a therapy session where Gastineau shared a story from his childhood. He said there was one time as a kid when he left his bicycle on his driveway, and his father backed the car over it. Even though he was crushed and crying, Gastineau's dad yelled at him, telling him it was dangerous and that this was his son's fault.

"I never got over that," he told me.

That wasn't in any of my research.

"Maybe that's why there's a toughness on your outside, but there's also a sensitivity to you deep inside," I said.

After finishing the interview, Gastineau went back to the Beverly Hills Hotel, and I assumed I wouldn't hear anything more from him. But the next day the hotel called us, saying that Gastineau refused to leave his room. We suddenly were worried about his health and if something terrible had happened. We called the police so they could figure out the situation. Fortunately, nothing dramatic transpired. No breaking down the door and barging in. Gastineau opened his door and told them he simply didn't want to leave his room just yet. He eventually decided to check out.

I felt bad for Gastineau. Some guys tried to intimidate you during an interview, but I thought there were some real issues going on with the football player. Stuff that research never could have shown me. That was the exciting and dangerous part about these free-flowing interviews—you never quite knew where they were going to take you.

• • •

THE BEST INTERVIEWERS MAKE THEIR GUESTS FEEL COMFORTABLE. Johnny Carson was a master of that. And so were others. Roy Firestone connected so well with his guests; his questions were probing and emotional. So were the ones Barbara Walters asked. She had wonderful empathy. And even though someone like Howard Stern was different in almost every way from Walters, he shared this trait of connecting with the people he spoke with. Stern has a way of making his guests open up to him.

What I've learned from watching these pros and others is that you have to know when to hold back and listen versus when you need to give your guest a little push. When do you lighten up the mood, or when do you go with the emotion? Every person is different, and every conversation is unique. I always made sure to never make the interview about me, to always stay in the middle, to always remain curious even if I was asking them about sensitive issues.

When I asked one guest what he least liked about Lou Holtz, the well-known coach at Notre Dame, he didn't hesitate to list the criticisms.

"The thing I like least about Lou Holtz is he's not particularly patient. He has high expectations and he doesn't worry about your feelings. He assumes we're all on the same team. We're part of a family, and you don't have a lot of time. And you just have to express what you feel and don't worry about feelings."

Lou Holtz might have been offended by these words if he hadn't said them himself. During the show while sitting across from me, the Hall of Fame coach was very quick with his assessment of himself, though he did add a caveat.

"At the same time, just like family, if you have a need or if you're down or you have a problem, he's going to be the first guy who's ready to help," Lou said.

Like any great coach, he wasn't there to be popular and have his players like him.

"My job is to get the very best out of people, make them productive, because when people become productive, achieve things they didn't think they're capable of doing, their self-image will continue to grow, and that's all we try to do."

• • •

UP CLOSE WAS FULL OF SO MANY LIFE LESSONS THAT GUESTS LOVED TO share. Lessons that were bigger than sports, that came as universal truths. So many times they were delivered with humor and heart.

"Chris, let me tell you something."

When Harry Caray says this, you lean in and listen. The beloved Chicago Cubs baseball sportscaster shared one of the most powerful things he learned.

"Anybody tells you that you have just as much fun not drinking as you can when you're drinking is lying," Caray said. "You go to a party. You drink these non-alcoholic drinks or drink water. You can't have quite as much fun as you can the other way. But when you realize if a guy knows the doctor told him don't drink, then if you go ahead and drink, you're stupid. And I'm not going to be stupid. I figured it out long ago. I'd rather be miserable and alive than very happy and dead."

I once asked NFL running back Jim Brown if there was anything he would have done differently in his life, if there was one thing he would have liked to have changed if he could.

"The thing about going back is that if you deal with the negative then you got to deal with the positive," Jim told me. "There is a balance of negative and balance of positive. And of course, I would hope that I did not do the negative things that I've done in my life. But you can't do anything about it, so I wouldn't go back and try to change that because we're on a journey and you have to make choices. And hopefully now with that knowledge, I can make much better choices."

I love to hear people's definition of happiness. During my *Up Close* interview with Bill Murray, I asked, "Were your happiest years doing *Saturday Night Live,* in terms of forming your showbiz career?"

"No, actually, a little bit before that. I worked on *The National Lampoon Radio Hour* before that. And it's kind of more fun when you're still a little broke and you're just having fun. Nobody's taking you too seriously because they're not paying you enough to take you seriously. You know, when you get on TV, they pay a little more and expect to be professional."

• • •

AS LARRY KING SAID, THE BIGGEST THING IN AN INTERVIEW IS LISTENING, of course. But I've learned over the years that you get a better response from the follow-up question than from the initial one.

While I was interviewing Hall of Fame defensive tackle Art Donovan, he demonstrated this very well. He was in his seventies when we spoke, and every answer he gave me was hilarious. Even when he wasn't trying to be. He had recently made some appearances on the *Late Show with David Letterman* and really connected with the audience.

"It was amazing how you bridged the gap, being an old-time football player connecting with the young audience," I said. "What's your secret?"

"I don't know," he said in his crusty Bronx accent. "Everything I said, they laughed at, so I kept saying things and they kept laughing."

"Does your wife laugh?"

"No. I was watching TV the other night with her and one of these promos came on. I said, 'Hey, Dottie. I'm really getting to be a star.' She says, 'You're a big jerk.' And you know—she's right."

I couldn't help laughing. "How long you've been married?"

"Forty years. Too long!"

"Forty—where did I go wrong?" I joked, knowing he was on a roll.

"I don't know. She wants to go away for our fortieth anniversary. She wants me to go to Australia. What the hell do I want to go to Australia for? To see kangaroos? I can go to the zoo to see kangaroos."

"No, but don't you want to broaden your horizons?"

"No—I've had enough horizons," Donovan said with a hint of amusement in his eyes. "Done everything you can possibly do."

"Everything? You've done everything you could possibly do? What's the one thing Art Donovan hasn't done that he needs to do before it's all said and done?"

"Ah, nah—to hell with what I want to do. A guy said, 'Well, how would you want to die?' I said I've got the tree all picked out—on the grounds of the Valley Country Club. I'm going to sit under a tree and I'm going to eat about fifteen or twenty kosher hot dogs. Eat a couple of pizza pies, drink a couple of cases of beer, and flat-out blow up. That's the way I want to go."

EIGHT

This Is Not *60 Minutes*

Everybody loved O. J. Simpson. But on the morning of June 13, 1994, everything about the star athlete's world changed.

"O. J. Simpson's Ex-wife, Man Found Slain," the headline for the *Los Angeles Times* read. "Football great O. J. Simpson's former wife and a 25-year-old man were found apparently stabbed to death outside her fashionable Brentwood area townhome early this morning."[1]

The story that unfolded has been well documented in popular culture. The details are now infamous, having been told in books, magazine and newspaper articles, documentaries, and a miniseries. ESPN did an incredible five-part *30 for 30* series covering this called *O.J.: Made in America*. I never imagined that a tragic Shakespearean tale like this could find itself on my doorstep in the middle of my career.

O. J. Simpson was a football star—a Heisman Trophy winner at the University of Southern California; the first overall draft pick in the 1969 NFL Draft; a Pro Bowl running back for the Buffalo Bills. At the time of this writing, he still holds the single-season yards-per-game average record in the NFL at 143.1 and is regarded as one of the best running backs of all time. When O.J. retired in 1979 after playing eleven seasons in the league, he was already a legend in the game, but he became even more famous and beloved when he ended up pursuing a career as an actor and broadcaster. And, of course, as the star of the memorable Hertz rent-a-car advertising campaign.

"He *was the guy* of the '70s," Joe DeLamielleure, O.J.'s former Buffalo Bills teammate, said. "Hank Aaron, Muhammad Ali, O. J. Simpson—and O.J. was the most popular of all of them. I didn't see them running through airports."[2]

On January 30, 1994, months before he was arrested and charged with the murders of Nicole Brown Simpson and Ron Goldman, O.J. was a sideline reporter for Super Bowl XXVIII, where the Dallas Cowboys beat the Buffalo Bills. He worked on the Bills' side of the field. Over the years, O.J. had been a commentator for ABC Sports, a role that included working as an analyst on *Monday Night Football*. But more than that role, O.J. had become known for playing Detective Nordberg in the *Naked Gun* comedies starring Leslie Nielsen, the third being released in March 1994.

O.J. was a football star and a movie star, a likable celebrity who was a natural on camera. Companies loved putting him in their commercials. He always came off as smiling and friendly, the kind of guy you'd want to hang out with. That's why when he was arrested in June 1994 and everything played out like it did, the nation was absolutely transfixed. It was unthinkable for someone of that magnitude to suddenly be charged with two horrific murders. There had never been anything like it in the sports world, and there hasn't been anything like it since.

Like everybody else, I was shocked and didn't believe it when I first heard the news about O.J's arrest. But once the facts came out, even people who were good friends with the athlete couldn't cover for him. With each passing detail, the public questioned how he could do something like this. I was left wondering the same question so many others asked.

Who is this guy?

Watching the so-called trial of the century, with its "Dream Team" of defense lawyers, I became convinced that O.J. was guilty. On October 3, 1995, after the nine-month criminal trial that became the most watched case in US history, a jury found O. J. Simpson not guilty. Then, after being sued by the victims' families in a civil trial that began in October 1996, Simpson was found liable for the deaths of Nicole Brown and Ronald Goldman and was ordered to pay $33.5 million in damages to the families.

Two years later, I would land the first live TV interview with O.J.

• • •

AROUND THE TIME OF THE RULING IN THE CIVIL TRIAL IN 1996, I INTERviewed Jim Brown on *Up Close*. When I asked the great running back about the dangers of placing athletes on a pedestal, Jim brought up Simpson.

"The danger is what you have now in the O.J. situation. You know, O.J. was made out to be the person we should all emulate. And—"

Jim chuckled for a moment, then continued.

"And he was made out to be this particular hero. And no one ever took a closer look—they didn't want to take a closer look. And even people that knew that O.J. wasn't as perfect as they wanted him to be did not stand up and have the courage to say that. Now you have people who are so guilt-ridden because they put their trust in him and they believed in this particular image and that image will always come back in failure. Because in order to be a true American, you have to rock the boat, because freedom, equality, and justice have to be for everyone. So if I just stay cool and make millions and deal with the image that white America wants me to have, at some point that shadowy background is going to come out and it's going to disillusion everyone."

"But the O.J. subject, and it may be a tired subject, but I'm still fascinated by it," I said. "I think you and I are the only ones who haven't written a book about it. And the question here is did O.J. lean on his color when it was convenient during this trial?"

"Of course he did . . . Unfortunately, in this country, Black people suffer so much from police brutality and racism until a person like O.J. can take advantage of that right now because a lot of Black people are hurting. So his skin color is Black even though he didn't live Black. So they embrace him in his fight against the establishment. And it's unfortunate because I would never be that weak. I don't think that all the people that think O.J. is guilty that are white are racist. I think there are a lot of people that care about two people, one being Nicole and one being Ron. And I think that these two individuals have been forgotten in this *whole* deal about O.J. It is so twisted—it's an American tragedy at this particular time. Everything about it is negative."

When I asked Jim whether O.J. would have been found not guilty if he weren't Black and weren't a celebrity former athlete, he gave his critique of the trial.

"Let me put it to you this way. The prosecution, to me, was the worst—it presented the worst case I've ever seen."

"And you followed this closely, I presume?"

"It was terrible. It was amateur time in Dixie. Therefore, an injustice was done because the state did not put forward the kind of prosecution that it should have. And I don't want to comment on the outcome of it, because when you deal with the ambiguous term of 'reasonable doubt' and you put people—a jury—up there, that jury is going to find reasonable doubt when the prosecution allows them to have so many areas to question."

Before changing topics, I asked Jim whether he had talked to O.J. or attempted to talk to him.

"I'm not going to talk to O.J.," he said.

"You don't think you could do him some good if—"

"No, I'm not going to talk to him. If he wants to talk to me and talk about the truth and stand up and be what I consider a man, then I'll talk to him, but I'm not going to talk to him."

• • •

IN MY EIGHTH YEAR AT ESPN AND MY FOURTH YEAR HOSTING *UP CLOSE*, O.J.'s agent reached out to us.

"O.J. watches the show and wants to come on. He thinks Chris is fair when he interviews people."

For a while we had been trying to get O.J. on the show, but once everything happened, we basically gave up. It had been about two and a half years since Nicole Brown Simpson and Ron Goldman were stabbed to death outside Nicole's home. After speaking with the bosses at ESPN, I told them I wanted to interview O.J., but obviously things had changed.

"I'm not going to talk to him about his Heisman Trophy," I said. "I have to ask him about the murders."

O.J.'s people said we could ask him anything. There were only two requests. The first was that the interview had to be live. That was why he had declined to be interviewed by Barbara Walters; he didn't want to tape it so the conversation could be edited. He wanted it live. His other request was that I couldn't ask about his children, a request I thought was fair and agreed to.

As word got out leading up to the interview that O.J. was coming on the show, there was a surprising amount of backlash. I received death threats from people. "I can't believe you're putting a killer on the air," some said. "You're going to glorify him." Even some of the announcers at ESPN seemed to silently agree with the sentiments. Others felt like the interview would be incredible but doubted that Simpson would show up. A few close friends and colleagues cautioned me that this could damage my career. But one person I was pleasantly surprised to get support from was my friend Bill Murray.

"You absolutely have to do the interview," he told me after calling to talk about it.

I opened up to him about being a little nervous about looking stupid during the live interview.

"There's a book you have to read," Bill told me. "It's called *How to Talk So Kids Will Listen & Listen So Kids Will Talk*. It'll help you from being thrown off or distracted by some of the stuff you talk about."

I bought a copy of the bestselling book coauthored by Adele Faber and Elaine Mazlish and read it. It provided some good advice on effectively communicating with your child, and ultimately with anybody you're having a difficult conversation with. Some of the most simple statements seemed perfect for my upcoming interview, like the following:

"Children don't need to have their feelings agreed with; they need to have them acknowledged."

I knew I had to enter the interview as unbiased as possible. I had to leave my personal convictions behind and be open-minded during the interview. I remembered the noteworthy details from Simpson's trial that had lasted 267 days:

O.J.'s arrest for domestic abuse against Nicole on January 1, 1989, eventually pleading no contest to beating and threatening to kill her.

The white Ford Bronco being chased by the LAPD.

O.J.'s blood and DNA being found at the crime scene.

The size 12 Bruno Magli shoes.

But the more I prepared for the interview, the more I became convinced that O.J. had killed Nicole Brown and Ron Goldman.

Someone connected me with Vincent Bugliosi, who had been a Los Angeles County deputy district attorney famous for prosecuting Charles Manson and his followers for the Tate-LaBianca murders in 1969. He won convictions against Manson and the others and wrote about it in *Helter Skelter*. Vincent was living in San Diego, so I spoke to him on the phone about interviewing O.J.

"Look, when you have O.J. live, this guy is going to make you look foolish," Bugliosi told me. "You can see in his behavioral patterns that he believes his lies. He knows the case and what really happened better than anybody."

Bugliosi was very helpful as he shared his view of O.J.'s mindset and personality. Years later in his book *Outrage: The Five Reasons Why O. J. Simpson Got Away with Murder,* Vincent wrote, "Simpson has got to be considered one of the most self-absorbed persons there could ever be, one whose narcissism is of jumbo proportions."[3] The prosecutor warned me that this narcissism was why O.J. wanted to do the interview live.

"Narcissists spin lies they believe in," Bugliosi said. "They'll make you look stupid."

Vincent was also helpful in reaching out to the two investigating officers for the case and connecting me with them. After I explained I'd be interviewing Simpson, I met with the detectives and asked them questions. How did they find out information, what sort of procedures did they follow? Philip Vannatter was one of the detectives. They didn't give me anything that wasn't in the police file. Everything showed that they had followed the rules and done everything by the book when it came to O.J.'s case. I also met with Dan Petrocelli, the attorney at the civil trial who ended up getting a liable judgment against O.J. He showed me additional evidence that they didn't see in the murder trial.

During the whole process, nobody ever sounded angry or vindictive toward O.J. There was never a sense of *We hate O.J.* and *We want to fry him.* They were disappointed that justice had not been done but understood that this was what the jury had decided. They wanted to help me since they knew what O.J. might say or think.

What shocked me the most were the photos I saw of Nicole Brown Simpson and Ron Goldman. They were gruesome. The jury in the murder trial wasn't even allowed to see the police photos of the murder scene. As I looked through them, I had to turn away because they were so horrifying.

All this additional evidence further convinced me that O.J. was guilty.

• • •

AS THE INTERVIEW APPROACHED, I BECAME CONSUMED WITH ALL THE details of the case as I planned the questions to ask Simpson. I spent so much time thinking and planning and preparing for the interview that sometimes I felt like I was preparing for a trial. I'd be having dinner with the family and someone might ask to pass the salt, and I'd blurt out, "I object!"

Relax, Chris, I told myself. *This isn't a trial. You're not a counselor or part of the jury.*

I had to remember that I was a sports broadcaster first and foremost. I didn't want to come out and attack O.J. I wasn't going to say, "Hey, you killed them." That wasn't my thing anyway. I planned on having a conversation with him and asking him questions everybody else wanted to ask. ESPN was careful as we approached the date. Their guidance with me was to not hype up the publicity about this. We knew it was going to be a different sports interview, but this wasn't *60 Minutes.* That's ironic since it ended up being almost sixty minutes long.

Days before the entire country watched my interview with O.J., one of his lawyers told me not to do it. It was early January 1998, and my wife and I were attending a function in the suburbs of Los Angeles when we ran into Robert Shapiro. He was one of the well-known members of the "Dream Team," the group of a dozen lawyers that represented O.J. in his 1995 trial. Before this Shapiro had become notorious for representing Erik Menendez in another highly publicized murder trial that unfolded before the nation.

Shapiro had heard about my upcoming interview and decided to warn me. He pulled me aside.

"Listen, Chris. I wouldn't do the interview. It's risky."

I was surprised to hear Shapiro's advice. I knew all the details and felt as prepared as he had been when he represented Simpson.

"But he won the case," I said, assuming he would have been excited to have O.J. on to argue for his innocence.

"Anybody connected to O.J. is bad news."

The way he said it, this could be a career killer for me, no pun intended.

The tone in Shapiro's voice and the expression on his face were foreboding. He seemed to be saying that there was something sordid about Simpson's case, about even being associated with it in any way. But nothing could change my mind.

This was a polarizing story, and it had left people talking and shaking their heads, unwilling to let go of it. It was an unbelievable series of events involving a monumental sports star. Everybody had an opinion on it and played judge and jury. The last news event that had riveted our country like this was the Lindbergh kidnapping.

There was no way I was going to pass up an interview with The Juice.

NINE

Are You Capable of Killing?

Nothing brings people together like big sporting events and national tragedies. My interview with O.J. is a combination of both. When I hear that he has arrived at the studio, I am actually a bit surprised; all of us have been wondering if he was really going to go through with this. Like I always do, I go to the green room to greet my guest. The only difference this time is that I won't stay around to have a friendly conversation.

"I appreciate you doing this," I tell O.J. "We'll be going live in a little bit."

As I go over my notes, I know I'm as prepared as I can possibly be, but I still have never felt more nervous in my life. I think of the mantra I've lived by my entire career: "Every night is the Super Bowl."

For me, this feels even bigger. I'm talking to a man found liable in the killing of two people.

Looking casual in a green sweater and white T-shirt, O.J. smiles at me and nods after I introduce him. So cool and so confident. I immediately bring up an article published in the most recent *Esquire* magazine.

"You were quoted as saying in this, 'Let's say I committed this crime. Even if I did do this, it would have to have been because I loved her very much. Right?' With a question mark and referring to Nicole in this. What exactly did you mean by that?"

My goal with starting with this quote is to see if he remembers making that statement, and then wanting him to explain exactly what he meant. When I first read it, I thought, *Who would even say something like that?* If you didn't kill your ex-wife—if you're totally innocent—why utter, "Let's say I committed this crime"? Why would you even think that way? I start with this because it sounded like he was rationalizing his behavior.

O.J. shifts in his seat, looking down for a moment as he slowly and calmly begins to explain his perspective.

"Well, it is curious, because so many very respected journalists in this country have heard me say this as a part of a scenario of things. Normally we talk about evidence and we go through a whole evidential thing when I'm talking to schools. I've talked to a number of law schools, and we get into an evidence thing. And I say, 'Well, what was the motive of this crime?' And then normally people jump out and say, 'Jealousy and control.' And I say, 'Yes. Petrocelli and Marcia made big points about that. So tell me what evidence was presented in the court that went towards jealousy and control.' And inevitably, there's no answer because there was none, right?"

"But for you in your situation, to link love and—"

"Well, hold on—let me finish, let me finish," O.J. interrupts, motioning with his hand for me to pipe down while flashing his famous grin.

He explains how money couldn't have been a reason since NBC and Hertz had both given him pay increases. Then he addresses someone saying that he had killed Nicole out of a sense of love.

"So why would I have to kill a person who is begging me to move back in with me, who has written me letters that you all saw publicly? 'I'll do anything for you. I'll move anywhere with you. I'll go anywhere. I just want to wake up and go to sleep with you.' It makes no sense. But of course, they [*Esquire* magazine] took this one thing out of the middle of there and made it as if it was an independent statement."

"But it sounds like you're reexamining your position in this crime when you say something like that," I say.

"I don't think so," O.J. states. "I disagree with you and I'm certainly not reexamining my position. I think that's incorrect."

I follow this up with the most quoted question of the interview.

"Are you capable of killing somebody?"

O.J. turns and halfway grimaces as he appears to think about the question.

"You know, I would say actually, I would say no, even though I'm sure—um, I'm sure if someone was presenting some imminent danger to my kids or something, I'm sure everybody would be capable."

I know he isn't going to admit that he killed Nicole and Ron, so my purpose is to show the information I've learned and ask him about it. Then people can judge for themselves whether he's lying or not.

"Would you kill for Nicole?" I ask.

"If I thought someone was going to hurt her. You protect the people you love. I mean, we dropped the bomb on Hiroshima and Nagasaki. I think most Americans supported that, even though we may, in retrospect, think about the lives that we took."

Woah, where are we going with things?

O.J. continues to talk, telling me a story about a time he found a guy in his house and how he ended up grabbing a baseball bat and leading the man out of his house without an incident.

"But, you know, you wonder," he says. "If my kids were there, if I walked into my daughter's room and this guy would have come upstairs in my daughter's room, I don't know what I would have been capable of."

My question comes before he can take a breath. "But love could cause you to go into a rage to kill?"

"I don't think so," O.J. says. "No—I don't believe so at all."

"Two criminal psychologists told me that that statement—two independent criminal psychologists—that that statement you made, even though you explained it, that they would interpret that if they were talking to someone as a form of an admission. Are you admitting something?"

"No I'm not admitting—" O.J. says, beginning an answer that twisted and turned and went all over the place without saying much of anything. Talking about hypothetical situations and prefacing things with "if." So I say that people could interpret this sort of talk as an admission or as a type of confession, but O.J. disagrees once again.

"Are you capable of going into a rage and not remembering exactly what you did?" I ask.

"I don't believe so, no."

"Have you ever done that?"

He shrugs. "No. I mean, I've been in rages, and when it was over, you kind of regret some of the things you might have said. Uh, but, uh, I don't feel that, uh, I've ever in my life done something that when it was over, I wasn't aware of what I, what I did."

O.J. gives a slight chuckle at the end of the comment.

I ask about the differences of both trials, how the criminal trial didn't convict him but the civil trial found him liable. Once again he doesn't directly answer me but begins to talk in circles about law until landing on his thoughts on justice.

"To this day, I'll never, never understand how you can find someone liable for a crime when they were found not guilty, which is innocent in

America," O.J. says with a confident smirk. "I hear these pundits always say, 'He wasn't found innocent.' Well, how can you say that?"

"No, because—"

"You're innocent until you're proven guilty!" O.J. states.

"Guilty beyond a reasonable doubt. It doesn't mean you're innocent. It just means they didn't have enough to convict you."

As I make my point, he looks over to one side in a way that says, *You have no idea what you're talking about.* Then O.J. continues to share his take.

"I just say, if you're a lawyer and you went to law school, the, the, the philosophy that, that our whole criminal justice system is predicated on is that a person is innocent until proven guilty. If he's not proven guilty, he's innocent. And nobody can argue that, unless it's me. Nobody can argue that. And so I don't understand how I ended up going to a second trial. I don't think it was fair, the second trial. I think the judge broke the rules of evidence. I think—I don't think anybody in America should have someone on the jury panel who said, 'I think he's guilty.' I think—I don't think that's—"

I have to interrupt.

"So you're questioning the judge and the jury. Were you questioning them in the criminal trial as well?"

He backs off and says he doesn't want to criticize the jury, that he prefers to do that in a court. Then he explains how he's doing the appeal and how he's been as "hospitable as humanly possible" to the sheriff's department. I ask why he didn't take the stand in the criminal trial and he tells me that Judge Ito warned everybody that they were going to lose the jury since the trial was going so long.

"So listen—I'm sitting here in jail. I know if I take the stand, that's going to be a month. I don't know how long I'm going to be on trial, but by the time we bring in people to verify what I said, they bring in people to verify what they have to say, the trial is going to go another month. We go on to twelve. It's like it was no trial. It's a mistrial. [Los Angeles district attorney Gil] Garcetti said he would retry the case. I'd be sitting in jail another three or four years with no money. Even Johnnie Cochran and these guys said they couldn't come back for *years* to help me. I had no choice."

I decide to press the issue.

"But when you're on trial for your life and people think you're guilty of something, and if you claim you're as innocent as you are, why not take the stand under oath and tell the world right there? Wouldn't that be important to you?"

"It would have been important to me. But I mean—" O.J. smirks and gives me a condescending chuckle. "It's almost, Chris, as if you hadn't heard what I just said."

"I heard—"

"I would have lost the jury panel," O.J. says, once again talking over me. "I would have been sitting my butt in jail for another two, three, four years before I could even get back to a trial. With two kids being raised somewhere else. I had no choice. I *fully* felt at the time we had proven to me beyond a doubt that I was innocent. That was my feelings, and evidently that was right."

"Well, the perception of the general public today is that you didn't take the stand because you wanted—you were avoiding telling the truth."

"Well, that's their problem." The million-dollar grin flashes again. "That's not my problem. I think in most cases, there have been many people have been found innocent that didn't take the stand. And the general public may think they're guilty or may *not* think they're guilty. I don't know. That's just the facts of life. The facts of life is, my lawyers advised me that if I were to take the stand, and Lee Bailey has made it clear, I fought my lawyers. Every lawyer I know has said, 'O.J. wanted to take the stand.'"

I agree with him and try to get another statement in, but he continues.

"They had to convince me that if I took the stand, that we were in danger of losing this jury. And if we lost this jury, I would be sitting in jail for years before I would be able to get back into the court."

"But ultimately, it was your call whether to take the stand or not. You call the shots."

O.J. nods. "Yes. And I didn't take the stand. I wish I had."

"You do? Why?"

He explains that a lot of the things that were said in the courtroom were stated when the jury wasn't present. Things that he thought hurt him. But Johnnie Cochran told him that this was a murder trial and they could only focus on the crime.

"You'll have plenty of time once you get out of jail to 'rehabilitate' yourself. But right now our job is to get you out of jail."

As O.J. quotes Johnnie Cochran, he says the word "rehabilitate" in a lower voice, as if to mock his lawyer. The whole idea of him having to rehabilitate his image is ridiculous, so I address this point.

"I don't think—I don't know how that's going—rehabilitating yourself in terms of the eyes of the public, because—"

"You see—you see," he interrupts. "You tend to put more importance on all my detractors. I try to focus on the positive people out there."

He goes back to the *Esquire* article I brought up in my first question, talking about how the interviewer took the time to get to know him. Then he says that so many reports out there about him are flat-out lies.

"Everywhere I go, people are nice to me. I have my two kids. I'm raising my two kids today. And basically, hey, you know, it's not the life I had before, but, hey, I laugh just as much and I miss Nicole. I miss the fact that my kids don't have a mother. But basically—hey. All you can do is the best you can under the circumstances."

The kids. He mentioned the kids.

This is the one topic O.J. had said was off-limits. But not anymore.

"All right. You didn't want to bring up your kids, but since you do, why do you seem to trash Nicole at every opportunity you get? The mother of your children. And you did in that *Esquire* article, talking about the friends she ran with and the things that she did."

He takes a sip of his coffee while his eyes shift in different directions as if he's surprised by my comment.

"Okay. I'd like you since you made that statement—and I find this a very irresponsible statement on your part—you read to the audience what I said that trashed Nicole."

His eyes shift from me to the desk, back and forth, the only display of fire that can be seen. I casually look through my papers, but I know exactly where the statement can be found.

"The *Esquire* article—the exact quote, I'm sure that we have it right here. 'I see these women on TV with their candlelight vigils for Nicole. Everywhere I've gone with Nicole women disliked her. They thought she was cold and snobbish. These women on the street with their candles, they all hated her before. It has nothing to do with Nicole. Everybody is just using her image for their own purposes.'"

Something strikes a nerve.

"Okay, how am I trashing Nicole?" O.J. asks, but when I try to answer he continues. "Hold on—let me finish. You heard every friend of Nicole, every single friend of Nicole who's ever talked about her on TV since her murder. They ask, what type of person was Nicole? 'Great mother, great mother, great friend. But when I first met her, she seemed cold. She seemed snobbish. I thought she was a cold fish.' Every single person, even people who became her friend."

The intensity is in O.J.'s voice and his stare and the way he speaks with his hands.

"But what's your take when you said she argued with people in the neighborhood or she had a hot temper and yelling at the help—" I start to ask.

"She did!" O.J. says, talking over me and shrugging. "She did."

"But why would you even bring that out now? Is that necessary?"

O.J. continues to try to make the argument that this is what other people have said about her, what other women have thought. So I have to bring up the obvious.

"If you don't bring that up, we don't know about that," I say. "If you don't bring that out. We don't need to know that, do we?"

My question makes him pause for a brief moment, as if it dawns on him who he is talking about and what he is saying.

"Well . . ." he utters.

"That she was snobbish or that people thought she was snobbish or cold," I say.

"Hold it, hold it, hold it, hold it," the combative athlete says with a grin. "I was focusing on these women. I wasn't focusing on Nicole. Every one of Nicole's friends have said this. Now, you didn't get on their cases. You didn't say that they were trashin' her."

He gives me his incredulous smile.

"No, but they weren't the ones who were charged with murder and went through two trials," I say.

"So what? You mean it's different? If somebody wasn't charged with murder, call her some horrible names, it's different?"

"My point is that you were married to her. That's the mother of your children. I just think it's something that at this stage you would avoid going in that area."

In his calm and casual demeanor, I know O.J. is still trying to intimidate me. Not answering the question, changing the direction of the conversation, getting away from the truth at the heart of this interview. I steer the discussion to another critical issue to cover with him.

"In the civil trial, you repeatedly said that you did not hit—when you were under cross-examination from Daniel Petrocelli—that you never hit, kicked—"

"I never punched her," O.J. interrupts.

"Okay, you said no to that. And then later in that trial and reading through the transcripts, there were numerous cases, including an incident in '89, where it appeared that that happened, that you had altercations with her."

"Well, let's see here once again, this is a problem I have with the media. Tell me numerous—'89? Tell me these other numerous cases. You throw this out like there's numerous times! Other than '89, what other time was it?"

"Isn't one enough, though?" I ask.

"Yes, once was too much," O.J. answers, continuing with the story of Nicole telling her mom about the incident, about Nicole admitting she was as much to blame as O.J. So I ask the simple question.

"But you hit her, right?"

"No, I didn't! I was very physical with her."

I continue to press him. "But we heard—we saw the pictures, the bruises—"

O.J. talks over me again.

"You think if I hit you, you'd be bruised?" he asks. "You'd be swollen. You'd be busted up a little bit."

As he speaks, the shot of Nicole from that night appears on the screen.

"But that picture, and I think it's—you know, we shouldn't be showing this out of respect—but I just think that looks like something that someone's gone through a pretty good beating."

He begins his answer once again in a controlled and serious manner, but with every word he speaks, the anger underneath seems to hiss out of him.

"Well, she had a bruise," he says. "If you saw a better picture, that's a Polaroid picture. And I—I cannot belittle—any bruise was too much. That's a picture with a Polaroid under flashing light at three o'clock in the morning, a woman who admitted she was drunk. I'd like to see your wife go take a picture and see what she looks like there. The point is, *any* bruise she had on her, I was responsible for. I told the court I was responsible for it. Went to court. I'm responsible. I had no excuse. The detective who testified in the case, the investigator, he said O.J. made no excuse. He knew he was wrong. He said it. The judge gave me exactly what the court recommended. I did it. Nicole and I went on with our lives. I don't understand why we're still talking about it."

There he is, the O.J. everybody was warning me about.

I know he's trying to push my buttons, trying to touch a nerve. And even though I think he's being a real asshole at this point, bringing in my wife for no reason, I don't want to lose my cool. I can't make this personal.

O.J. tries to once again explain the 1989 incident. She was pushing him, he was pushing her. But he makes it sound like some simple skirmish. And once again he asks a question that shows his complete detachment from the reality here.

"And why are we talking about it now?" he repeats.

We remain on the incident, O.J. refusing to back down, refusing to admit that he did beat her or hit her even though the evidence is clear as day.

"Well, she wrote about it in her diary," I say. "And we heard her—"

"Aw, come on," he says, closing his eyes in disbelief. "You guys—you guys are so full of beans. She didn't have a diary."

O.J. continues to talk about Nicole denying what happened, about the media refusing to tell the truth. He won't budge on this. Eighteen minutes into the interview, I announce that we have to take a break and that we'll be back in a moment. As we do, O.J. chuckles and moves in his seat like some kid in middle school who's about to go to recess.

Right after we break, O.J.'s publicist comes out of the green room, hollering at me.

"You can't be talking about this," she says.

O.J. waves her off.

"It's okay, I got this," he says. "Go back in there. It's fine."

As she walks away, he shines his big grin.

"I like this kind of stuff," O.J. tells me. "The only way I can get my point across to people is to have this type of interchange. Otherwise they're going to say you were soft on me and gave me softball questions and stuff."[1]

There are a thousand different things that I might have imagined O.J. saying next, but what comes out of his mouth during our commercial break truly stuns me.

"I have a tee time at the Riviera next week," O.J. says as if we're close friends. "Right now there's only three of us, so let me know if you want to play some golf with me and my buddies."

I politely tell him no thanks as my mind reels in disbelief.

We just showed pictures of his battered ex-wife and now he's asking me to golf?

It's surreal.

• • •

WHEN WE COME BACK FROM THE COMMERCIAL BREAK, I BRING UP O.J.'s statement about vowing to dedicate his life and resources to finding the "real killers," and I ask him what he's doing to find those "quote-unquote 'real killers.'" He answers by referring to random things like investigators and volunteers and books coming out by people in the trial that might "collect information." Then he ends up talking about Faye Resnick, one of Nicole's friends who became noteworthy for writing her own book published four months after the murders.

"Her credibility was so bad, they couldn't put her in either trial, even though they based much of what they tried to do to me on what she had to say," O.J. says. "I've always felt—I feel in my heart—that the key to the deaths of these two people was through Faye Resnick."

"Really?"

Several times as O.J. continues to talk about Resnick, I try to insert a question, but he just talks over me.

"In your mind, there's no doubt—"

"No."

"—that you had any involvement in the death of Ron Goldman or Nicole?"

"I didn't," he says.

"You're not responsible—"

"I didn't do it."

"—in any way?"

"I'm not responsible in any way, shape, or form," O.J. states with a stern glare.

O.J. doesn't answer my question about how much money he is supposedly spending on people to find the real killer, so then I ask if he has any moral obligation to pay the $33.5 million civil settlement against him.

"I don't feel I have a moral obligation to pay because morally I've done nothing wrong."

When I bring up O.J. taking the stand at the civil trial and not having an explanation for his blood being at the crime scene and Ron Goldman's blood being in O.J.'s Bronco, he launches into a summary that sounds like one of his former lawyers arguing the case.

"They had no explanation as to, for instance, the person, even though they lied, is who collected the blood. No explanation. This person testified under oath on at least two occasions that she processed it, they let it dry overnight, and then she folded [it] up in a bindle. Now, a bindle is a piece of paper. She wrote her initials. Now, we know chain of custody. She wrote her initials on each and every one of those bindles. And no one at L.A. said they touched it—"

"But when you were on—" I begin to ask.

"Hold on, let me finish here, you're missing the point here," he stops me, giving me that controlling smile. "When those blood samples went to these various places to be tested, miraculously, her initials had disappeared. So where are they? Is this the same things she collected? Obviously not."

"All right, but the point is, when you were under oath on the civil trial, you didn't say that. You had no explanation."

"How can I talk about what they collected? How—how I—how do I—how do I know what they collected?"

Once again, I lead us back to the big picture, to the reality of this story.

"You explain—you say you have people looking for the real killers. How do you explain that all the evidence so far points just to you? We have not seen one shred of evidence—"

He interrupts me once again and starts denying this, shaking his head as I ask for any evidence. Then he begins to talk about items from his defense—hair and fibers found not belonging to him, EDTA (a blood preservative) discovered, the FBI getting involved and hiding evidence that would have helped him in the civil trial.

We're already twenty-five minutes into the interview, so I know we're close to finishing. I tell viewers we'll take a quick commercial break, and then when we're back I'll address the famous white Bronco chase that everyone talked about. The one 95 million people watched that involved O.J. being driven by his friend and former football player A. C. Cowlings. The guys at the home office of ESPN in Connecticut tell me to keep going even though the thirty-minute window is almost finished. I'm glad because I still have a lot more questions to ask O.J. And the next question is one that a lot of people have wanted to ask him.

"Some of the questions that people have asked want to know [about] the Bronco chase following the murders. Why would someone run in that scenario? I know you said you were going to visit the grave."

O.J. at first seems to want to argue, but then he composes himself and answers in a calm way.

"One, I didn't run. I was depressed. I'd gone through, obviously, a tough week. And then I heard I was being arrested. And at one point I looked at A.C. and I said, 'Take me to Nicole's grave.' I was very depressed. I just wanted the pain in me to stop. He drove me to Nicole's gravesite down in the Laguna area. We drove up, we looked at the gate. There was a cop car covering the entry to the—to the cemetery, which how would we know unless we were there? We went and parked for a while. And then A.C., I think, got out of the car to use the restroom or something. And then when he came back, he noticed I had a gun, and he said, 'I'm taking you home.'"

"Why'd you have a gun?" I ask.

"I was just depressed," O.J. says. "I had a gun in the beginning that week with somebody that just killed my former wife and, from all indications, had been at my house, because we were hearing about a bloody mask and all of this junk behind my home at that particular time. But by this time who knows—you know, I was very depressed."

"So you were considering suicide?"

"Possibly, yes, I can't—yes, I probably was. I just wanted the pain to stop."

He explains being chased by the LAPD while his friend was driving him home, saying they were going to stop, that they wanted to stop, that they were doing what they had told the police they were going to do. I remind him that in the civil trial, the Bronco chase came up, and it was revealed that Simpson had a disguise and passport with him. He discounts the "stupid little mask thing" and then says he always keeps his passport in his travel bag, so he wasn't thinking of going anywhere other than back home.

"But the American public is not stupid," I say. "It looks guilty when you're driving away with a gun and disguise and a passport. You can't blame people for thinking that you were running from this."

I want to ask about his feelings toward the public reaction to him, so I mention a poll ESPN did about O.J.

"Seventy-five percent of the people overall, regardless of the criminal trial or the civil trial, say that you're guilty. And 77 percent of the white people, 25 percent of the Black. What is your response to this? Do you care?"

"You know, you wish it wasn't such. I feel that I've had one person to answer to originally—I mean eventually—is my Lord and Savior. And since I know inside that—that's the only thing that really matters. And I've looked throughout history, and when I read the Bible from Moses to Jesus to whoever you want to name—Job—they all went through similar things."

O.J. just compared himself to Moses and Job and Jesus. What the hell is he thinking?

"And I think that's what the Bible was for me, an example," O.J. continues. "It was like a map that says things like this can happen in your life and you can overcome it. I think I've overcome it by getting so much of the hate out of me, and I had a lot of hate in me and anger in me."

"But there's a hate in a lot of people towards you," I quickly state.

"Well, that's their problem."

I bring up the public backlash we've had about having him on *Up Close* to be interviewed.

"For someone who's such a public person, can you live like this? Can you live as a pariah?" I ask.

"Well, you know, I live as a pariah on TV," O.J. answers, saying that in his real life he is accepted and treated as he's always been treated.

When I ask whether O.J. thinks he's going to convince people that he's innocent, he says all he can do is give his side of it. Especially in forums like this—live and not edited interviews. He says he doesn't have a P.R. person and scoffs at the suggestion that he's trying to make a comeback.

"That's the perception, that you're trying to make a comeback," I say.

"I'm trying to raise my kids," O.J. says. "I'm trying to get my golf handicap down. And hopefully, eventually we'll get enough information together to get the D.A. to reopen this case."

He says he just wants to live his life, that people on TV say anything and everything, that you can always find somebody who has something negative to say about someone.

Another blatantly obvious question comes to my mind.

"But it doesn't look like you're consumed with finding the real killer. Somebody murdered someone you love so much."

"Well, I can only do what I can do. Wouldn't you think that Fred Goldman—anybody—well, they think I did it."

O.J. literally has the audacity to start to suggest that Fred Goldman isn't concerned about finding the right killer.

"He was consumed," I remind O.J.

Once again, O.J. defends himself, wandering down a path where he says friends of Ron Goldman have been murdered, saying that he's not just sitting on his butt doing nothing. He claims that drugs definitely played a part in the murders of Nicole and Ron, so I ask when was the last time he ever did drugs, a rumor that has followed him throughout the trials. He says it was the late '70s and early '80s, blaming the time and the culture but saying it was something he grew out of.

After one more commercial break, I bring up the issue of race that has become such a pivotal part of the trial.

"Do you think that clouded the question of justice at all?" I ask.

"You know, I think race has been a very convenient, a convenient issue for certain people in this country. Obviously, when Mark Fuhrman got involved in this case, it was impossible to avoid race. I find it curious that I can see Marcia Clark and these pundits I see on TV. They'll talk about the nanny trial or the schoolteacher that had a baby with the sixth grader. And they said, 'Well, if they were Black, they'd be in jail.' And I said, 'Well, isn't it interesting how they're now saying things that I happen to agree with, but when a Black lawyer says it, he's playing the race card. It's unethical.'"

As we get to the subject of his public image and how much it's important to him, he says that he's gotten rid of a lot of the anger that's been inside of him.

"And where did that come from?" I ask.

"This whole case. I feel I got screwed big time in this case."

"You still firmly believe that?"

"Oh, yes," O.J. says, going on about how dishonest the media has been in reporting about his life now.

"When you say you want to get your life back in spades, you believe you will?" I ask.

Somehow he brings up Job once again.

"In the Bible you read about, about Job, and about if you keep the faith in it all, you get it all back. I don't know if it's material you get it back or if it's not material. It's unimportant to me. What I want to get back is the feeling that I had for life, which I think I have. I think anybody who has met me over the last two years, especially the last year, would say—hey, he's a nice guy. I've always tried to help people. No one has had a bad thing to say to me—about me—before this."

"You talk about the Bible," I say. "There are many people out there that feel you're getting your punishment on earth by, because you're such a public figure and enjoy that so much, being shunned by a large percentage of the population, that is difficult for you."

He laughs and grins and says under his breath, "I don't care what you say." Then he talks about the great time he had yesterday with his friends. The great time he had last night watching his son win a basketball game. The great time he has every day. His voice is agitated once again.

"Nobody sees me moping around and crying," he tells me. "Matter of fact, all you people in the media seem to get upset when you see that I'm out there living my life, socializing with my friends and raising my kids. So if they think this is punishment, great."

Nicole and Ron will never have another moment to live out their lives.

For our last brief segment after a final commercial, O.J. says again that he can't live in my world, the world where people dislike him and think he's guilty. He can only live in the world that he lives in. He begins to tell me about a commentator on a prime-time show going out to dinner with him recently.

"He was shocked at the reaction of the people in the restaurant, the women, white women—" O.J. says.

This time I have to interrupt.

"I'm shocked at the negative reaction that we got to having you appear on the show, even though we could ask anything we wanted. Let me ask—if you could change one thing about your life currently or something, what would you change?"

O.J. asks me to clarify the question, then he says, "I think that what really first comes to mind is that I don't think I would have ever been unfaithful to either one of my wives."

"Okay," I say, pausing for the first time in the interview, knowing I only have one or two more questions left. "Would you trade your life for Nicole or Ron Goldman now? Would you give your life?"

"I would have put my life certainly on the line for Nicole. I mean, I would have died for her. Yes, I would have. I loved her. I—I truly, honestly believe that a kid needs a mother more than they need anyone. The most important person in my life was my mother. I wish—I don't think I can do the job with my kids that Nicole was doing and has done with my kids. All I can do is try the best that I can. Yes, I would trade for Nicole, but I would be certainly lying if I said I would trade with Ron Goldman. I don't know Ron Goldman. People die every day."

People die every day? Did he really just say that?

"Is there any chance that you could have been involved in these murders and blocked it out?" I ask.

"Absolutely not. No."

"Are you in denial?"

"Absolutely not. None at all. Not at all."

It was time to wrap it up. "All right. O. J. Simpson has been our guest here on *Up Close*."

O.J. grins and raises his eyebrows as if this has been a fun ride at the amusement park.

"Nice talking sports with you," he says with a chuckle.

I don't smile. And for the first and only time while doing the hundreds of interviews on *Up Close,* I don't shake his hand after we're finished. Maybe this is my one way of showing the viewer my real thoughts regarding his guilt.

• • •

I'VE NEVER WATCHED MY INTERVIEW WITH O.J. EVEN THOUGH I'VE seen clips, I don't want to view the whole thing again. As I mentioned, I usually watch every show back and grade it, and I've been doing this going all the way back to when I did local TV. People would sometimes wonder what I was doing in the editing room after the show each night. I wanted to watch the shows to see what worked and to find what things I could improve upon. But this was one time when I didn't want to judge my performance.

Maybe I figured I'd never do an interview quite like this ever again.

If there is any regret I have about the interview, it's that I wish I could have asked him a couple of other questions. Somewhere I should have said, "Could you have had help?" But even more than that, I sometimes have wished that at some point I simply said, "Look, O.J. Did you kill your wife? Did you kill Ron Goldman? Did you do it?" But I never wanted to appear one-sided, as if I had already made up my mind on him (even though I had). I wanted viewers to make up their minds based on O.J.'s answers.

The feedback I heard and saw came back very positive. I heard Fred Goldman say in the press that he thought it was one of the best things somebody could watch since O.J. never took the stand in the criminal trial. Vincent Bugliosi told me, "Kid, you did okay." One TV critic commented that it was a hard-hitting interview and it made for great television. They went on to say, "Who would have guessed that Chris Myers, a sports talk show host, would have provided millions of viewers with a spirited set-to with Simpson, who has become something of a master at deflecting questions and defusing them with smoke-and-mirror side stories."[2]

That's the question I kept asking myself. Who would have guessed? I have to admit that I was quite flattered by much of the praise.

Talk show hosts like Howard Stern and Jay Leno complimented me on the interview. The *Baltimore Sun* newspaper even had a write-up that said, "In the biggest moment in his career, Chris Myers did himself, his network and his profession quite proud."[3]

While I knew the magnitude of my interview with O.J. because of the trial and everything else, I don't think it really hit me until after we finished. It felt a bit like what I felt after the bombing at the Olympics. There was this high-pressure intensity from being live and reporting, and then afterward there was a sense of relief at getting through it. Once I began to see the write-ups and hear people talking about it, that's when it really hit me how many people had watched the interview. For years I've heard many people telling me they can remember where they were when they watched me interview O. J. Simpson live.

It truly was one of the most talked-about water-cooler moments in sports television history.

• • •

A FEW YEARS AFTER THE INTERVIEW, I WAS VISITING THE KERLAN-JOBE clinic in Los Angeles for a follow-up procedure on my knee. I had injured my ACL/MCL while playing touch football with the television crew and had gotten surgery on it. After I got into an empty elevator and pressed the floor number, another figure stepped in.

It was O.J.

"How's it going?" I said.

O.J. looked at me for a moment and then smiled. "Hey—I remember you."

"I'm getting my knee done," I told him. "How about you?"

"Well, I got this problem with my hand. I got surgery for it a while ago, but it looks like I'm going to need more to clear things up." He pointed to a gash. It was unbelievable.

Did that really just happen?

After he got off on his floor, I couldn't help thinking of O.J.'s injured finger after the murders of Nicole Brown Simpson and Ron Goldman. Of how he told police he at first couldn't remember how he had cut it, and how he later claimed he had injured it after smashing a drinking glass at the hotel when he heard the news about his ex-wife's death. A statement O.J. had made about his finger to the LAPD after being interviewed by detectives for the first time always stuck out to me.

"I just kind of went bonkers for a little bit."[4]

That might have been one of the most honest statements O.J. ever made without even realizing it.

TEN

Where Are the Tigers?

I f you don't jump at unexpected opportunities, you won't get more than what's expected.

In 1998, after working at ESPN for a decade, I made the decision to join Fox Sports. I had always thought of myself as a company guy. When I first started at ESPN, I pictured myself being there for thirty years. Those days, however, were in the past. People rarely stayed at one company for decades until they retired anymore.

Just a little corporate background. After ESPN was founded in 1979, ABC acquired it in 1984. Then in 1996, the Walt Disney Company acquired Capital Cities/ABC, Inc., ABC's parent company. After ESPN became a subsidiary of Disney, I started noticing changes. It reminded me of a bit the comedian George Carlin once did:

"We used to listen to rock 'n' roll. Now everybody's listening to rock. Whatever happened to roll!? It's the same feeling I get when I'm walking through Sears, wondering what they did with Roebuck."

To many, the environment began to feel more corporate and more of a layered business as opposed to the atmosphere of fun and creative sports television that made *SportsCenter* and helped ESPN thrive. The vibe amongst people who worked there was that we went from celebrating Mickey Mantle to celebrating Mickey Mouse.

So far in my career, I had fulfilled every contract I ever had. This has always been something that was very important to me. It bothered me when players signed contracts and then wanted to be traded or wanted more money in the middle of the deal. Going all the way back to my two-year deal in Miami, I worked there two years. Just as that was coming up, I moved to New Orleans, where I signed back-to-back three-year contracts. With ESPN, my deal with *Up Close* was coming up, but they told me they couldn't guarantee the show would still be in L.A. if I signed on with them again. ESPN talked about having me come back to Connecticut to do other things.

Our family couldn't imagine leaving California.

That's when Fox came along. In a lot of ways, they reminded me of those early years at ESPN when you could have a lot more fun and be creative. Fox said they would love for me to join them, and they made a very enticing pitch.

"Whether it's football, baseball, or NASCAR, as long as you know what you're talking about, you can have fun and be yourself. Viewers want that. They can tell when someone's authentic."

Their offer nearly doubled what I was making at ESPN. But perhaps more important, working for them would mean our family wouldn't have to move back to Connecticut.

I didn't immediately jump ship, however. I felt like I had been a really loyal and hardworking employee for ESPN, but I also knew they had given me many opportunities and I was grateful for that. So I went to ESPN and told them what was happening. I said I wasn't planning on leaving, but this was what Fox was offering me and they were also guaranteeing certain years. With two young kids, this sort of stability was important.

I had hoped for a dialogue, but instead they thought I was making this up. Even though I had an agent, I was making direct calls so I could talk to the executives. I told the president of the company that this wasn't some negotiating ploy, that it was really where things were at.

Look, I told them, I realize you guys have budgets, too, and I'm not looking for it to be more than what Fox is offering, but maybe if it's closer, then it makes sense. They were a bit dismissive. They didn't really believe I meant this. And when I told them I was going to leave, they basically communicated a hard truth to me.

We are all replaceable.

Maybe that was true, but nobody likes to hear it. Especially when you have somebody else who wants you badly. The decision to leave was still tough. It was one I labored over.

I can credit Al Michaels for giving me the nudge to go for it. While he was in the *Up Close* studio for a taping, I mentioned to him that I was wrestling with the decision. I shared that I wasn't unhappy at ESPN, but that Fox was offering more opportunity as a growing network. Michaels gave me the usual *you have to weigh your options* thing, but as I pressed him for career advice, he said I should go for it at Fox.

When I committed to Fox, ESPN came back and said they could give me more money. But I told them it wasn't about the money, it was about more than that.

"I'm sorry—we made the decision," I said.

There was my family to think about, and future chances to take, and a fun network on the rise.

We all have moments in life when we have to start over again, when it takes a while to settle in and find our spot. Starting high school. Going away to college. Getting that first job. Moving into your own place. Getting married. Moving out of state.

Starting over is an adjustment, but you try to do the best you can and make the decisions at the time based on what you know, based on what's important to you and your family. I still had my list of goals on those notecards. There were still lots of different jobs I wanted to do. Roles I wanted to play. Sports I wanted to be involved with. Athletes I was still interested in getting to know.

Fox would give me those opportunities.

• • •

ONE OF MY FIRST MAJOR INTERVIEWS FOR FOX WAS WITH MIKE TYSON. The last time I had seen him in the ring was on June 28, 1997, when everybody came to Vegas to witness Tyson face off against Evander Holyfield at the MGM Hotel. It was a rematch between the fighters. Seven months earlier, Holyfield, the underdog, had knocked Tyson down in the sixth round and eventually won the match after the referee stopped the fight in the 11th. Everybody had eagerly wanted to see a rematch, perhaps nobody more than Tyson.

Two hours before the fight, Showtime held a prefight party that included a who's who of famous actors, athletes, musicians, and TV personalities. Everybody from Whitney Houston and Tiger Woods to Eddie Murphy and Nicolas Cage was at the party, mingling or at least attempting to mingle. I was among those on the guest list. I had been invited to the fight, so on this evening I was a fan and not a sportscaster. None of us knew how infamous this fight would become.

I was accustomed to interacting with athletes like Shaquille O'Neal and Dennis Rodman, but running into someone like Madonna was quite another experience. She was a big basketball fan and enjoyed watching ESPN. I knew the pop star had recently had her first child, so I was curious about what motherhood was like for the Material Girl.

"So, do you actually change your baby's diapers?" I couldn't help asking.

Madonna gave me a dry and hilarious reply. "No, I never see the kid. What do you think I do? Just go out and sing and dance?"

We all know what happened during the fight. In the third round of that bout, Mike was disqualified after biting Holyfield twice, first on the right ear and then the left. Tyson ended up losing his boxing license for fifteen months. But the chaos in the ring spilled out shortly after the fight. While spectators exited the MGM Grand Garden, gunshots rang out and spooked everybody, resulting in a mini-riot. People stormed through hallways trying to get out of the hotel. Restaurants shut their doors to keep people out. In the melee, as two hundred hotel security guards and cops worked to clear the area, twenty-three people suffered minor injuries and one individual suffered a heart attack.[1]

During the craziness, I got trapped in a clothing store with a group of people that included one of the Baldwin brothers. At first I wasn't sure which one it was. I knew it wasn't Alec, the best known of the actors. I soon figured out it was Stephen Baldwin, star of '90s hit movies like *The Usual Suspects*. After the crowd heard supposed gunshots and began to swarm out of the hotel, I had snuck into a store, only to see them close their doors. Now we couldn't get out.

As if the night wasn't surreal enough, Stephen Baldwin decided to grab a clothing rack to try to knock open the door. Eventually we were let back out. Hotel sources would later say they believed the gunshot sound had actually been either a champagne cork or broken glass.

When I interviewed Evander Holyfield on *Up Close* shortly after the fight to get his perspective on it, he told me he never would have thought that someone would bite him on the ear. Maybe you could get bit somewhere else, but not on the ear.

"A piece of your ear is still missing," I said to him. "They said they found it afterwards but then it was missing when they went to sew it back on."

Holyfield told me it was amazing how it came up missing.

"Came up missing meaning somebody stole it," I said.

"What I hear is someone took it for a souvenir," he said with a chuckle.

"But that's a little strange, don't you think?"

"I would think so. I wouldn't think that your ear would be valuable."

"Well, yours is, because apparently somebody's—a collector—bid $30,000 for a piece of your ear. That is funny."

I brought up some of the great headlines the day after the fight. "Bite of the Century." "The Real Meal." "Pay Per Chew." Then I asked Holyfield if he'd been able to find the humor in this.

"When you look at incidents like this and it's behind you and you have a true forgiveness, you can laugh about the situation," Holyfield said. "You know, you laugh about the things that you did as a kid. This wasn't funny at the time, but once you got it behind you, it becomes funny."

Years later when I interviewed Tyson for the first time, I discovered he hadn't gotten over the bite fight. Laughing about it was the last thing he wanted to do.

• • •

OF ALL THE YEARS I COULD HAVE SAT DOWN WITH TYSON, 1999 WAS not a good one. In the two years since losing his boxing license, Tyson crashed his motorcycle and broke some of his ribs, filed a $100 million lawsuit against fight promoter Don King, and was sentenced to a year for assaulting two motorists in a road rage incident. He had already served three years for being convicted of rape in 1992. The prosecutor on the road rage case wrote in a memo to the judge that Tyson was "nothing less than a time bomb."[2] He would end up serving four months and eventually be let out on parole.

None of this had stopped him from stepping into the ring for the first time since the Holyfield match. He faced Francois Botha on January 16, 1999, and knocked him out in the fifth round of the fight. In his post-fight interview, Tyson was asked whether he had lost any confidence and any of his anger since everything had happened.

"I need respect," Tyson said. "If you show me respect without writing trashy articles about me then I'll show you respect. I'm a man . . . No one's going to disrespect me and no one's going to write about me without me retaliating back."

Nine months after the bout with Botha, Tyson was scheduled to step into the ring against Orlin Norris, a cruiserweight champion who had only fought one round in over a year. The twelve-round fight on October 23 would be at the MGM Grand in Las Vegas and televised on Showtime. Days before his match, I went to Vegas to interview the famed boxer. The goal was to sit down with him and have a friendly chat.

His gym was on the outskirts of Vegas. It was your typical sweaty, smelly, grimy gym. Maybe a little more so since it was in the desert. Tyson had an entourage there that seemed a bit indifferent to our crew. We had to wait and watch him finish up practice. The boxer looked like the same Tyson in the ring, moving well. Our crew set up everything for the interview, but at the last minute, Tyson decided to change the location.

"He wants to do it at his house," someone told us.

We were forced to pack up everything and go to the mansion he was living in. The boxing champion had purchased the eleven-thousand-square-foot mansion in 1995 shortly after being released from prison in March of that year. He reportedly paid $3.7 million for the seven-bedroom home that resembled a French chateau.[3]

I rode with one of the guys from Tyson's entourage. I think his name was Gator or Crocodile. He wore Army fatigues and jumped in a Jeep pickup that he drove with the windows down and dust flying everywhere. I half wondered if Tyson was going to want to change the location again once we got to his house.

After waiting for the gates to open, we drove down the winding driveway past a sprawling estate that included a tennis court and a guesthouse. The mansion resembled Tony Montana's in *Scarface*. The front door had crystal handles, and there was a fountain in the entryway. The pool outside was surrounded with more fountains and statues of historic figures like Alexander the Great and Genghis Khan. We decided it would be an ideal place to do the interview by the pool.

Tyson had once been interviewed at this mansion and shown playing with his white Bengal tiger named Kenya. As I approached Tyson for the first time, I tried to lighten the mood with a little humor.

"So where are the tigers?" I asked.

He jokingly responded, "I had to get rid of them. They don't like white people."

I decided to refrain from any more conversation while our producer, cameraman, and crew set up for the interview. There were several people around Tyson; I wasn't sure if they were assistants or bodyguards. The concept for our discussion was that I'd show the boxer *Sports Illustrated* covers that spanned his career and get his reaction on them. As I sat down across from him, I began working my way through the stack of magazines, starting with the first cover from 1986 that showed a beaming young fighter.

"They're calling you 'Kid Dynamite,'" I told him. "The headline says,

'Mike Tyson: The Next Great Heavyweight—And He's Only 19.' What did you think about making the cover of *Sports Illustrated* for the first time?"

Mike shared a few thoughts on each cover I presented him.

From 1986: "Dynamite! Mike Tyson: The KO Kid Is a Champ at 20."

From 1988: "Too Much! Mike Tyson KO's Larry Holmes," and "K.O.: Mike Tyson Demolishes Michael Spinks in 91 Seconds."

Also in '88: "Will Love Marriage (And His Mother-in-Law) K.O. Mike Tyson?"—showing a happy Tyson while his then wife, Robin Givens, leans on his shoulder, a pensive look on her face.

From 1990: a "KO'd" Tyson lands on the mat after a hit from Buster Douglas in the 10th round.

From 1991: "Tyson: Is the Fury Gone?"

From 1992: "Guilty."

With each passing magazine cover, Tyson grew more intense and shared fewer thoughts. I knew he wouldn't love seeing the cover from November 1996 titled "Giant Killer: Evander Holyfield Stuns Mike Tyson," but I still wanted to hear his thoughts about that match.

We finally got to the famous ear-biting incident. The July 7, 1997, *Sports Illustrated* cover showed Tyson right after taking a bite, on the attack and his jaw clenched, while Evander Holyfield grimaced in pain. I handed Mike the magazine with the title that read "Madman! A Crazed Mike Tyson Disgraces Himself and His Sport."

Before I could even ask him a question, he started cursing at me.

"You m—f—er. You're trying to provoke me."

I froze and tried thinking of a response. Tyson was sitting only a couple of feet across from me. Before I could get a word out, he lunged at me and continued spouting obscenities. When someone whose trade is knocking people out, and has been known to have some anger issues, comes at you like that, it can be scary.

For a brief second, I realized that your life flashing before your eyes wasn't just a cliché; it actually does happen. Tyson got to his feet, but just as he started to swing his fists the two assistants or bodyguards held him back, locking his arms as he got inches away from my face. Thankfully he wasn't in the best shape of his life, because they could actually hold the irate fighter back. While he fumed, I panicked and took in my surroundings, looking for a way out of there.

I could always jump in the pool.

The boxer dubbed "the baddest man on the planet" was inches away from me, being restrained from kicking my butt. The fighter who once said, "I'm the most brutal and vicious, the most ruthless champion there has ever been," wanted to knock me out.

I was already white from never being out in the sun, but somehow I turned whiter.

As my producer stepped in to sort things out, Tyson finally relented and sat back in his chair. Everybody was silent for a moment as we listened to Mike breathing heavily. I remained in my seat, trying to appear calm and collected, giving my inner self a pep talk to stay composed: *Don't let him intimidate you, Chris. You interviewed the greatest boxer ever when you were only in high school, and Ali didn't intimidate you. You sat across from O. J. Simpson and grilled him about the murders of his ex-wife, Nicole, and her friend Ronald Goldman, and he didn't intimidate you.*

Of course, Ali and O.J. never tried to come after me.

After glaring at me for a moment, Tyson finally spoke.

"You're a real prick. You're hitting me with all these disgusting pictures."

I shook my head. "No—if you don't want to comment on it, don't."

"I will comment on it, but you're a prick," Tyson said.

I really wanted to go hide behind the Genghis Khan statue.

"If you don't want to comment on it, you don't have to," I said again.

"I am going to comment on it, but you're a prick. Just letting you know. Continue."

Nothing in me wanted to continue. I wanted to get the hell out of there. As I tried to get us back on track, Tyson started up again.

"You're unsensitive. You have no sensitivity to anything. I'm not—it doesn't affect me, I'm just saying, you have no sensitivity. You don't know how it affects me."

"No—I'm sorry," I said, and I meant it. "I didn't mean to offend you. It's just your life. The point I was making—I'm going to ask you about it."

"All right, and I can give you my opinion what I think about you," Tyson said.

I knew very well what he thought of me.

"You know, Mike—if you don't want to answer the questions, just tell me." I glanced at my producer, who looked stunned. "Maybe we should pack up and leave."

I wasn't trying to be a jerk about this. I honestly questioned whether or not he was going to freak out again. Mike waved off the idea.

"No, no, no—let's finish this."

We continued with my set of questions based around the magazine covers. I didn't really hear what he was saying because all I wanted was to get out of there as quickly as possible. But just as we were finished and getting ready to leave, Tyson surprised me.

"Let me give you a tour around the house."

Just a few minutes earlier, this guy wanted to strangle me, and now he wanted to show off his mansion? I tried to be polite and get out of it, but he wouldn't have it. "Come on, let's go," he told me, and I really couldn't refuse. And I'm glad I did it. I got to see a whole other side of Tyson as he showed off parts of his house.

As he guided me from room to room, commenting on this particular piece of art or some type of furniture, I was baffled by his sudden change of demeanor. He asked if I wanted a bottled water. He made some jokes. We had what seemed like a relatively normal conversation. During these moments, Tyson was no longer the guy who wanted to pulverize me. He was a really nice guy.

• • •

BEFORE WE LEFT TYSON'S ESTATE, HIS PEOPLE BEGGED US NOT TO show the part of the interview where Tyson lunged at me. That footage was never shown. I think they ultimately destroyed those tapes. I wish I still had that as a memento of surviving my first and only "fight" with the great boxer.

When I finally got back into the safety of our car and we headed back to our office, I was struck by two things in the interview. The first was when Tyson mentioned that the two places he felt most comfortable in this world were in jail and in the ring. Those were the two places he felt the most safe and secure. I couldn't help feeling sad.

Tyson echoed this years later in an interview he did with former NFL stars Channing Crowder, Fred Taylor, and Ryan Clark in *The Pivot Podcast*.

"I had the best three years of my life in prison," Tyson said. "I had peace. That money doesn't mean anything if you don't have your peace, your stability, and your balance. You need your sanity to dictate any part of life."

The other statement Tyson made that struck me was a comment about happiness. I had talked to him about the levels of happiness in his life, and he told me there wasn't really any happiness whatsoever. He didn't even know what that very word—"happiness"—meant because of all the bad things that had happened recently in his life. Happiness was something foreign to him. Tyson would eventually be diagnosed with bipolar disorder in 2017, and would go on to battle bigger opponents outside the boxing ring such as depression and alcohol abuse.

Tyson once said that he was the best boxer ever. "No one can stop me," he said in his post-fight interview after knocking out Lou Savarese 38 seconds into the bout in June 2000.

No one but himself.

ELEVEN

The Intimidator

They called him "the Intimidator." Dale Earnhardt had been given a lot of nicknames over the years, such as "the Man in Black" and "Iron-head," but "the Intimidator" was perhaps the best known and most fitting for the driver from North Carolina. The moniker came from The Winston All-Star Race at Charlotte in 1987 when he battled Bill Elliott and won by his famous "Pass in the Grass."[1] He was an aggressive driver who had his share of controversy on the track, but he was also one of sports' most beloved heroes. Not just in NASCAR, but in all of sports.

I witnessed Earnhardt's charisma and personality before the 2001 Daytona 500. This was the first Daytona 500 for the Fox broadcast team, and I was the host for the pre-race and post-race coverage. Leading up to the big race, we had almost two weeks called "Speed Weeks" where we did daily reports. I'd speak to drivers about the race and their cars and the sport itself. For me, it was a great primer on NASCAR.

While I'd interviewed people like Dale Earnhardt and Dale Jarrett and Jeff Gordon in different formats through the years, this time was different since we were part of the network that was broadcasting the event. We weren't just bystanders to the race; we were almost a part of it since Fox had the exclusive rights for it. So I was able to get caught up on drivers, rules, cars, and other aspects of the sport. It was almost like NASCAR boot camp.

Dale Earnhardt was the face of NASCAR. The forty-nine-year-old had won seventy-six Winston Cup races and earned the Winston Cup seven times. He had finally won the Daytona 500 in 1998. In many ways, Earnhardt was a folk hero. He reminded me of that old-fashioned type of cowboy like John Wayne or Clint Eastwood. Even though he had earned the Intimidator nickname because he could be a bully on the track and did whatever he could within the rules to win, he often helped out other drivers, and he kept his successful life simple. Even with all his money and rewards. You knew all about the legend, but then when you met him, he seemed like a regular sort of guy who knew what he wanted to do in life.

Days before the race, Earnhardt spoke to Jeff Hammond and me. We asked him how he was feeling entering his twenty-third Daytona 500.

"Victory lane's where you want to be," Earnhardt said in his gentle southern accent. "It took me twenty years to get there. But I do feel good. I feel better this time than I did last year. Really. I feel more relaxed. Maybe it's because I've had such a great time—the last twenty-four hours. And this week leading up to the Daytona 500. The whole thing."

Earnhardt had had neck surgery a couple of years earlier, so I brought it up. In 1996, he was involved in a major crash at Talladega when he and Sterling Marlin slammed hard into the wall. Earnhardt hit almost head-on, destroying his car and needing to be cut out of it. Unbelievably, he was able to stand on his feet and give a thumbs-up to the crowd despite having a broken collarbone and dislocated sternum. At the end of 1999, after rupturing a disc during the racing season, he had spinal column surgery.[2]

"After the surgery—I mean, you can drive for another ten years," I said. "What's your plan?

"Yeah, it put ten years on my career. Really, I'm in good shape. The race cars are handling great, but I needed to get the surgery straightened out with my neck. And I had a great year last year, so I'm even stronger this year. I'm working out and staying in shape. So I'm focused. I'm determined. I'm going to go out here and give it our all this year."

It was a good interview, but I couldn't have imagined at the time that it would be one of Earnhardt's last, and that we were on the verge of NASCAR being changed forever.

* * *

THERE WERE SO MANY STORYLINES HEADING INTO THE RACE. FOX WAS broadcasting the Daytona 500 for the first time. Seven-time Cup champion Dale Earnhardt was looking to win his second Daytona 500. His son Dale Earnhardt Jr. and Michael Waltrip were both driving for Earnhardt's racing team. Waltrip was trying to finally break his streak of 462 consecutive Winston Cup races without a victory. His older brother, NASCAR Hall of Famer Darrell Waltrip, was calling the race in the Fox booth.

It was a bit of a shock when Fox ended up getting the rights to broadcast NASCAR. In a deal finalized at the end of 1999, the broadcast and cable rights for NASCAR were sold to Fox, NBC, and their cable partners, effective for the 2001 season. This marked a big transition from NASCAR's longtime partners of ABC, CBS, ESPN, and TNN. NASCAR's premier event, the Daytona 500, would rotate annually between Fox and NBC. With Fox gaining experience and success with the NFL and Major League Baseball, they wanted to expand and add NASCAR to their portfolio. They saw the popularity of car racing and had lots of creative ideas on how to continue to grow its sizable audience.

When the executives at Fox first approached me to host their pre-race and post-race coverage, I had to state the obvious.

"Look, guys—I'm not a gearhead. I'm not a car guy."

The irony of that statement was that I came from a family of car guys—my younger brother, Frank, my older brother, Dan, and my father. Before moving to Florida and working at the post office, my dad had worked in a car manufacturing office. All three of them loved to work on cars, and they always seemed to be talking about them. When I was younger, they dragged me to races when we weren't watching baseball or football. They were fans of NASCAR and had followed it over the years.

Since we didn't have a NASCAR track in our area when I was a kid, my brothers took me to drag races in Miami and Fort Lauderdale. The crowds were large and excited. When the loud engines drowned out everything, I could feel their vibrations trembling through me. I had an enthusiasm for the sport and started choosing between drivers and manufacturers like everybody else. Our family were Ford guys while our cousins in Ohio were Chevy guys. It was similar to any big rivalry in sports.

While I was at ESPN, I interviewed a variety of NASCAR drivers, but I was still new to the sport. So when Fox told me I was their choice to host the pre-race and post-race coverage, I took it as an exciting challenge. I knew I wasn't their first choice, but I also knew what they were looking for. They already had a NASCAR champion with Darrell Waltrip, and they also had a former crew chief in Larry McReynolds. What they wanted from me was a television sports guy who approached NASCAR in the same way I had approached every sport—with an interest and a curiosity. They didn't need a gearhead; they wanted me to engage with drivers and with the other analysts.

"You're going to cover the race and the rules, but we're not going to get into the weeds," the executives told me. "We want you to talk about personalities and promote the sport itself."

I have always appreciated how Fox likes to do things a bit differently. I thought it was great for them to want somebody who wasn't a NASCAR person to come in and ask questions that were broad enough for anybody to understand. We wanted to reach a wider audience. I found it to be an appealing challenge to take a sport that was perceived to be regional and show that everybody could enjoy it. The viewer didn't have to be a car fanatic to love watching NASCAR. This mindset motivated me to think creatively.

For example, that first year we created a thing called "10 Laps," which was a short interview that consisted of ten quick, rapid-fire questions that didn't always have to do with car racing. Fun stuff like "Boxers or briefs?" and "Chocolate or vanilla ice cream?" It's become commonplace now, but back then we were among the first to do this sort of thing.

The goal was to give viewers a chance to get to know these drivers. David Hill, the president of Fox Sports, wanted me to focus on these guys and what made them tick. To talk more about the mindset of race car drivers than the motors inside those race cars. At the time, a lot of the drivers hadn't been able to show a lot of their personality, so that was our plan. I found it an exciting challenge to take a sport that was very different from football and baseball and still focus on the athletes themselves. Not to take away from the machinery and mechanics of the sport but rather enhance it.

As I entered the world of NASCAR, I discovered a tight-knit community that loved to call it "our sport." NASCAR had a very loyal audience, and the appeal was only growing. This was an era where the sport really grew, and the Fox team was instrumental in that growth. For me, I never tried to be anything other than myself, and I'm thankful that for an exclusive sport like NASCAR, the drivers and the fans welcomed me with open arms.

• • •

ALL ROADS LEAD TO THE DAYTONA INTERNATIONAL SPEEDWAY. WHEN I first arrive, I feel the magnitude of this track. It is a massive concrete structure that has its own lake in the middle of it. They call it a super-speedway for a reason because of its size and speed. It resembles a steel city with all the roadways and the seating arrangement. Daytona smells like action. You can smell oil and rubber like you might in a garage, but it's a garage on steroids with multiple cars being worked on. The sound isn't simply loud, it's ground-shaking. Even if you're not into racing, there is an adrenaline rush being here.

These drivers resemble superheroes, complete with their helmets and neck devices. They climb into their rocket ships and blast off going 200 miles an hour. Hitting each other and drafting and spinning out of control. It's incredible to imagine cars going that fast at that degree of banking. To show the degree of banking, we'd drop a bowling ball from the top and let it roll down and it would gather a real head of steam. Everything about Daytona was designed to make a big, in-your-face statement. There are other notable tracks that people loved for their intimacy or racing style, but nothing is bigger than Daytona.

Nearly a quarter of a million people pack this legendary speedway waiting to see forty-three drivers start the race. As I welcome viewers to the race, I also welcome two others on my broadcasting team: Daytona 500 winner Darrell Waltrip, and his former crew chief who was with him then, Jeff Hammond.

For Waltrip, this marks the first time he's in the booth versus being on the racing track. He's a legend himself, having won eighty-four NASCAR Winston Cup races, including the Daytona 500 in 1989.

During one section of the pre-race coverage, we show footage of Waltrip's Daytona victory.

"I never get tired of watching it," Waltrip says. "That's what you live for. That's what every driver here lives for, to drive into the victory circle here at the Daytona Speedway. It's one of the most emotional wins you'll ever have. You beat everybody when you're at your best. And it's such a relief. It's just a relief to win a race so big."

Back when he won it in '89, he received around $175,000 for coming in first place.

"Now it's over $1.3 million," I say.

"Basically chump change today," Jeff Hammond adds.

I nod. "But it's a memory that's worth a lot; it's priceless."

The Fox preshow brings its tradition of interviewing drivers, discussing the race, and looking at the various aspects of the sport. We also have a little fun by bringing in a face familiar to Fox Sports viewers. I set up the segment that airs.

"Speaking of great, this weekend, we had one of the greatest quarterbacks to ever play the game with us. Fox's own Terry Bradshaw stopped by last night. Terry and Dale Earnhardt tried to give us a little tour of this historic track, but it turned into a bad episode of *The Dukes of Hazzard*."

NASCAR had asked Bradshaw to serve as grand marshal of the Daytona 500, so he would be giving the ceremonial command for drivers to start their engines. The night before the race, Earnhardt decided to give Terry a ride around the track. And even though Dale was only driving a pace car, the experience still terrified the usually jovial NFL analyst. Earnhardt joked about crashing into the wall while driving, jerking the wheel to rattle Bradshaw, and he finished by spinning the car on pit road and hopping on top of its hood with Bradshaw by his side.

Forty-five minutes before the race, while discussing the issue of safety, I speak to the man I call NASCAR's version of Dick Clark. Ken Squier had been the lap-by-lap commentator for NASCAR for over twenty years.

I ask him, "We showed the drivers meeting earlier and the race director said, 'Hey, be safe out there today. This is not Talladega.' What did he
mean?"

His response is significant.

"Well, NASCAR can preach, but they can't reach. They told them on
Thursday, you can't run more than two wide going into turn number one.
But the pictures in all the papers in America—one of them points five
wide into turn one. That's what we're going to see today at 190 miles an
hour."

We're able to do live interviews with some of the drivers before they
climb into their cars. So many of them look relaxed and ready to go. One
of those is Dale Earnhardt, who lounges in a chair with his feet propped
up next to his RV. Matt Yocum asks if he can win his second 500 today.

"Well, we've got a good shot. We got a good race car. I wasn't really excited about the car yesterday afternoon, the last practice, but the car came
around. I think it's going to be okay. We've got a good engine in it, but a
little wind today. A little exciting. I think it's going to be some exciting
racing."

The Intimidator nods his head.

"You're gonna see something you probably hadn't never seen on Fox,"
Earnhardt says as a grin spreads underneath his thick mustache.

• • •

BEFORE THE RACE, DALE EARNHARDT HUGS KYLE PETTY.

"I love you and I'm thinking of you," Earnhardt says.

Kyle is part of NASCAR royalty as the son of Richard Petty, who was
the face of NASCAR before Earnhardt. Kyle and his family were looking
forward to that history continuing in a fourth generation with his son,
Adam, but a tragic accident back on May 12, 2000, changed that. Adam

Petty died in a crash during practice at New Hampshire International Speedway. He was nineteen years old.

Earnhardt had avoided talking to Kyle for nearly nine months after Adam's death. He wasn't sure what to say, and the loss was personal since Adam had raced and hung around with his own son Dale Jr. They eventually reconciled and were able to talk things out.[3]

Now at the start of the new racing season, Kyle is honoring his son's memory by driving Adam's number 45 car. Before the race, Kyle is asked how he's feeling.

"It's incredibly emotional to be here," Petty says. "It was incredibly emotional rolling through the gate down here with the 45 Sprint car without Adam here. And it's been pretty emotional all week long. Couple of autograph sessions, I've kind of broken down a little bit, I'll have to admit. It'll be emotional when the race starts. In church, it was a little emotional this morning, but, you know, I wish he was here, but he's just not."

Since Adam's accident, NASCAR has had two other tragedies. In a July practice in New Hampshire, Kenny Irwin Jr. died in a crash, and then in October of the same year, Tony Roper died in another crash at Texas Motor Speedway. Three deaths in the last year.

The dangers that have haunted the history of NASCAR are part of what makes it such a thrill to watch. The stakes are high, and these great drivers battle with each other. "You're going to block me? Then I'm going to block you." "You bump, I'll bump." The risk and reward . . . the high speeds and the challenges . . . they're daredevils who go 180 or 200 miles an hour within inches of thirty other cars. And if there is an accident, it is exhilarating to see everybody walk away from it.

The most devastating thing is when one of them doesn't.

• • •

A CRASH—A BIG ONE—COMES WITH THE CARS HEADING INTO TURN two with 25 laps to go. Twenty cars are involved. Tony Stewart takes the worst hit, his car going sailing before it lands on another car and begins to flip over a couple of times. Thankfully Stewart is okay along with the rest of the drivers. The race continues.

The exciting storylines entering Daytona play themselves out to the very end. Fourteen different drivers lead the race amidst the forty-nine lead changes, including Earnhardt, who takes the lead four times. With 17 laps remaining and the Intimidator in the lead, he lets the two cars he owns pass him: Michael Waltrip with Dale Jr. close behind him. Then Earnhardt begins to block anybody from following those two cars.

On the final lap of the race, Earnhardt continues to block for Waltrip and Dale Jr.

"Here they come, gang," Darrell Waltrip says in the broadcast. "I told you. You think these guys are gonna settle down and take it easy? Say, 'Hey, everybody's gonna get a good finish'? No way. They're gonna race their hearts out."

Soon he and Jeff Hammond scream out a collective "Woah!"

"Look at Earnhardt. Sterling got into Earnhardt."

"Dale is doing everything he can to keep Sterling behind him because Dale knows that Sterling's got a fast car."

As they approach the white flag, Darrell can't help but become a fan cheering his younger brother on.

"You got him, Mikey. You got him, man. You got him. Come on, man!"

And then suddenly . . .

"The 3 car down—"

"Woah!"

"Big trouble."

So close to the finish line between turns three and four, the left rear corner of Earnhardt's car makes contact against Sterling Marlin's right fender. Earnhardt tries to get control, jostling to the left and then pivoting hard to the right and shooting up the track where he slides into Ken Schrader's car. This makes Earnhardt's out-of-control number 3 car angle as it slams nose-first into the wall.

As Michael Waltrip finally earns a Winston Cup victory after 462 races, Darrell Waltrip screams a triumphant "You got it, you got it, you got it! Mikey!" There are tears in the big brother's eyes as he hoops and hollers. Then he utters five haunting words.

"I just hope Dale's okay."

• • •

SILENCE. ALMOST COMPLETE SILENCE.

As the race ends, fans see the face of NASCAR hit the wall in a brutal accident. They know what we know in the booth: it was bad but we don't know just how bad. Even those who know the sport much better than me know it was a tough wreck, but guys have walked away from a lot worse. Tony Stewart *just* walked away from flying and flipping his car over.

It's amazing how things can change in a split second. The mood swings dramatically with so many emotions. The jubilation of winning suddenly begins to fade as Dale doesn't climb out of his car. The usual hysteria of the crowd blowing horns and yelling and partying is suddenly gone. Everybody is quiet. As I see the reactions from those around me like Darrell and Jeff, then the faces on the drivers, it's obvious that something bad has happened. But we don't have any official information right away from anybody down on the track or from NASCAR.

Fans stare in silent shock as an ambulance carrying Dale Earnhardt drives away. Some linger while others begin to file out of the speedway. It's the only sporting event I've seen where more than a hundred thousand fans walk out with just the sound of footsteps. Feet shuffling and hardly a word spoken. They feel it and don't want it to be true.

Their silence out of respect tells the story.

Our broadcast is scheduled to end soon, so we finish without any official word. We remain waiting, knowing we can't break into network programming even if we receive information. There's a sick, empty feeling waiting to hear news. Knowing that such an amazing day and race turned into this.

Two and a half hours later, an official announcement is made.

"Seven-time Winston Cup champion and former Daytona 500 winner Dale Earnhardt has died from a crash suffered in Sunday's Daytona 500. The accident occurred on the final lap of Sunday's race. The tragic news came Sunday night, two hours after the race ended, from NASCAR president Mike Helton."

Like everybody else, I'm shocked. This was the star of the sport. Earnhardt was forty-nine years old, a father and husband, and he was still winning races. He was still the face of NASCAR.

In reporting the news and discussing Earnhardt's death, my goal is to communicate effectively and be as authentic as I can be. My job is to deliver information to the viewers, so whatever emotions I'm feeling inside need to be under control. In my mind, I'm asking what the person watching wants to know. I don't need to tell them how I feel; I just need to deliver the details as respectfully as I can.

Words can't do it justice, yet as a sports broadcaster, that is exactly what you attempt to do. So our crew of Mike Joy, Jeff Hammond, and Ken Squier all try to put this tragedy in perspective for the viewers. As I direct the conversation to Hammond, who worked with and competed against Earnhardt many times, he speaks slowly with a full heart.

"I was fortunate enough to watch Dale get in his first car way back when we were racing in Concord, and his daddy was still helping Dale," Jeff says. "A competitor—I don't think I know of anybody I've ever been around who epitomizes the word. The man was relentless as far as his competition was concerned. We had a lot of good times together. We raced together on his dirt tracks at home. We used to go to his place and ride in the back of his boat, go tubing together, hunting together. But through all our relationship and friendship, he always was a competitor."

I turn to Mike Joy, who called most of the races throughout Earnhardt's career.

"Nicknamed the Intimidator, but it was hard not to like that in him," I say.

Mike's words resonate with everybody listening.

"You had to respect him. You had to like him. The compass of this sport has lost its true north. Dale Earnhardt defined the limits of on-track behavior. And every time he pushed that limit, the limit moved with him. But more importantly, Chris, he set the standard and the goals for every driver who followed him."

I now address the dean of NASCAR.

"Ken Squier, you saw all of his Daytona 500 performances. This was his twenty-third consecutive start. And it's difficult to describe or put into words what Dale Earnhardt did for NASCAR racing."

The job might be difficult, but Ken delivers a poignant and poetic summary of Dale's life.

"Well, whatever stock car racing is, Dale Earnhardt was. He was the child in the back of a pickup truck at the Charlotte Motor Speedway with his dad watching those cars in the Coca-Cola 600 and dreaming someday of being in Winston Cup racing. He was the teenager whose equipment was a T-shirt and a crash helmet. Bumming rides, building cars, trying to prove that he could handle those short tracks in the Carolinas just as well as his father, Ralph Earnhardt, did, who was a national champion. He was the guy that came along in 1979 and became a rookie of the year in Winston Cup racing and one year later was the Winston Cup national champion. And through it all, he seemed quiet. He became the Intimidator, one who didn't have much to say, but he did it with the deeds on the racetrack."

Squier describes Earnhardt's wife, Teresa, changing his demeanor, how he became easier with the media, and then how losing his best friend in the world, Neil Bonnett, in a crash changed him again. How he came out of that dark period and eventually won the Daytona 500.

"Now we come to this point in his career going down the backstretch in the final lap out in front," Squier continues. "Michael Waltrip in one of his cars. His son is running in second place. And two of his colleagues, two of his racing pals, are right in there beside him, going for a photo finish for third spot. There's Ken Schrader from Missouri on the outside. There's Sterling Marlin from Tennessee on the inside. And as they went into that turn and he saw what was coming about, I would consider that Dale Earnhardt died happy."

• • •

THE DEATH OF DALE EARNHARDT CHANGED NASCAR FOREVER. THE issue of safety that had been discussed more and more with each passing year suddenly couldn't be ignored. As Kyle Petty said in the ESPN documentary *Intimidator: The Lasting Legacy of Dale Earnhardt,* "When a star disappears, then people pay attention."

Over time, there were many safety improvements. One of these was the use of the HANS device, a head and neck support device that reduced head or neck injuries in a crash. Many of the deaths in NASCAR over the years had been from a basilar skull fracture. Earnhardt's death was one of those. But it would take another accident later that year to finally convince NASCAR to make the HANS device mandatory for all racers.

On October 4, 2001, twenty-five-year-old Blaise Alexander crashed his car head-on into the wall at the Lowe's Motor Speedway in Charlotte, North Carolina. The violent accident also happened to involve Kerry Earnhardt, Dale Earnhardt's eldest son. Blaise and Kerry were battling for the lead when their two cars made contact. After Alexander's car smashed into the wall, the two cars struck each other again. Kerry Earnhardt's car flipped over and then slid down the track with flames spewing from under its hood. Earnhardt was fine, but Alexander died from a basilar skull fracture.

Even though Alexander was driving as part of ARCA (the Automobile Racing Club of America), it didn't matter. This was the fifth death of a driver in seventeen months. Soon after this, on October 17, 2001, NASCAR mandated the use of the HANS device for its top three series. They also made safety improvements on things like the walls, installing safer barriers on oval tracks and concrete walls.

Even with Dale Earnhardt's passing, he had made a mark on NASCAR. He had finally forced the changes that have saved lives ever since. Over the years, there have been twenty-eight drivers killed in crashes in the NASCAR Cup Series. There have been zero deaths in NASCAR since we all lost Earnhardt.

● ● ●

WHEN I THINK BACK TO THE 2001 DAYTONA 500, I WILL NEVER FORGET seeing Earnhardt during the week before the race in his garage as the sun was setting. Usually we weren't on the track late in the day, but for some reason today we were. A lot of people had gathered around Earnhardt and I was trying to wrap things up to go back to the hotel. He was standing there staring at me, so I greeted him. He nodded his head.

"Life looks pretty good from here, doesn't it?" he said.

I looked out to the vast, sprawling stands of the Daytona International Speedway in the glow of the evening sun. Here's the great American race driver before the great American race. I think for a moment about how someone had the idea to begin racing cars on the hard sand of Daytona Beach before moving here.

As the sun was setting behind him, Earnhardt looked like an all-American cowboy. Maybe he always had this sort of aura around him.

• • •

MY OWN SUMMARY OF LOSING EARNHARDT CAME BEFORE SIGNING off the air that night.

"Drivers used to say the worst thing to see on the track was Dale Earnhardt in your rearview mirror. Now we all realize the worst thing is not to see Dale Earnhardt at all."

TWELVE

Why Not Us?

We love the epic battles. The games that will forever be memorialized. And in the long history of baseball lore, the 2004 American League Championship Series matchup between the Boston Red Sox and the New York Yankees became one of the all-time great series.

It's the bottom of the sixth inning in Game 3 at Fenway Park, and the Red Sox look bloodied and beaten. The Yankees took the first two games in New York, and now Boston is down 13–6. The weather is cold and damp, and the mood is gloomy. This has all the makings of a horror movie, one we've seen way too many times. So it's fitting that I'm interviewing the "King of Horror" and one of the biggest Red Sox fans in this stadium.

"I'm in the seats with Stephen King, author. How horrifying is this for a Red Sox fan?"

"Oh, you always ask me the same question," King tells me. "For a Red Sox fan, it's terrific just to be in the playoffs."

For someone known for killing off his characters in creative ways, King seems particularly charitable. Donning a navy Red Sox cap and a red team coat, the famous novelist looks like any other diehard in the seats. I'm the sideline reporter for the night, hovering in the camera well behind the New York Yankees dugout. It's cramped in there—it's not like roaming the sidelines at an NFL game; the teams will let you jump in the dugout between innings. The fun part is getting to run up to the stands every once in a while to interview people like King.

"Coming into the series, I'm sure you were a little bit more optimistic given the history and how well guys like Curt Schilling and Pedro Martinez pitched this year," I say.

"Sure, well, of course," King replies. "The wild card's that you never know what's going to happen when somebody's injured. And I think that what we saw happen this year was the injury to Curt Schilling was like the first domino, and it put a strain on the pitching staff that we didn't expect. And it's changed things since then. So that is—there's been a little more adversity, let's put it that way."

With his natural ease of talking into a microphone about his team, King is giving Joe Buck and Tim McCarver a run for their money in the broadcasting booth.

"If you were writing about this game tonight, what would you write?" I ask.

"What I'd write is probably a seven-run rally in the bottom of the ninth inning with a walk-off David Ortiz home run. That's how I'd write it."

I laugh. "All right—optimistic."

"Because I believe in suspense, but I also believe in happy endings," King interrupts with a good-natured grin.

"And maybe not reality, though, right?"

Maybe I'm not as much of a believer as King. He continues his sports narration.

"Well, I mean, I think that the Red Sox are America's team in a way. And of course, one of the things that I believe in very strongly is that one of the reasons that the Red Sox are America's team—for instance, you take the Phillies, when they finally won the World Series, they were just another baseball team."

"I think the Yankees would argue with that," I say to him.

As we go back to the broadcasters, Joe Buck adds to the conversation.

"Chris better watch himself. That was an antagonistic Stephen King coming back at him. He might find himself in one of those novels with some sort of spell being put on him before the end of the night."

It turns out the Red Sox are the ones who have the spell put on them. They end up losing 19–8.

· · ·

WE LOVE HISTORY. UNLESS YOU'RE THE BOSTON RED SOX, WHO WOULD love to forget the decades of futility. Eighty-six years, to be precise. Red Sox fans want to change history, and that means finally reversing *the curse*.

I'm not a big believer in curses, but athletes are very superstitious. Fans can be too, especially those long-suffering ones rooting for the Red Sox. Maybe the "Curse of the Bambino" is just something to rationalize the losing and the suffering for Boston Red Sox fans. But for so many of those devoted followers, it's very real. And looking over their long, illustrious history of failure, there is something quite eerie about some of their infamous losses.

These losses, this curse—this tradition for torment—have become a Red Sox trademark. After experiencing the blowout at Fenway Park in person for Game 3, I have to admit that there's something in the air. Some mystique for misery.

Did Boston's decision to sell Babe Ruth to the New York Yankees in 1919 truly curse them? They had become a great team, winning five of the first fifteen World Series. But the story goes that Harry Frazee, the Red Sox owner, needed money and sold Babe Ruth to their rivals, changing the fate of both teams forever. The New York Yankees ended up winning four World Series with Babe Ruth, while the Boston Red Sox fell into a deep decline. By 2004 the Yankees had won twenty-six World Series; the Red Sox hadn't won one since. They had reached the series four times, and had lost each one in the seventh and final game.

Red Sox fans have their team's misfortune tattooed on their psyches.

There was Game 7 in the 1946 World Series with the St. Louis Cardinals when Dom DiMaggio tied the game in the eighth inning after a two-run double but pulled a hamstring and was replaced by Leon Culberson. The next sequence of events in the ninth inning became part of the legend of the curse. With Culberson out of position, a hit by the Cardinals' Harry Walker resulted in Enos Slaughter scoring all the way from first base.

Then there was the game in the 1978 American League East between the Red Sox and the Yankees. In a season where the Red Sox had one of their best teams ever, they ultimately had to face off with their rival in a tiebreaker. Nobody expected the Yankees' shortstop Bucky Dent to do anything, but he hit a three-run homer in the seventh inning to prevent the Red Sox from going to the World Series. As a newspaper headline the next day said, "Destiny 5, Red Sox 4."

Then there was 1986, perhaps the most cursed moment in the entire history of the Curse of the Bambino. It was Game 6 of the World Series against the New York Mets, and the Red Sox were leading 5–3 in the 10th inning. This was when a routine ground ball went through the legs of Red Sox first baseman Bill Buckner and the tying run got to the plate. The Mets won the game and the series.

And then we reach 2003, where there was yet another Game 7 in

My first broadcasting job as a teenager. Looks like I could have been a backup singer for the Bee Gees.

In the newsroom at WTVJ in Miami where I got my big break as a weekend anchor and reporter.

On air at WTVJ— covering local sports was our primary job, but we also emphasized the national sports scene.

Eighties sports television. Yes, it was a gamble for me to go to New Orleans, but it turned out to be my launching pad to ESPN and Fox. I was likely telling the viewers that the Saints had lost again.

With Chris Berman and Bob Ley at the earthquake World Series at Candlestick Park in San Francisco.

Cohosting late-night *SportsCenter* during the peak growing years of ESPN.

At the ESPY Awards, hanging with the all-time headliners of *SportsCenter*: Dan Patrick, Charley Steiner, Linda Cohn, and Bob Ley.

The historic first live interview with O. J. Simpson after both of his trials. Our interview continues to be talked about today.

Some of the most enjoyable and heartwarming conversations I've ever had were with Coach John Wooden. I always came away feeling better about my life and the world we live in.

Author Stephen King at Fenway Park during the Red Sox 2004 World Series run. Just thinking about him still scares me.

With outfielder Johnny Damon and the self-proclaimed "idiots" after the Red Sox curse finally ended.

Fighting through the crowd to interview the greatest quarterback of all time, Tom Brady, after the greatest Super Bowl comeback of all time. (And how about our hair?)

Charles Barkley, my buddy since the '90s. I'm always waiting for him to say something outlandish or controversial.

One of my favorite things to do is call an NFL game, and I've been blessed to work with some outstanding analysts such as former Cowboy Daryl Johnston, a three-time Super Bowl champ.

Always enjoyed my time with Hall of Fame Buccaneer Ronde Barber.

Four-time NASCAR Cup champion Jeff Gordon was a driving force in the rising popularity of NASCAR.

Auditioning for a remake of *Three's Company*. Off-season day at the beach with Troy Aikman and Erin Andrews.

Our son Christopher, gone too soon. Thankful for the time we had. He lives on in our hearts forever.

My friend Bill Murray told me my golf swing is amazing: "You do everything wrong, and the ball ends up in the fairway."

This is not an audition. This is just Bill Murray being Bill.

Bill Murray came on my show the week of Super Bowl XLVIII. Afterward, he brought me along for his appearance on the *Late Show with David Letterman* and then to a Kings of Leon concert.

yet another ALCS with the Yankees. It was the 11th inning and the score was tied (yet again). And just like everybody expected, disaster struck when Aaron Boone blasted a walk-off home run to win it for the Yankees.

The comedian Steven Wright sums up the sentiments for all Boston fans:

"Being a Red Sox fan is like a Charles Dickens novel. Everyone is just trying to survive the situation. For me, it's a psychological war in my own mind dealing with each season."

So close, again and again, only to see the ball fly over their heads or between their legs.

Boston is a city steeped in American history, from its English Puritan founders to its national folk hero, Paul Revere. It's an exciting city to explore and Fenway Park is such a cool park, where you walk through the neighborhood to get to this stadium that smells like boiled peanuts. You have the thirty-seven-foot-tall left-field wall known as the Green Monster and the pole on the right-field line known as the Pesky Pole. The fans sing in unison to songs like "Sweet Caroline" as if somebody is in the stands leading them.

Being here in Boston at Fenway Park is a reminder of why we love the game. You can't help but be a fan of baseball at a place like this. But after Boston loses their third game, the town suddenly feels like a tomb. It seems like the energy and life have been sucked out of this energetic and fun-loving Red Sox team. During a conversation with Boston's manager, Terry Francona, I refer to the vibe I'm feeling.

"It feels a little like a morgue out there," I say.

Managers are always going to put a spin on things, even when things look as dire as they do now. But Francona appears a bit offended by my comment. In a respectful way he disagrees.

"The players and I don't feel like it's over," he says. "We're going to be all right. We haven't given up."

I apologize for my assessment of that situation and explain that I'm just going by what I'm seeing and sensing.

"I'm not in the locker room so I can't see that," I tell Francona. "I'm just a broadcaster."

I'm also being realistic. Sure, there's the dreary weather and letting one slip away to your bitter rivals, but there's the hard truth about being down by three games.

I don't believe in the Bambino Curse, but I do believe in historical facts. Facts like Paul Revere rode a horse in the middle of the night to inform the American militia about British movements. And facts like no team has ever come back from a 0-3 deficit in a playoff series. Twenty-five teams have tried and failed.

Terry Francona and the Red Sox still believe. Not only do they plan on proving me and the rest of the world wrong, but they also plan on making history and finally breaking that damn curse.

• • •

WE LOVE THE LONG SHOTS. THE IMPOSSIBLE ODDS. THE TEAMS AND the players who never give up no matter how bad it looks. When Boston wakes up the day after Game 3, they realize just how bad those odds look. Bob Ryan writes about them in the *Boston Globe*:

"They are down, 3-0, after last night's 19–8 rout, and, in this sport, that is an official death sentence. Soon it will be over, and we will spend another dreary winter lamenting this and lamenting that."

That sounds like a classic Red Sox statement if I ever heard one. But the statistic is one that nobody can argue with.

On this night New York plans to keep the hits coming. Last night they had 22 hits with 19 runs scoring. With the game still scoreless in the third inning, I report what I'm hearing on New York's side.

"In the Yankee dugout, you can hear the phrase 'Keep the line moving, keep the line moving.' That's what the Yankee players are telling each other when they come off the field in between innings. It's a phrase they've latched on to. They won't be moving like last night when they scored 19 runs. But they think they can hit Derek Lowe even though they say Lowe's cutter is cutting pretty hard tonight."

The Yankees plan to do what they did last night: take those hometown Red Sox fans out of the game. Terry Francona told me that fans were wacko in this time of the season and they went bananas from the first pitch, but all those hits silenced the crowd last night. By the top of the eighth inning, with the Yankees leading 4–3, the crowd seems to be taken out of it once again.

"The chill in the air is not just what the Red Sox fans are feeling," I tell viewers from my vantage point. "The temperature has dipped in the low forties down on the field. I noticed when the Red Sox were batting, a number of their players were going back in the tunnel, getting near the heater. In fact, Curt Schilling was really one of the few Red Sox players that was vocal at cheering. Meanwhile the Yankee bench—A-Rod, Jeter—very vocal, very attentive. Maybe the difference between 3-0 and 0-3. Or the difference between being a Yankee or a Red Sox."

Francona would probably disagree with me once again. But unlike so many of those signs in the stands, I don't quite **BELIEVE**.

At the top of the ninth inning in Game 4 at Fenway Park, things look bad for the Boston Red Sox. They are down 4–3. Coming back into play after a commercial, Fox shows more of the assortment of signs being held by fearful and frustrated fans.

"Make History or We're History!" one sign says.

"I can't believe we fell for this again," declares another.

"Patriots 20 in a Row! Red Sox 4 in a Row! Let's Make History!!"

"IT AIN'T OVER YET!"

A man has a paper bag over his head with the words "Who's My Daddy?" and an unhappy face drawn on it.

A woman has a sign that says "YANKEE HATER" that's pointed at her.

The screen fills with Red Sox fans. There are the hands on the head. The fingers over the eyes. The grimaces and the sighs. The mouthed curses and shut eyes. The stares of disbelief and regret.

All of these images play out as U2's "I Still Haven't Found What I'm Looking For" plays in the background. If there is any song title that sums up the Red Sox, it's this one.

The Red Sox are hitting against Mariano Rivera, one of the greatest closers in baseball history, who is looking for his thirty-third save.

The clock strikes midnight, and there is life for the Red Sox with a leadoff walk for Kevin Millar. Dave Roberts comes in as the pinch runner. Goes out for a huge lead, then jumps back to first base twice after Rivera tries to tag him out. A third time is close—too close. Even Roberts knows he was almost tagged out. Then just as Rivera throws home, Roberts takes off and steals second.

Bill Mueller's single straight up the middle brings Roberts home. The crowd erupts. There are still no outs. But Mariano has already given up more than enough. The inning ends in a tie.

By the 11th inning around 12:45, Joe Buck says, "I don't think it's going to be a very productive workday tomorrow across Boston. There's a lot of people staying up late."

The question is whether there will be a Game 5 tomorrow afternoon.

With two outs in the bottom of the 11th, Johnny Damon comes to the plate. He's batting a dismal .056 in this series, and he's 0 for 5 tonight with one run batted in. After being walked, Damon steals second, but a high bouncer to Jeter ends the hopes for the Red Sox to score.

With the temperature continuing to fall, the Red Sox reach the bottom of the 12th. With Manny Ramirez at first, Ortiz swings and—

Stephen King is prophetic.

A walk-off David Ortiz home run.

History holds its breath. The curse remains quiet.

After five hours and two minutes, the Red Sox are still alive.

• • •

WE LOVE THE MISFITS, THE REBELS WHO MARCH TO THE BEAT OF A DIF-
ferent drum. This Boston team is certainly full of them, as the *New York
Times* professes:

"The Red Sox are a ragamuffin group composed mostly of self-
proclaimed cowboys who sport cutoff tank tops and garish tattoos, either
grow their hair down to their shoulders or cut it close to their scalps, and
shave their beards in a fashion that could scare children."

Last year this Red Sox team made it to Game 7 of the ALCS with a
mantra of "Cowboy Up!" But coming into this year, the team was tired
of that slogan. Johnny Damon began to call them "idiots" based on their
fun-loving personalities and their choice to ignore things like the curse
and the Red Sox history. As he once said, "We are not the cowboys anymore—we are just the idiots this year. So we are going to go out and try to
swing the bats, find the holes, and, hopefully, good things happen."[1] That
includes refusing to count themselves out even though they were down by
three games.

At the start of Game 5 in Boston, I share something on the air that I
discovered earlier that day.

"Just when you think that maybe things were calming down in the
Red Sox–Yankee rivalry comes this," I say. "Today's Boston paper has a
picture of Gary Sheffield. Doesn't say where or when, but he's quoted as
saying—talking about the Red Sox—'They're a walking disaster. They
act like they're tough and how they care so much about winning but it's
all a front. They're just a bunch of characters.' Caught the eye of Red Sox

players. A staff attendant told me it wasn't just pinned up on a bulletin board in the locker room. It's posted all over the Red Sox clubhouse."

After last night's game ended at 1:22 a.m., Game 5 in Boston starts at 5:11 p.m. Pedro Martinez is the starting pitcher; in his 31 starts against the Yankees, he is 11-20. But Martinez starts strong, pitching a scoreless first inning. The Red Sox go up 2–0 in the first inning. The fans are boisterous and energized, showing no hangover from yesterday's marathon match. But this game will turn out to be a long one—even longer than last night. It also might be even more thrilling than Game 4.

In the sixth inning, the Red Sox get a nasty case of déjà vu from last year's Game 7 in the ALCS. Everybody remembers it well. In the 2003 game versus the Yankees, Pedro Martinez was pitching. In the eighth inning, Boston led 5–2. Martinez had already thrown 100 pitches, but he was left in. That's when things fell apart for the Red Sox. Even after the Yankees scored a run and got runners on second and third bases with only one out, Martinez was still left to pitch. Soon it was tied up and the Yankee fans were going out of their minds. An exhausted Martinez was finally taken out of the game. In the 11th inning, Yankee pinch hitter Aaron Boone hit a walk-off homer to end the game.

So when Red Sox fans see Martinez still on the mound in the sixth inning, they start to wonder. Boston is leading 2–1, but suddenly the tides shift and the Yankees go ahead 4–2. The energy is sucked out of this crowd as the whispers of yesteryears begin to start humming. But in the bottom of the eighth, Ortiz does his magic again, blasting a ball to the Green Monster and pulling them within one run. They tie the game before the end of the inning, setting up another tie game heading into the ninth.

As we enter the 10th inning, then the 11th, the masses at Fenway Park are mentally exhausted. I can only imagine what the players are thinking and feeling. There's an edge to every pitch, to every swing, to every crack.

The big moment can come at any time. But with each passing batter and each out, everybody is starting to ask the same questions.

Is this ever going to end?

We're all experiencing history. Watching it and living through it. But you can't help thinking about tomorrow and running through what you have to do and the fact that fans are drained and delirious and that this has suddenly become the longest game *ever* in the postseason.

As we get to the 14th inning, Tim Wakefield is pitching. He was the losing pitcher from Game 7 in the American League Championship Series last year, but he still manages to have three consecutive outs in this inning. Terry Francona recounts that Wakefield is pitching on fumes, that "he pitched the last inning on heart."[2] Wakefield is a true gentleman to be around. His tireless arm allows the knuckleball to be a marvelous part of the Red Sox magic.

In the bottom of the 14th, with two outs and two on base, David Ortiz comes up. Johnny Damon looks ready to storm off second base. Ortiz doesn't hit a walk-off homer, but instead ends the game with a single to center field. Damon dances to home plate. The Red Sox survive one more night.

• • •

WE LOVE THOSE BIG HITS. THEY ARE THE MOMENTS THAT YOU IMAGINE when you first learn how to play baseball.

Twelve-time All-Star David Winfield described to me on *Up Close* what it felt like to hit the big shot that ultimately wins the big game. He would do that in the 1992 World Series when his two-run double in the 11th inning gave the Toronto Blue Jays a 4–3 lead and ultimately a victory over the Atlanta Braves.

"Every young kid growing up, when they finish playing on the playgrounds . . . they say, 'I'm up. Men on base. World Series. Here's the pitch.

Bam!' You get a hit, your chest is a little bigger, and there's a smile on your face—that's what it was. And that grown man—years—twenty years after I started playing—I fulfilled that dream."

• • •

WE LOVE THE GUTS. THE MENTAL AND EMOTIONAL FORTITUDE THESE athletes have. In the middle of the spotlight with all of America's eyes on them, these baseball players can stand and somehow deliver.

Tonight all eyes are on Curt Schilling and his bloodstained sock. Game 6 in the 2004 ALCS will forever be known as "the Bloody Sock game."

In the first game of the division series, Schilling injured his right ankle, so the day before this game the right-handed pitcher agrees to do a radical surgery that temporarily binds his ankle tendons into place. Schilling gives viewers a brief synopsis of the procedure, explaining he had two choices when he weighed whether or not to get surgery.

"It was either this or not pitch. This was the choice. Basically, what they did was—it didn't take long—they just went in and they sutured the skin down to the tissue on the bone between my two tendons—the dislocated tendon and the tendon in the normal place—to keep the dislocated tendon out of place so it wouldn't pop back in and out there."

The question on all of our minds before the game is whether or not he can pitch. As Schilling steps onto the mound in the first inning, there is blood already soaked through his sock. Joe Buck explains the risk that Schilling and the Red Sox are taking by him playing tonight.

"The danger for Schilling is—when that tendon crosses that ankle bone, if it were to rupture, it is a big deal for a guy about to turn thirty-eight in November."

When I talked to Curt Schilling years later, we spoke about this famous game and some of those who said he was making the entire thing up.

"I was there—I can vouch for you on that one," I told Schilling. "You were in pain. Once again, you get people saying he's overdramatizing the moment."

"That's one of those conspiracy theories.... To think that I would, first of all, fake it. Secondly, to think that I would think about it far enough in advance to literally, like, make blood appear on my sock. People don't grasp how hard it is to play this game."

I asked Schilling about Terry Francona's decision to allow him to play. Was he going to be damaging his career? How could Francona make that big of a decision?

"Terry and I've been here long enough that I think he to a point he trusts me. And that was really—we had no options at that point. We really didn't. We had to have Derek Lowe for Game 7. *If* we had a Game 7. And, you know, we did the surgical procedure the day before. So I had twenty-four hours to walk around and see if it was going to work and I felt like it was going to. I looked at that as—I wasn't a twenty-six-year-old future Hall of Famer. I was a guy, a veteran player, who if that would have ended my career, I was at peace with that because, you know, I really honestly just put my faith in God. A lot of people got upset about me talking about my faith after the game, but it really was a case of faith. I didn't want him to help me go out and win. I just wanted to pitch."

That's exactly what Schilling does in Game 6. For seven innings the pitcher shuts down the Yankees, allowing only one run. All of Boston's runs come in the fourth inning, with Mark Bellhorn's three-run homer. The Yankees try to fight back, but eventually they lose to the Red Sox 4–2.

The Bloody Sock game became famous. Even after he came in off the mound, we all knew this was one of the all-time great feats in baseball.

As for his bloody sock, Schilling told me, "I think one of the club-house guys probably pilfered it. I never even thought about it at the time. But the one from Game 2 of the World Series is in the Hall of Fame."

• • •

WE LOVE THE MINDSET. THE CALM IN THE MIDDLE OF THE STORM. THE chess moves constantly being played by pitchers. So much of baseball is centered around what they do.

Over the years I've had the opportunity to interview some of the all-time great pitchers, and I've always been fascinated about the pressure they're under and how they can remain so focused.

Bret Saberhagen played for a number of teams in the major leagues. The right-handed pitcher known for his fastball and his accuracy was the MVP of the 1985 World Series when his Kansas City Royals beat the St. Louis Cardinals. When he visited me on *Up Close,* I asked him about such a mindset.

"Take us inside your head, pitching that seventh game at that young age. The kinds of things that you were going through, physical things going on and nervousness."

"I had won twenty games that year and I was nervous all the way up to that game," Saberhagen said.

"Is that sweaty palms, shaking—"

"Sweaty palms and just realizing that the whole season—this is it. The whole season is riding on tonight's game. We either are world champions or we're not world champions. And at that time I felt like that was a lot of pressure. But once I got out there and started pitching, all that pressure kind of went away and I just went about my game."

The Royals beat the Cardinals 11–0 in that game.

The best pitchers in the game have always managed to make the pressure go away. They actually seem as though there *is* no pressure, that they're going about their business. Greg Maddux was one of those. Playing with the Atlanta Braves and Chicago Cubs, "the Professor" won the 1995 World Series with the Braves and also earned the Cy Young Award four years in a row. The list of his awards and accolades is very long. He was known for his control, but more than that, as one of the smartest pitchers to ever throw the ball. When he was a guest on *Up Close,* I wanted to understand what was going on inside Maddux while he was on the mound.

"How come you don't show more emotion when you're out there pitching?" I asked.

"Well, I do; I might not show it—maybe I just hide it good," Maddux said in his understated tone.

"But that's by design?"

Even then his mind was searching for the perfect answer to my question.

"I don't want to act surprised if I get somebody out. That's one thing. And, you know, I'll get upset when I hang a pitch or the guy has a good at bat off me. I'll get upset at those times. But, you know, I just really expect to get guys out. And when I do, I don't want to act surprised."

"Very businesslike," I replied. "And one of the things that makes you successful, you don't panic when things don't go right, when sometimes you have to deviate from your plan or your plan isn't working. How do you maintain that composure?"

This is what we all long to have as a player. Especially in the game of baseball.

"Well, I think you have to understand that there's going to be peaks and valleys in this game, and especially over the course of the season. You throw over 250 innings, you're not going to throw a shutout every time you go out there. You're going to get hit. You're going to give up runs. You just try to limit it as best you can. And, you know, when you give up three or four in a game, don't give up four or five. And I just try to take that."

Tom Glavine was another great Atlanta Braves pitcher and the MVP on the same team with Maddux that won the World Series. During an interview I asked similar questions about the mindset he had pitching in Game 2 of the World Series.

"I knew after the first inning I had good stuff, I had good location, and it was just a concentration thing of not thinking too far ahead as far as hitters or innings. Not thinking too far ahead, of *Gosh, if we win this game, what's it going to mean to everyone?*"

I asked Glavine if this was something he battled on the mound or even before and after games.

"Once you realize as a pitcher, you've got your stuff and you have the things you want going on out there, then it becomes kind of a personal battle with not getting caught up in all those things," Glavine told me. "The big thing for me, like I said, was I knew the stuff was there, and now it's a matter of mentally staying where I am and not thinking down the road as to what is this all going to mean if you keep doing what you're doing and we win. Because as soon as you start doing that, you lose track of what you're doing. You give up some runs."

"Why weren't you nervous?" I asked.

"I don't know. I think because I had been there. I think that obviously helps pitching in those situations. The more you do it, the easier it gets. I mean, it's never totally easy, but I think you learn to deal with everything else a little bit better. I don't know. I think there was so much talk about what this game meant both for the team, for the organization, for the city, and that's all everybody wanted to talk about it. And all I wanted to do, I know I made up my mind—I wasn't gonna think about that. I was just going to think about the game."

This was exactly the same mindset that the entire Boston Red Sox team had in 2004 when they were down three games and left buried underneath the Curse of the Bambino. They all knew what making history and beating the New York Yankees would mean to the city. But they continued to just focus on the game at hand. And they had one left.

Game 7. The number where the curse usually reared its ugly head.

. . .

WE LOVE THE COMEBACKS. IN THE FINAL GAME IN THE 2004 ALCS, THE Boston Red Sox complete their miraculous and improbable comeback. Fittingly, before the game the team watched the film *Miracle* about the 1980 US men's Olympic hockey team that took the gold. But the miracles in this series had already happened. Tonight the Red Sox went out there and took care of business.

After going ahead 2–0 in the first inning, a grand slam by Johnny Damon in the second made the score 6–0. Boston never slowed down or looked back. In the ninth inning, with the Red Sox leading the Yankees 9–3, Fox put up a graphic that listed the major upsets in sports history. There was Clay beating Liston in the 1964 heavyweight boxing match. Super Bowl III when the Jets beat the Colts. The '69 World Series when the Mets beat the Orioles. The aforementioned 1980 USA men's Olympic hockey team that beat the USSR. And the 1985 NCAA championship where Villanova beat Georgetown.

This Boston Red Sox team weren't underdogs coming into the series; in fact, they were favored. But after being down three games to none, they were one out away from the season ending. Batter after batter and inning after inning, Boston kept holding its breath and playing from behind. There were so many opportunities for the Yankees to send them home, but the Red Sox remained.

The only hit to be added tonight is another one by Boston. The comeback is complete and the Red Sox defeat the Yankees 10–3.

Anyone watching this series knew that it was special. With each Boston victory, we knew we were watching history. We were watching a team do the unthinkable and come back from the most impossible odds. For me, I witnessed firsthand how people can overcome difficult challenges. The situation had become desperate for the Red Sox players, and the series seemed lost. But they came back stronger than ever.

Joe Buck sums up this moment.

"For people in New England, they will always remember where they were when the Red Sox finished off four in a row against the Yankees at Yankee Stadium on Wednesday, October 20, 2004."

• • •

WE LOVE THE FANS. WITH THE RED SOX IN THE WORLD SERIES, THERE IS a feeling that they've already won, that they've already beaten the Curse of the Bambino. They still have to play the St. Louis Cardinals, but the momentum they are carrying is unstoppable.

History is made as the Red Sox sweep the Cardinals in four games.

Throughout the series, both at Boston and St. Louis, I'm able to talk with the exuberant Boston fans. There is eighty-six-year-old Sam who attended the 1946 World Series. Teresa who is a big Red Sox fan living in Sweden. Then there is seventy-nine-year-young Annie, a forty-year season ticket holder. I talk to Annie during the game.

"Did you ever think you'd see the Red Sox be this close in a World Series?" I ask Annie.

"They've been close before. Only one pitch away in '86. One strike away. We should've had it."

"You've seen a lot over the years," I say. "Your husband used to come to the game with you."

"Yes, he came up until about two years before he got too sick. Except he died on the thirtieth of June."

"He'd love to see this ballclub, I'm sure. How would you describe this group?"

Annie begins to do her own broadcasting, giving a detailed rundown of the games. I can't help but chuckle as she talks about taking pitchers out too soon and analyzes the Red Sox team.

Another two guys I talk to in the Green Monster are Jimmy Fallon and Tom Hanks. Fallon has been shooting a movie about the Red Sox with Drew Barrymore for the past three weeks called *Fever Pitch*.

"We're rewriting the ending 'cause all this is all happening," Fallon tells me. "'Cause this never happens as Red Sox fans all know they are the toughest in a postseason. This is amazing and so great to be here right now."

I ask Tom Hanks if he is a Red Sox fan.

"Well, I grew up in Oakland. In Cleveland. I'm an American League boy born and bred. And I—look, I'm an American. And when the Boston Red Sox are finally in the World Series—there's nothing wrong with the city of St. Louis. They are lovely people. They have lovely colors on their baseball uniforms. But come on! I want Bill Buckner to have a good night's sleep, for crying out loud!"

Before throwing it back to Joe Buck, I ask Jimmy Fallon to do his best Boston accent to describe what's happening in the stands. Fallon doesn't disappoint with his thick Boston drawl.

"It's a wicked pisser up here. Having a great time. Boston rocks!"

This is the general mood. The fear and trepidation I felt at Game 3 of the ALCS are long gone. In Game 4 in St. Louis, I interview a father and son who are Red Sox fans. The teenage son brought a friend to watch the game.

"You guys are missing school for this?" I ask him.

"Yep, and I'm loving it." Then he adds, "I'm from Boston and I can't wait to go back and brag about how I got to see the Red Sox win the World Series."

It's wild to see a confident Red Sox fan.

"I hope your teacher's okay with that," I say. "Pretty cool that Dad brought you here. You know, you're setting him up possibly for a lot of disappointment given the Red Sox history."

The father gives me a knowing smile. "I realize that it's a risk, but we decided to take it."

* * *

WE LOVE THE CELEBRATIONS. THE CELEBRATION IN BOSTON FEELS bigger than any tea party to Red Sox fans. Seconds after this historic win, I'm able to stand on the field with the jubilant Red Sox players. The first I reach is Johnny Damon.

"The historic march completed with Johnny Damon," I say. "Congratulations. The Red Sox—the Idiots—are World Series champions."

"Absolutely. I mean, we know we're idiots. We know we're cowboys, but we also know we're world champions. We just overcame what a lot of people could not even realize. So I know there's a lot of happy people back home in Boston."

Outfielder Kevin Millar is with us as well.

"How important was it given the history, Kevin, to finish it off and not let it go to a fifth game?"

"I tell you right now, man, this is a big-time team we're playing with. A big-time bunch of guys. I'm so proud to be a part of this organization."

I put the microphone back over to Damon.

"Take us back to 0-3 Yankees and how it all began and what you guys did to get through that."

"Well, we're just so carefree," Damon says with a beaming smile. "Huh? We're down. We're like, okay, let's go out and win Game 4. And then we knew we had Pedro and Schilling for 5 and 6, so we knew we were going to Game 7. We had confidence. We gave them due respect to the other teams. The Cardinals were a great team. And you know—we did it."

"And for the Red Sox fans, not only in Boston, across the world, watching in Baghdad, Iraq, across the country, what do you say, Kevin?"

"I'd like to say thank you for being there, man. We were just we wanted to do so bad for the city of Boston to win a World Series . . . So rip up those 1918 posters right now."

"All right," I tell them. "Congratulations. Stephen King is smiling somewhere, and a happy ending."

THIRTEEN

The Sidelines

When you approach Lambeau Field from the outside, driving past homes and businesses in the neighborhood, you see a monument to pro football. As you enter it feels as if you're walking into a shrine to the sport. You can almost hear the voices of Curly Lambeau and Vince Lombardi. And then you stare at the same hallowed ground, knowing there is a modern-day NFL game to be played.

As I found myself at a playoff game at Lambeau Field in January 2004, I wasn't thinking about the history of this stadium. I was looking for a hat. Brett Favre and the Packers were playing against their former head coach Mike Holmgren and the Seahawks. I was the sideline reporter for the Packers for this game. With a wind chill of seven degrees, I realized that I hadn't dressed warmly enough for the weather. It was cold enough for a cup of hot coffee to start turning to ice. I found a thick beanie, but since it didn't have a Fox logo on it, I ended up wearing it underneath a Fox Sports cap along with a heavy coat over lots of layers.

After the start of the game, I was standing close to one of the large gas flame heaters they had on the sidelines. Nowadays they have better ways for players and coaches to stay warm, like heated benches, but at the time they only had a couple of heaters on each corner of the sidelines. The only other player close to me was the Packers' punter, trying to stay as loose and warm as possible. At one point in the middle of the action the punter walked up to me.

"Are you all right?" he asked me.

"Yeah, thanks," I told him, thinking he was just being polite.

"Are you sure?"

"Yeah, I'm just really cold."

The punter looked a bit concerned.

"You know—I think you're on fire."

I thought he was joking, but as I looked down I could see smoke coming from the hem of my coat. There were no flames, but somehow the back of my thick winter jacket had caught on fire because I was standing too close to the massive heater. Nobody else had noticed. I stood there smacking the back of it, making sure the sparks went out.

Later in the game, when Joe Buck and Troy Aikman came to me, they laughed at my winter apparel and told me to stay warm. The second time the guys came to me for a sideline report, Buck couldn't resist.

"And now let's go down to Chris Myers and his hat and that Elmer Fudd look."

I've never heard Aikman laugh so hard.

$\bullet$ $\bullet$ $\bullet$

THERE'S A DIFFERENT VIBE AND VIEW ON THE SIDELINES, WHETHER it's football or baseball. You feel the physical presence of the players, the crunch of pads, the force of fighting over turf. Hits sound harder. Whistles sound louder. Plays seem faster. You hear the chatter, the screaming and scheming, and the trash-talking. The game feels more real, more raw. This up-close view gives you a deeper appreciation for the game and for great competition.

Even though there is a monitor nearby to watch replays, you can easily miss things as you move to observe sideline interactions by the team's bench. You prepare for any moment, having something you can add on every play, but you are given barely any time. You only get about thirty seconds for each live report, so you have to make them count. That's why you're on the constant prowl. Sometimes the role of a sideline reporter requires a greater awareness and understanding of health and medicine. You always have to be ready to explain something to the audience, whether it's an injury or about something you heard from the field. Beyond injury information, you are looking for the mood of the team, any interesting observation about a player or a coach. You can set up an anticipation for the viewers, but you can't clutter what the guys in the booth are doing. Instead your job is to enhance and support. Get in, get out. Keep your role on the flow of the game.

At halftime you get to talk to the coach and bring out new inside information to the audience. The key is to make it look easy and casual, but it's high pressure because the crowd is loud. Anytime you're on during the quarters, you don't want to talk through the snap. Then the postgame interview always has a frenzied atmosphere around it, with celebrations and hugs and handshakes and conversation. In the middle of the mayhem when the players' jobs are finished, you still have a job to do and ask what the viewer would want to know in a two- or three-question time frame.

I have always believed that there is an art in reporting from the sidelines. I've seen it change over the years and become something different. Nowadays a reporter might tell the backstory to an athlete or an anecdote that's not taken from the flow of the game. But for me the goal has always been to get information in the moment of play directly from the field. Sometimes it's summing up the general mood of players on the sideline. Sometimes it's telling the audience what a coach had to say, but doing it in a creative way. Enhancing it somehow.

"Sean McVay came out smiling from ear to ear because his team drove for a touchdown that last time. He was buzzing like a kid at Christmas over there."

Instead of simply saying how disappointed a coach might be, I might tell the viewers at home that steam was coming out of his head. Sometimes I would need to paraphrase so the coach didn't make any next-day headlines. Like Mike Singletary's comment once after I asked him about his quarterback: "If I don't bench him I'm going to kill him!"

At times the fan in you pops up, moments where you get caught up in the excitement of a great play or a tightening of a game. In these times you quickly check yourself back in to your job responsibilities, sometimes channeling that fan in you to make sure you're reporting what the viewer wants or needs to know. The most important thing is to help share the enthusiasm and excitement with viewers at home. They can't fully appreciate just how loud the crowd sounds, and they can't see all the sights and sounds inside the stadium. You do your best to help the television audience be there with the players and the fans.

• • •

"EVERY NIGHT'S THE SUPER BOWL."

I've been saying that ever since I started in broadcasting. Maybe it's a corny saying, but it's something I was taught early on. No matter what game I might be doing, it needs to be the most important thing I can possibly be doing because it's for the people watching at home. It can be a preseason game or feature a winless team or be a lopsided score. And I've applied this mentality to every sport, not just football.

On February 6, 2005, that line literally became true. As part of the Fox team, I was at Alltel Stadium in Jacksonville, Florida, for Super Bowl XXXIX. This was Jacksonville's first time to host the event. It was fitting that I was back in the state where my sports broadcasting journey started. The New England Patriots under head coach Bill Belichick were coming into the thirty-ninth Super Bowl as the defending champs and were trying to win their third Super Bowl in four years. The term "dynasty" kept being mentioned. They were playing Andy Reid's Eagles from Philadelphia, a city craving a Super Bowl championship.

The pregame ceremonies included a tribute marking the sixtieth anniversary of the end of World War II. As the military band played their drums and trumpets, a host of heroic veterans were introduced: soldiers from the 101st Airborne; the Tuskegee Airmen; Marines who were in the Battle of Iwo Jima; a Medal of Honor recipient; and the Navy WAVES, representing thousands of uniformed women who served and died in the war to help keep the world free. The forty-first and forty-second US presidents—George H. W. Bush and Bill Clinton—also walked on the field to hear the combined choirs of the Army, Navy, Air Force, and Marines sing the national anthem.

While the chorus of voices filled the stadium, I couldn't help but think of my father. Like some of the soldiers on this field, he had rushed onto the beaches of Normandy, seeing death and destruction all around him. As I mentioned earlier, he had never spoken much about the war, except for the time after we watched *Saving Private Ryan* together, and later in life, when he began to attend reunions with World War II veterans.

Even though he had never been that interested in sports, I knew he was proud of me being here. My dad valued hard work, and it was that work ethic he taught me that had carried me all the way to this Super Bowl. Surely he never could have imagined me being on the field for this big game. But then again, when I was a kid, I never could have imagined that either.

During the commercial break before kickoff, we received instructions from our producer, Richie Zyontz. I was on the field ready to interview Patriots' Troy Brown when Zyontz said, "Chris always says, 'Every night's the Super Bowl.' Well, Chris, you're finally right. You're here."

Those words really struck me. This was really happening.

"Just be quick and get a brief comment from him," Zyontz said about my interview.

As I stood next to Troy Brown, I could feel his energy.

"No need to be nervous even though there are millions watching," I told him. "I know you've got a game to play, so I'll just ask you a couple of quick questions."

But just as I uttered those words, I was the one who suddenly became nervous.

This is the most-watched event on television and I'm about to go live.

After all the interviews over the years both on the field and in the studio, this felt different. This truly was bigger than others.

With the show coming in from commercial break, I heard Joe Buck through my headset.

"With the kickoff seconds away, standing by with Troy Brown, let's go down to Chris Myers."

For a moment, I froze. In my ear I heard them yelling, "Chris! Chris!" as I suddenly stopped in my tracks. It felt like minutes passed, even though it was barely seconds.

"All right, thanks very much, Joe," I said. "With the most veteran Patriot. An intense look . . ."

Then I lost my train of thought. It actually felt like I froze for an entire minute. I could hear them yelling my name in my headset. Troy Brown tapped me on the toe to keep going. Of course, it was just a second that I paused. It certainly didn't *feel* like a second.

I finished the thought: ". . . this close to kickoff. What's going through your mind?" Brown had been here before; this fourth Super Bowl didn't seem to intimidate him a bit.

"Just coming out and playing a great game," he answered. "You know, you don't want to go out and turn the ball over and have any mistakes and give them opportunities for some points on the board."

Yeah, and you don't want to go out and suddenly freeze and make a mistake in front of millions.

"You are Mr. Versatility. What concerns you the most about this matchup?"

As Brown answered me, I finally fell back into the oldest thing you learned in broadcasting school: you're speaking to one person even if you're speaking to millions.

"All right, have fun tonight," I said. "Thanks, Troy Brown. He will be catching the ball, playing defense, and also returning punts."

After all these years and interviews and time spent around athletes in studios and stadiums and fields, I couldn't help still getting some pregame nerves. But they didn't last long. The kickoff happened right in front of me and the thirty-ninth Super Bowl had begun.

Coaches and players try to act as if the Super Bowl is just another football game, but you know when you walk into that stadium . . . You know it's bigger than any game you've been around. The lights, the colors, the people. And then they play and you feel the magnitude in every snap.

All these years later, I still get that rush at an NFL game when the ball is kicked off and the microphone is turned on. It never gets old; Sundays just aren't the same without it. Just like when I was a fan, as a broadcaster there is always an excitement and anticipation of what's to come before the game starts. There are nerves and tension. But when the game arrives it's worth it all. That's why I do feel like every football game is like the Super Bowl.

I've always lived with this "every night's the Super Bowl" approach, pushing myself to win, treating each new task at hand like it's important, like nothing else at the moment matters except this game. Sometimes I've rationalized that middle ground is a compromise in life—that you have to go all out for everything. That's when I have to be reminded to come back down to earth. To walk out of the football stadium back into the garage at home.

My family sometimes says to me, "Every day is *not* the Super Bowl." You need to have average days, too, calm days to balance out the crazy ones. But in terms of approaching my job and work assignments, this is how I've always done it, giving it the best that I have. In a world where you're surrounded by others who do the same, that's the only approach to take.

• • •

ON THE FIRST NIGHT OF 2007, LOVE IS IN THE AIR. THE LOVE FOR COL-lege football and the Bowl Championship Series. For bluebloods and long shots. For running backs coming back from injury and first-year head coaches. And for New Year's Day watching a bowl game in person.

Set in a brand-new stadium, an epic David versus Goliath battle is taking place. The University of Phoenix Stadium in Glendale, Arizona, is host to the Fiesta Bowl. The No. 7–ranked Oklahoma Sooners come in as the giant program with seven national championships under their belt. They are excited to have their Heisman-hopeful running back Adrian Peterson playing once again after breaking his collarbone three months earlier. The No. 9 Boise State Broncos are seven-and-a-half-point underdogs despite their 12-0 record and Western Athletic Conference title.

Fox is broadcasting the game this evening, and I am on the sidelines reporting. Coming into this matchup, few give Boise State any chance—other than Broncos fans. I interview Boise State coach Chris Petersen before the game and ask about this perception.

"Your team—America's underdog, the little guy. Do you feel like you're playing for more than just Boise State here?"

"Yeah, we're playing for a lot of things," Petersen tells me. "We're play-ing for the city of Boise, our university, the state of Idaho, and anybody else out there that thinks they might not have a chance. We're playing for everybody."

"You're undefeated, but you said you hadn't seen anybody as big and as fast as Oklahoma. What's your approach?"

"Yeah, they're an excellent football team. They've got great tradition and history. We're just going to play hard. We're gonna leave it all out here on the field tonight."

This is one of those overused phrases in sports, but on this night, Petersen is absolutely correct. Both teams leave *everything* out there.

With three minutes left in the game, it feels like we are watching another entertaining college football bowl game, but it hasn't reached the status of classic. Not yet. Then Oklahoma drives 77 yards with the clock ticking down. With 1:26 remaining, QB Paul Thompson hits a jumping Quentin Chaney to make it 28–26.

Oklahoma goes for the two-point conversion and fails! But wait . . . Boise State is called for pass interference. So they try again.

Oklahoma goes for two and they make it! But wait . . . The Sooners are called for an illegal shift. So they give it a third try.

Oklahoma makes the two! It's tied 28–28.

With 1:13 on the clock, Boise State begins their drive to win the game, but Jared Zabransky's first throw is intercepted for a pick-six! This indoor stadium erupts. The crowd is jumping and shouting and electric. Boise is down 35–28.

We have reached classic game status.

Zabransky makes a first down at the 43-yard line with 40 seconds left. Then he's sacked. Then a dropped pass. Then an incomplete pass.

After three plays, it's fourth and 18 with 18 seconds left in the game.

A mere 18 seconds.

You can just feel the tension and the wild anticipation.

Zabransky hits Drisan James at the 35-yard line with a line of Oklahoma players playing prevent in front of him. James darts right and goes backward, then quickly laterals it to Jerard Rabb, who sprints to the left and jumps into the corner for a touchdown! The hook and ladder trick followed by the extra point ties the game again at 35 with seven seconds left.

"It's not the size of the dog in the fight, it's the size of the fight in the dog," Fox commentator Thom Brennaman says, quoting Mark Twain.

When a Mark Twain quote arrives in a broadcast, you know you're suddenly approaching a "greatest ever" game.

Adrian Peterson opens overtime by running the ball into the end zone and putting Oklahoma up by 7, 42–35.

Boise State drives and once again faces a mighty fourth down. The snap goes to wide receiver Vinny Perretta, who runs an option play and throws a touchdown pass to tight end Derek Schouman, putting them within one point. An extra point attempt will tie the game, but Boise State doesn't want a tie. Coach Petersen decides to go for two to win the game.

"We're playing for everybody," he'd said.

Coach Petersen also has another trick play waiting for the world. The snap goes to Zabransky, who executes a perfect Statue of Liberty handoff with one hand in the air and the other at his side before giving it to Ian Johnson. Boise State's star running back is untouched as he runs into the end zone and straight into the ecstatic crowd.

Emotions have been spiraling for the last hour. Now it's an explosion of emotions. People are stunned and in disbelief. Others are exuberant as they celebrate.

"Congratulations on one of the greatest college football games we've ever seen," I tell Zabransky as I interview him in the midst of the celebration.

"Oh, it's unbelievable," Zabransky says. "You know, these guys just kept believing, kept believing. And I saw where they got it. We got it right here. We just kept battling from that last play of regulation all the way to that play. Unbelievable."

"Biggest win in the history of Boise State football. What about that final play, the fake without hesitation to go for two?"

With a sweat-glistened face and a confident grin, Zabransky talks while taking in the scene around him.

"I mean, we wanted to come out here and win. We weren't going to hold anything back. We've been practicing that play all season long. Actually our backup quarterback put that extra fake in. It was just—when it worked out, we ran it against Idaho and it was good, and we just held on to it until now."

"You threw an interception that looked like it would cost you the game. Did that cross your mind? How did you get over that?"

"It is not over until it's zero zero zero. And I knew that. And the guys came up to me and they said they believed in me. That's all I needed."

"Perfect season. Do you deserve a shot at Ohio State?" I ask.

"I think we do," Zabransky answers. "I think you got to look at it. We go 13-0. We beat everybody out on schedule. Now the media talked about Oklahoma being such a great team and they battled, but we let them come back into it. And you know what? We deserve a chance in a national title."

An epic game with an unbelievable outcome. You can't top this . . .

Then again, anything can happen in sports.

Wild finishes can become even wilder.

Mike Burks is the producer in my ear, and he tells me the stage isn't set yet for the trophy presentation, so I look for another Bronco to talk to. I spot Ian Johnson still celebrating with fans, so I head over to the mayhem and ask if he's willing to do an interview.

"I'll do it, but I want to propose," Johnson tells me.

In the chaos and commotion on the field, I assume he's wanting to propose a better playoff system for college football. Zabransky just told me they deserve a chance to be in the national title game, so that's probably what Johnson's wanting to talk about as well. I tell the running back that's fine.

When Mike Burks tells me we're on and I talk to Johnson in front of fans who are still cheering, his girlfriend, who is one of the Boise State cheerleaders, comes running over. I will learn later her name is Chrissy Popadics, and she's the team's head cheerleader. At this point, I'm thinking he has a different kind of proposal in mind.

"Talk about the game and the finish," I ask Ian.

"We played real hard to get here. And then once we got here, we wanted to come out here, show them that they're in the game with us and show them that we deserve a little respect. We had a bit of fumbles. But we wanted to show them how we play ball and we showed them. And it came down to who had more heart, and we had it."

The Boise State fans right behind us are literally shouting in Johnson's ears.

"And you didn't waver even after the interception runback and you were down," I say as one of the fans gives a loud "woooh!"

"I mean, if you looked on the sideline, our guys started smiling afterwards," Johnson says.

"Do you deserve a shot at Ohio State after a perfect record?"

"I mean, we're not going to say that because—hey, we got our bowl game. We're happy with our bowl game. I mean, we went 13-0. We deserve a little bit more respect. We're just out here to win and get a little bit of respect."

I ask him if he thinks Oklahoma took them lightly. Just as I ask this, Burks comes over the line and tells me we have to wrap this up and go.

"We know they did," Johnson says. "The way they're talking about us, the entire game. The way they're talking to us when they were down. I mean, the whole entire week, we felt like we're the little brothers."

"How about that final play, the guts to go for two?"

With Mike Burks telling me we have to go, Johnson still hasn't said anything about a proposal.

"I mean, we just felt amazing that our coach had enough confidence in us to go for two to win this game because we're playing to win, not to lose."

I'm nodding, knowing we have to go and realizing that I have to make a split-second decision on live television, so I go for it.

"I know you're going to propose to your girlfriend. Congratulations."

This is really the only thing I can do in order for this to happen. My producer doesn't know anything about the proposal, so I have to tell him about it and give Johnson the opportunity. He immediately moves in front of Chrissy and takes her hand, then bends down on one knee.

"Hold on, wait a minute," I say on the broadcast as Ian proposes to a shocked Chrissy.

I put the microphone in front of her as she shares an ecstatic "yes!" with the country, then puts her hand over her mouth as tears fill her eyes. When Johnson stands and reaches in to hug her, Chrissy jumps into his arms and embraces him while the crowd behind erupts once again.

"She said yes!" I say. "Ian Johnson, proposing to the head cheerleader at Boise State. Does it get any better than this in college football? I don't have anything else to say."

The story has a happy ending. Ian and Chrissy married on July 28, 2007. I did receive some criticism about stepping on his proposal reveal, but if I had just thrown it back up to the producer, that moment would have been lost on live national TV. Thankfully I played a small part in their fairytale story.

• • •

AS MUCH AS I LOVE SPORTS, THE PULL OF SPORTS BROADCASTING IS not the games but rather the people. It might sound corny, but my interest is in these athletes. And I'm not only fascinated to know what a winner is thinking and feeling, but I'm also curious about what is going through the minds of the losing players and coaches. Half of the audience is usually on the losing side, so they want to hear from their heroes. My job is always to ask what viewers want to know. Without being too sappy about it, I want to feel these players' emotions.

How's it feel to blow a 20-point lead?

What's it like to fumble the ball and have forty other teammates looking at you and costing them the game?

What were you thinking when you blew your cool and then your guys blew the game?

For me, it's always about the human element behind the hero. How do these professionals handle losing?

Some have mastered it better than others.

History is about to be made. I'm on the New England Patriots sideline for their Super Bowl XLII matchup against the New York Giants. The Patriots came into this game with an undefeated record of 18-0, hoping to join the 1972 Miami Dolphins as the second team to have a perfect season. They are 12-point favorites, but after a tough defensive battle, New England has a narrow lead of 14–10 with 2:39 left in the game. Eli Manning and the Giants begin their drive on the 17-yard line.

Once again I had been watching the brilliance of Tom Brady on the field. After he connected with Randy Moss for the go-ahead touchdown with 2:42 remaining, I had been ready to storm the field and battle the mob to interview the quarterback and wide receiver. I had already pictured the confetti raining on top of me as I elbowed and pushed in the celebration mayhem. I also couldn't help but see the irony in this story.

I grew up in Miami and experienced a city cheering on its undefeated Dolphins team. Now I'm here to witness history being made once more in the very same town.

The crowd roars as Eli connects with a receiver for a first down. Then he completes another. Then Brandon Jacobs rushes on a fourth and one to continue this impossible drive. Manning has to run with the ball and then nearly tosses an interception. It's third down and five with 1:15 left on the clock.

Of course, in a tight game like this, anything can happen with one minute left in the game. Sometimes you need a perfect strike to win the game. But sometimes you need to make a perfectly impossible catch. That's what happens on the third-down play with 1:15 remaining. When Manning gets the ball, the pocket around him starts to collapse, forcing him to step up and move around. The back of his jersey is being held as he avoids four Patriots and shuffles out to avoid a sack. He spins, almost going to the ground, then launches the ball.

History indeed will be made today, but not because of the Patriots' perfect season. It's because David Tyree makes what will later be dubbed the "helmet catch." As the wide receiver leaps for the ball at the 25-yard line, Patriots safety Rodney Harrison leaps with him. Tyree catches the ball with two hands, then has to secure it against his helmet with only his right hand after Harrison knocks his left hand off the ball. When Tyree lands on top of Harrison, he still miraculously has the ball clutched against his helmet.

It's one of the greatest plays ever in a Super Bowl.

Moments later, Eli Manning finds a wide-open Plaxico Burress to give the Giants the lead with 35 seconds left. There is still always the chance that Brady can pull off some more magic—we've seen it happen so many times—but this night belongs to New York.

Things change in the snap of a finger, or the snap of the football.

As the Giants celebrate their win, I realize what I'm going to have to do.

Ask Bill Belichick about this loss after they were so close to being undefeated.

I go from feeling like a kid in a candy store to a kid getting a root canal with an angry dentist.

I know the last thing Belichick wants right now is to be interviewed, but we both don't have a choice. The coach of the losing team is required to give an interview after the Super Bowl.

As I stand in the echoing silence in the hallway near the Patriots' locker room, Belichick appears to be in shock.

"Coach, you haven't had this feeling for a long time. How would you describe it?"

"Not a very good one. You know—we're disappointed."

He doesn't look at me or the camera as he gives his answer.

Oh boy. He really does not want to do this.

"Where did the game get out of hand, in your opinion? Or you want to talk about the last drive?"

He pauses for a second, then gives a gloomy shrug. "Well, we had our chances on the last drive they made. You know, they made some plays, and they made big ones at the end."

The coach is still looking down, then he tightens his lips and gives me a pained look.

This is tough. Let's see if he can open up some more.

"Did you expect this kind of game in terms of a defensive, low-scoring game?" I ask.

Again comes the dismissive shrug.

"Well, it's a three-point game the last time we played them, so, you know—we knew it was gonna be a tough, hard-fought game, and it was."

Yeah, but the last time wasn't in the Super Bowl. Can you please give us something interesting for the audience and football fans? Something about this extraordinary moment?

Having covered him over a number of years, I know Belichick isn't going to open up and suddenly be different than he always has been. I just can't decide if he's unsure how to handle this sort of situation, too stunned to speak, or if he is intentionally being difficult. Or a combination of all three. All I can do is ask questions and be respectful; viewers will interpret his attitude in whatever way they want.

"Can you talk about what the defensive plan was in that last drive?" I ask. "It looked like Eli Manning was going to get sacked. Obviously, he got away and completed it—"

"Yeah, we got our hands on a few balls and we had some pressure on him. But, you know, in the end they made those plays and we didn't. So— that's a difference in the game."

Of course, we already know that. There are a thousand things we *don't* know.

Did you think you had Eli Manning sacked?

Do you think there should have been a call by an official?

How is the team feeling emotionally after all the talk of the perfect undefeated season?

For a guy who is so detailed in the way he coaches, Belichick doesn't want to share a single thought. I decide it's time to abort with a hundred million people watching.

"I know this is difficult," I say. "What do you tell your team after, you know, a perfect season up till this point?"

"Yeah, well, we're disappointed."

We're disappointed? That's it? After you had a chance for a perfect season? After the chance to make history and surpass the Dolphins? I'm sure it's a bit more than just disappointed.

Of course, all that runs in my mind in milliseconds before I end the interview. I don't say any of it. I want to be respectful and give him space.

"Okay, Coach, thanks very much."

"Okay, Chris. Thanks."

"Appreciate it," I say before he goes. "Thanks for a great season."

The interview lasted an entire fifty-seven seconds. As he leaves, I realize I would have been better off talking to the players. But coaches need to have at least a moment with the broadcaster. I can't help but feel for

Belichick. I don't feel like he was being rude. That's just how he handles losses. That's how I take it.

He acknowledged me by saying my name. That shows his human side. He's just reeling.

I have to put myself in his shoes. He and his team are in a bit of shock. They expected to win the game and they almost did. They got so close. But the Giants managed to go the distance and pull out a win.

Later on when we have a small group gathering at Fox and I feel a bit disappointed to have not gotten more from Coach Belichick in the interview, my boss tries to lift up my spirits.

"You're a f—ing hero to be able to handle a jerk like that," he tells me. "He was so rude and you were just doing your job."

I'm not bothered by Belichick's interview. I was a little thrown off, but he's still a person like all of us. Except in this case, he resembles the kid in Little League who'd never lost before and now was trying to accept a defeat for the first time in his life.

• • •

BEING ON THE SIDELINES CAN MAKE YOU FEEL LIKE A KID AGAIN, LIVing out your childhood dreams. That's why one of the most special parts about getting to do that has been bringing our sons to the games.

Once while I was covering the Baltimore Ravens, our son Christopher accompanied me to the game. We arrived at the field early. The temperature was cold and felt especially frigid since we were coming from the West Coast. I was able to introduce Christopher to Joe Flacco, the Ravens quarterback. Baltimore's coach, John Harbaugh, came out to greet us as well.

"This is my son, Christopher."

Harbaugh gave him a firm handshake. "Nice to meet you."

Christopher was clearly excited to meet the coach and they struck up a conversation. As the wind whipped around us, Christopher began to shiver, and Harbaugh noticed.

"Where's your jacket?" Harbaugh asked.

"I'm guilty," I said. "We just came from California. I didn't tell him to bring a coat."

"Look—go to our locker room and tell Skip that Coach Harbaugh told him to give you a Ravens jacket. That's yours. You keep it."

Christopher lit up when he put on that Ravens jacket for the first time. He ended up coming into the booth and seeing how everything operated. During the game he watched me at work and got a glimpse into my world of broadcasting.

Growing up, Christopher had never been much of a sports fan. A part of him resented sports because it took his dad away from him, and he had other interests. He was a really smart kid who was into history and music, and he loved video games. His friends were the ones who eventually got him into sports. They'd tell him when they would see his dad interviewing some famous athlete, or talk about games they'd seen and teams they were following. Over time Christopher became more engrossed in sports. He would sound like I did when I was a teen, rattling off statistics, facts, and scores. By the time he traveled to Baltimore with me, he was in college, and had become a big fan of the NFL. This trip cemented his love of the game. So did another road trip he took with me to a Vikings playoff game where he had a chance to meet Brett Favre. These trips also allowed him to see how hard I worked.

"Wow, this is a lot tougher than I thought, Dad. But it's really cool."

FOURTEEN

Dreams Brushing by You

On October 22, 2006, the Hendrick Motorsports NASCAR team won the Subway 500 that was held at the Martinsville Speedway in Ridgeway, Virginia. After battling rookie driver Denny Hamlin in the final six laps, Jimmie Johnson emerged victorious at the short track. Two years earlier, Johnson had won the same race, but the victory had come under a shroud of unbelievably difficult circumstances. After climbing out of his car now, the driver immediately referred to that 2004 win.

"I just don't know what to say—I'm kind of out of breath. I want to wish Mr. Hendrick and everyone back in North Carolina—as part of N501RH going down a couple of years ago, we didn't have a chance to celebrate then because of the loss," Johnson said, referring to the registration number of the plane that crashed, killing everyone on board, including members of the Hendrick family and organization. "For close friends and I, we're just happy to be here today. And it doesn't ease the pain, but it maybe put a smile on all those families' faces."

Since Rick Hendrick started Hendrick Motorsports in 1984, they had become the most successful auto racing organization competing in the NASCAR Cup Series. To date they have set records for fourteen NASCAR Cup championships and 307 wins in Cup Series races. I knew about the tragedy that occurred two years earlier right before this race, so during the post-race show I mentioned the anniversary on the air.

"You know—as a dad, this has to be a touching moment for Rick Hendrick, who two years ago lost his son Ricky when the plane carrying him and nine others crashed while on the way to this track."

In fact, the Beechcraft Super King Air 200 headed to the Martinsville Speedway in Ridgeway for the Subway 500 was not only carrying Hendrick's only son, but also his brother, two of his nieces, and several of his best friends and closest business colleagues. Ten people—eight passengers and two flight crew—died when the plane registered as N501RH crashed on Bull Mountain. Pilot error and heavy fog were listed as contributing factors for the crash.

After Jimmie Johnson's Subway 500 victory, it was a bittersweet moment for Rick Hendrick. This win signified something special for Rick as both a father and the team owner. Since it was on my mind, I decided to mention it even though it was a sensitive topic. Once again, I wanted to highlight the human element in sports.

It turned out that Rick saw my comment and decided to reach out to me to say thanks. We had never really met, so he asked people for my number in order to contact me personally. When we spoke, he explained how much it meant for me to mention the loss of his son.

Twenty-four-year-old Ricky Hendrick, a former driver in the Busch Series, was being groomed to take over Hendrick Motorsports while his father backed away from daily operations. After his son's death, Rick Hendrick doubted if he could continue in the business. As he told ESPN, "The hurt was just so bad, and it was so much grief. The crash made all these holes, and all these people had meant so much to me."[1] Yet eight days after the crash, Hendrick stood before the organization and assured them they needed to carry on.

"This place is going to go on, and we're going to take care of each other," Hendrick told every single member of the Hendrick Motorsports team.

They weren't just a business organization. These employees were family, and as a family they were going to do anything it took to get through this. For Rick Hendrick, this was a rallying call to press on and go the distance.

"It was like I was with my extended family," he said. "And the love and support in that room was just overwhelming, how we all were so emotional. But it gave me tremendous strength. I fed off of that."

I never could have imagined how one day Hendrick would use that same strength to help someone else going through an overwhelming tragedy. That person was me.

• • •

"WE JUST DON'T RECOGNIZE THE MOST SIGNIFICANT MOMENTS OF our lives while they're happening. Back then I thought, 'Well, there'll be other days.' I didn't realize that that was the only day."

Of all the memorable lines in *Field of Dreams,* these spoken by "Moonlight" Graham may be the most significant. Burt Lancaster played the character of Archie Graham, a New York Giants baseball player in 1922 who only played in one inning in one game yet never got to bat. These words spoken to Ray Kinsella, played by a young Kevin Costner, reflect the hopes and the regrets we all carry in our lives.

Whenever I hear this quote or think about it now, I can't help but think about our eldest son, Christopher.

On February 16, 2012, shortly before I was scheduled to fly to Florida for the Daytona 500, I planned to have lunch with Christopher. He was an honor student in his second year at Moorpark College, so after his classes he was going to drive out to the house to meet me. Christopher was deciding which university he wanted to attend after graduating from Moorpark—either UCLA or Columbia. I knew the subject would come up during lunch. As someone growing up in a house full of dogs, Christopher was starting to consider going into animal research or something related to that. He had a love for animals and had been active as a volunteer with a rescue program.

As the minutes passed and I didn't hear from him, I assumed that something had happened with school. It wasn't like him not to call or leave a message. *He's probably with friends and just got delayed,* I thought. But when a police officer showed up at the door, I immediately suspected that something was wrong.

"Is there a Chris Myers here?" the officer asked.

"That's me."

What he said next—what he explained had happened—is difficult to remember or talk about. The police officer said that a vehicle registered in my name had been involved in an accident and the driver had been killed. The police initially thought that was me, but I instantly understood the horrific truth. The vehicle was my old car, the one I used to drive before I got a newer car, and the one that Christopher now drove.

The news came as a shock. The rest of that day and the days that followed were a blur. It was devastating to have to go to the site and identify things. The phrase "unspeakable tragedy" doesn't do justice to what happened. I don't know how we got through it all. Yet as I look back at everything and wonder how to write about this, I can say that the only way you get through something like this is by coming together with your family.

That's exactly what Susan, Alex, and I did. You also need others to come alongside of you. I was humbled and grateful to see how many people provided comfort and support.

Right away my brothers and sisters, who were scattered all across the country, traveled long distances to be with us. We had relatives and neighbors who reached out to us. My Fox Sports family was there for me, too. Eric Shanks, the CEO and executive producer of Fox Sports since 2010, happened to be driving with his wife the day after the news, so he called me and asked if I wanted some company. I hesitated at first but then told him sure. Shanks, an Indiana native, is a bright, talented executive who is quiet and practical. When he came over we just sat out on my back patio and didn't say a lot. This small, kind gesture meant a lot to me.

Comfort came from many others, too. I saw the best in people. My Fox colleague Troy Aikman flew out right away to see me. Larry Fitzgerald, star Arizona Cardinals wide receiver, called me all the way from Africa where he was on a safari just to ask me if I was okay. Peyton Manning sent me a personal note. Bud Selig, the former Major League Baseball commissioner, phoned me with his consolations. Kyle Petty, who lost his own son Adam, reached out to me as well. At the time I was doing a program for Showtime called *Inside NASCAR* with Kyle and Michael Waltrip. Kyle provided much firm support to help me deal with my loss.

Since Christopher had done volunteer work with Life Animal Rescue, that's where we told people to send money and donations in honor of him. Once again we were touched and grateful when the Tampa Bay Buccaneers and the Minnesota Vikings were among the first teams to make donations in Christopher's name. It was incredible to see strangers giving to this group just to support us during this time. Many made donations and were quick to do so with sizable amounts.

I found another huge supporter in someone else in NASCAR: Rick Hendrick. When he heard the news of Christopher's passing, he instantly reached out to Fox Sports and asked what they could do to help. The first thing he did was to fly members of the Fox crew out in a private plane to attend the small funeral we had. Every one of the crew who I worked with made the cross-country trek on the Hendrick Motorsports plane. Since this was the week of the Daytona 500, all of them had to turn right around and go back to Florida. Despite the storm of emotions and grief, I was grateful to see my teammates there. It was an incredible gift from Rick Hendrick.

Fox Sports told me to take as much time as I needed to be with my family and to heal. Mike Helton, the president of NASCAR, told me that whenever I was ready to come back to work, I could bring my entire family with me. The France family, who own and operate NASCAR, personally reached out and told me to let them know anything I needed.

Rick Hendrick ended up becoming more than just a sympathetic friend. In many ways, he has resembled the guardian angel Clarence from *It's a Wonderful Life,* one of my favorite films. Over the years, Hendrick has kept in touch with me. He understood what I was going through, and he knew how important it was for me to be around someone who understood. He offered me a hand on the shoulder, knowing the difficult days that lay ahead.

Days where you question your own existence and real purpose.

Days when you need some space.

Days when you need some company.

Days when you don't know what you need.

Hendrick came alongside me to be a gentle compass. He offered advice without telling me what to do or not do. All he could do was speak of his own experiences.

"I'm years ahead of you," Hendrick told me. "Here are some things that are going to happen and here's how we dealt with it."

He gave me suggestions for ways to deal with the grief and told me to call anytime. When I was nearby, Hendrick told me to reach out so we could get together for lunch or dinner. Here's a busy and successful guy who's not only running NASCAR's most successful racing team but also had car dealerships and businesses that employed thousands of people. Yet he was there for me, showing me how he had found a purpose and a reason to keep going on. Encouraging me to keep living my life despite the loss.

Hendrick says we're part of a club nobody wants to be in. We share a special bond and I owe him and his family a lot. We began a tradition of having lunch every year at Daytona before the big race. His guidance and encouragement have truly helped me throughout the years.

"You're allowed to be happy," Hendrick told me. "You're going to have sad moments, but you have to go on. You have to be thankful for the moments you had with Christopher. And you have to know that you're going to see him again in some form."

That belief that we're going to see Christopher again is what I live by and what my family lives by to get through. Because when you lose a child like this, you can feel like packing everything in. You start to question your purpose, your existence, your faith . . . all of those things. But you still have a heartbeat and you still have a life to lead. Not just for yourself but for others.

Hendrick has helped me remember this. But others have come along the way to help in their own unique ways. One of those was my favorite comedian, who decided to bring some cheer our way.

• • •

BILL MURRAY UNDERSTOOD GRIEF. HIS FATHER HAD PASSED AWAY when he was seventeen years old. Since he was on a movie shoot outside the country when he heard the tragic news, he couldn't attend the private funeral we had for Christopher with family and friends. Several of the Murray brothers were able to come, however, and Bill made plans to visit us a week later.

"I'd like to come out and just talk to you guys," Murray told me. "To go out to lunch with you and your family."

After flying out from the East Coast to Los Angeles, Bill rented a car and came by the house. Susan was gone but Alex and I went to a local deli where Bill spoke candidly to us. He was just there to support us, not saying much at first but easing into talking about his father's death when he was younger and how his family responded. He didn't go into a lot of details, but he did express how they dealt with everything. The main point he made was that when someone close to you dies, the important things to remember are the time you had with them and what they meant to you. The rest of the conversation was Bill chatting with Alex and helping us move on and ease the pain of a tragic loss.

I had gotten to know Bill over the years and had seen various sides of him—the comic, the competitor, the showman, the prankster, the fan. But this was a new side to him. There was never a moment where he told us this was how we should feel or this is what we should do. There was just a vibe of comfort and understanding from a guy who has made a career out of making people laugh.

After lunch, Murray turned back into the comedian on the drive back home.

"I have this corned beef sandwich left over and I can't take it with me on the plane," Bill said.

I glanced at him, not sure why he was bringing it up.

"It's not going to go to waste," he said. "Let's drop it off at one of your neighbors' house."

"Really, Bill?"

"Yes, absolutely. Who do you think would love a corned beef sandwich?"

I honestly had no idea.

"Come on—there has to be someone," Murray said with a straight face.

I shrugged. "I don't know—there are the Delgados who live close by."

"All right. The Delgados. I'm sure they would love a little corned beef. Let's drop it off there."

So we pulled up in the driveway and Bill climbed out of our car with the takeout box in his hand. We watched him as he stood at the door and rang the bell. When the mom of the family opened the door, she looked both surprised and amused to find Bill Murray standing there.

"The Myers have a leftover corned beef sandwich that they wanted you to have," Bill told the woman.

As she took the box in her hand, still looking perplexed and speechless, she glanced over at Alex and me watching in the car. We waved at her. Bill soon got back in our car and nodded.

This has always been the gift of comedians, how they can break the tension and sadness in our lives. This small display of Bill's humor by doing some random impromptu thing was exactly what our family needed. We needed this comic relief during a season when there was little to laugh about.

• • •

EVERYBODY HAS THEIR OWN TIME CLOCK FOR GRIEF. THERE IS NO guidebook, no ten-step program to getting back to life. At a certain point, I spoke to our family about when we should start to get back to regular life. When I should go back to work and when Alex should start attending school again. Nobody was pressuring us. But after a couple of weeks of dealing with our loss and after having so much support, I decided to go back to work. The people at Fox Sports and NASCAR were very careful about making sure I was being taken care of. They had told me that at any point if I needed to step away, they would get somebody to fill in for me until I was back.

When I went back for the first time, NASCAR sent a private jet to bring me to the second race of the NASCAR season. It would be the

Subway Fresh Fit 500 taking place at the Phoenix International Raceway in Avondale, Arizona. Bill Richards, the Fox Sports pre-race producer, accompanied me on the trip. He and his longtime girlfriend, Lex, had both known Christopher when he was younger. They were part of the game night tradition and had attended one of Christopher's plays in high school.

Coming back to my Fox Sports team brought some normalcy to my life. It felt good to be back. As I greeted viewers to the pre-race program, I had to fight my emotions and do my job.

"Blue skies. Temperature in the eighties. A great day for racing. And we're getting ready for the start of the race at Phoenix. This is where America gathers every weekend for NASCAR. Hi, I'm Chris Myers, and it's good to be with you for the second race of the season. Alongside me in what we call 'the Hollywood Hotel'—Michael Waltrip, two-time Daytona 500 champion, and of course, our NASCAR Hall of Famer, Darrell Waltrip."

"Man, it's good to have you back, Chris," Darrell said with a heartfelt glance. "We missed you. Glad you're here with us, buddy."

"It's good to be back. And thanks to NASCAR, the Fox family, all the fans who sent support. My family is deeply indebted. Difficult to talk about. But we get back to the here and now and the challenge ahead. And I know drivers themselves after what we all witnessed last weekend are seeking some sense of normalcy. Will they find it here in Phoenix today?"

I was among those seeking some sense of normalcy. The truth was I was choking back tears and on the verge of losing it. Usually whenever I was in front of a camera regardless of the circumstances, I could always handle things. But this was the most difficult situation to push through. Thankfully I made it through with the support of the people around me.

One huge show of support came in the Hollywood Hotel, a portable studio we used for pre-race coverage, from the very start of Fox broadcasting NASCAR. It was a mini-trailer with a picture window that'd become very popular with the fans and viewers over the years since we were right there at the track where the action was. The race car drivers could walk right in at any point, like if they were involved in a wreck or had engine problems. There had been some classic rain delays where we had lots of fun in the Hollywood Hotel.

For this first race back in Phoenix, I had wanted to be as private as I could about what had happened. But I found all these fans had gathered outside to show their respects. They gave me a sympathy card to show their support. When I opened it, I saw countless signatures—names of viewers I had never met—people I didn't know letting me know they were thinking about me and my family.

Words can't do justice about how much this meant. It was very heartfelt for these people to have had that connection to what had happened. You expect it from your family, but to experience this firsthand from NASCAR fans truly showed the loyalty and the hearts of these people. I had seen that with Dale Earnhardt's death and how people reacted on that day for years, and how they still have strong feelings. But I'm not Dale Earnhardt. I'm not a driver or an owner. Yet the fans thought enough to recognize my loss.

This was the sort of thing you might see in a movie. I almost didn't know how to act. I told them thanks but then stepped away for a moment since I was overcome with emotions. The fans weren't pushy and gave me my space. It was tough, but this meant so much to me. That's why I have always been so indebted to NASCAR Nation.

Remembering this brings me to tears.

For my entire career, it has never been about me. Covering the game and the players was always the priority. But suddenly, this story *was* about me and my family. It was one thing to receive some attention or acknowledgment for the work you've done, but this was something different. It was nice for people to show appreciation for what you were doing, but this ran a lot deeper. This made me appreciate this sport and the fans even more.

Looking back, I wish I had said more when I returned. But I worried that I wouldn't be able to make it through, that I would break down live on the air. I knew I had the support of the men sharing this desk with me and the crew surrounding me. People knew I needed some space and wanted to keep things private. But this was another thing Rick Hendrick helped me with. He helped walk me through getting back into my world without feeling guilty about everything I had gone through.

*   *   *

A LOT OF PEOPLE EXPECTED SUPER BOWL XLVIII ON FEBRUARY 2, 2014, to be a cold game. It was the first Super Bowl to be held in an outdoor stadium in a city with frigid temperatures. The Denver Broncos were playing the Seattle Seahawks in MetLife Stadium in East Rutherford, New Jersey. I was there as a sideline reporter along with Pam Oliver and Erin Andrews. This was one of my first big NFL assignments after Christopher died.

With the two-year anniversary of his passing two weeks away, I still couldn't help but become emotional during the singing of the national anthem. As Grammy-winning soprano Renee Fleming began to sing, I started to think about Christopher. He had always been a sharp kid, someone who was smart and funny. He loved showing his wit, especially when the whole family was together. As he had gotten into high school and college, Christopher's engaging personality really showed. He had my kind of personality, being a bit of a showman but also driven.

As I stood by myself with cameramen at my side and everybody's attention on the American flag and the singer, the waves of memory hit me and I began to cry. There was so much deep inside that had built up—feelings and emotions I didn't even know were there—that all of a sudden poured out of me. For one of the few times in my professional career, I couldn't pull myself together for a few moments. This could have happened at any given time, so thankfully it was one that would go unnoticed.

I wiped the tears away and readied myself to do my job. And when it came time to do it, I delivered.

During grief counseling after the loss of Christopher, the counselor said we were going to have these moments when a connection or a memory hits you. It was strange to have it happen right before the Super Bowl, since I was always very focused at times like this. But having lost my father a year earlier, the swell of the patriotic anthem and the memories of my father and my son all seemed to hover around me and moved me to tears.

I had been raised with a strong sense of faith and spirituality, and that certainly was helpful in continuing to move forward through such a tragedy. But the truth about grief is that it is something you have to process yourself. Other people can tell you what to do and what might happen. You can talk with others who have gone through something similar, but sometimes there are no answers to be given. That's just the reality of life and death.

• • •

MY MOTHER DIED IN HER FIFTIES AFTER YEARS OF BATTLING CANCER. On her deathbed, she gave me some advice: "Try not to have many regrets in your life."

She said other things to me, but that particular statement struck deep and stayed with me. It meant even more when we lost our son at age nineteen.

I have always tried to look forward and push ahead. Not to live in the past but rather to learn from it. But there's a lot to be said about two things.

First off, stopping to smell the roses. Living in the moment. Taking in the moment. Processing the moment.

And second, reminiscing about the good times. The good feelings. The optimism. And even reminiscing about some of the bad times, the adversity and challenges overcome.

There have been melancholy moments when I realize that I was a workaholic just like my dad. We sometimes live in extremes, not realizing how it affects those closest to us the most. I wish I had had more time with Christopher. But then I remember, between the travel for games and research for interviews and radio shows in my profession, there were vacations with the family and backyard swimming pools and hikes and Daddy Days at school when my sons were young and Little League and soccer and so much more.

But still—there wasn't enough time. Just like Moonlight Graham reminds us in *Field of Dreams*.

"Back then I thought, 'Well, there'll be other days.' I didn't realize that that was the only day."

Moonlight Graham gets into only one major league baseball game and that's it. As he explains, "It was like coming this close to your dreams and then watch them brush past you like a stranger in a crowd." But Graham goes on to be a children's doctor and has an impact on many lives.

No regrets.

It's funny how things intersect in a person's life. Back in 1989 during my first year at ESPN, one of my first assignments was to report on the making of *Field of Dreams*. I interviewed the producer, Phil Alden Robinson. The film was about to be released, so I had only seen some of the clips. It turned out to be a great baseball movie, one I saw with my dad.

Years later, as I found myself interviewing Kevin Costner at the 2014 Super Bowl for his upcoming movie *Draft Day,* I had to ask him about working with Burt Lancaster, who played Moonlight Graham. Of all the movies and scenes I could have asked the Oscar-winning actor about, it was this particular scene that has always drawn me in.

I didn't just get close to my dreams—I've been blessed to have seen my professional dreams come true in becoming a network sports broadcaster. And my dreams also came true by having our two sons.

Sometimes I think of the boys sledding down that long winding driveway in Connecticut. I remember taking them to the beach during the day or driving ten minutes to Malibu to watch the sun setting over the Pacific. Breathing in the salty air alongside my sons always felt therapeutic and calming.

The sea and the sun are still there. So is my family. And so are the memories of those moments we shared with Christopher. Losing Christopher still feels like the time with him brushed by too quickly . . .

I'm still grappling with "no regrets."

FIFTEEN

The Faith of a Saint

Luck. Destiny. Superstition. Curses. Breaking the curse. Sports can bring out the strangest notions and irrationalities in both fans and players. And while I don't believe in curses in sports, I can say that I've seen a lot of magical games and moments in my career. Especially when it comes to my onetime hometown team, the New Orleans Saints.

In 1987, I reported on a bizarre story involving the Superdome. As I said earlier in the book, 1987 was the year when the New Orleans Saints finally made the playoffs. This was the year when Coach Mora and I made the bet that if they made those playoffs, Susan and I would get married. In the same year, construction crews began work on expanding a shopping mall right next to the Superdome, and they ended up making a startling discovery. They found the remains of bodies that had been in the old Girod Street Cemetery. Thus the "Superdome Curse" began.

The actual truth was that the only section of the Superdome that sits on any part of that cemetery is two of its parking garages.[1] And for the first eight years of the Saints' history, games were played in Tulane Stadium since the Superdome hadn't been built yet. We also know that New Orleans finally won the Super Bowl in 2009 with Sean Payton and Drew Brees.

Just as the 2004 Boston Red Sox and 2016 Chicago Cubs teams showed, you finally put talk of curses behind when you win. In 1987, New Orleans made big strides toward that when they finally got into the playoffs. This was the start of a magical run with those Saints.

• • •

LOUISIANA AND FLORIDA. IT'S FUNNY HOW THE TWO STATES I HAD lived in ended up colliding when the Saints finally got into the playoffs. Their December 6, 1987, victory came against the Tampa Bay Buccaneers in the Superdome. They had won their sixth straight game and would end up winning three more to end the season at 12-3. On my television show *4th Down on Four,* we had a special celebrating the win to clinch a playoff berth. Stan Brock, the Saints' number one draft pick in 1980, who played right tackle and had been through the toughest years with the team, joined us for this momentous occasion, and I had a chance to get his thoughts.

"This is a great feeling. You know, being 1-15 at one time in our career and thinking, *God, this thing's never going to end. We're jinxed.* We've got a great franchise now, a lot of winners on our team, got some guys out of the USFL that are helping us tremendously, and I don't know—it's hard to put it in words. Been through the thin of it. Now we're right in the thick of it."

Stan's first season in fact had been that dreadful 1-15 season. I asked the tackle what was the biggest difference in this Saints team and how had things turned around.

"I don't know," Brock told me. "It's like I say, it's hard to put your finger on it. It's something that we work hard every year. You come into the season, you think you're going to win. And as the season goes on, your dreams begin to fade out. Now our dreams are alive and everything is going good."

Everything was good for the moment. In the home playoff game versus the Minnesota Vikings, everything was *not* good. The Vikings would go on to beat the Saints 44–10. Yet at the end of this blowout, with two minutes remaining, the fans in the Superdome did something unexpected: they gave their team a prolonged ovation. Saints team owner Tom Benson walked onto the field and led the cheers. If you didn't know the score you would have thought the Saints were the team blowing the Vikings out.

The Saints lost that battle but won the war by making it to the playoffs.

As their magical and strange history has played out, I've found myself in the middle of a lot of crazy moments.

•   •   •

IT'S FUNNY LOOKING BACK ON MEMORIES AND SEEING THE WAY things sometimes line up a certain way. As if the stars are aligned. Cool moments—twists of fate—things that happen that bring you full circle. The 2009 NFC Championship Game is one of those.

So many years after that 1987 Wild Card game between the Saints and the Vikings, the two teams found themselves battling each other once again in the Superdome. The two major storylines coming into the game were the Saints hoping to capture their first-ever conference championship less than five years after Hurricane Katrina, and the Vikings' quarterback Brett Favre playing in what could be his final playoff game.

It had been two decades since I left New Orleans, yet I still felt a kinship with the Big Easy. One of the greatest compliments I ever received was after I had moved on to ESPN and someone from New Orleans said that they were happy "one of their own" had made it big. I hadn't forgotten those early years with the "Ain'ts," those fans that were both loyal yet frustrated and vocal in the old days. Sean Payton and Drew Brees had shifted the standard. They had moved the Saints from simply trying to have a winning season and getting to the playoffs to now winning it all and being an elite team in the NFL. Payton and Brees weren't just guiding the team to victories, but they were also actively involved with the community and had embraced the New Orleans fans, community, and entire region.

The game was thrilling, with the two teams going back and forth. Neither side led by more than a touchdown at any point. With the score tied 28–28 in the fourth quarter, the Vikings famously imploded. First there was a penalty for twelve men in the huddle, then a hobbling Brett Favre rolled out and threw a pass across his body instead of simply running to go out of bounds or to make a first down. That ill-advised pass was intercepted with only 33 seconds left in the game, leading to overtime.

There were no bad omens or mojo when the Saints won the coin toss and got the ball first. After a field goal won it for them, New Orleans was headed to the Super Bowl for the first time ever. In a way, it felt better to be in the Superdome to celebrate this Saints win than to be in the Super Bowl.

In another one of those crazy ironies, Terry Bradshaw was supposed to do the trophy presentation for the winning NFC team, but he had been battling a sore throat and woke that morning with laryngitis. So Fox asked me to do the presentation. Under a gentle shower of confetti and a rooftop of bright glowing lights, I stood on the stage with an exuberant group of players.

"After more than four decades," I said above the roar of the crowd, "the New Orleans Saints are going to their first-ever Super Bowl. Tom Benson, the owner, is here. We have Deuce McAllister, the Saints' all-time leading rusher. Of course, Sean Payton. Drew Brees we'll get to. They're hollering for you to present the NFC trophy as the headline of the *Times-Picayune* says 'Super Saints.' So Deuce, take it away."

There were lots of moving parts here. The table in front of me with the trophy and players reaching out to touch it. The newspaper I had just held up. Tom Benson next to me. I had to make sure to guide all of this along in the chaos.

"How about dat, New Orleans?" Deuce shouted. "Mr. Benson, on behalf of the NFL, it's my honor to present to you the George Halas Trophy as the NFC champion!"

Deuce and I held the massive trophy up along with the Saints owner. After we put the trophy back on the table, I put an arm around Tom. I thought how special it must have been for him, to celebrate in New Orleans and the decision to not move the team after Katrina.

"All right, Mr. Benson. I know you're glad you kept the Saints here in New Orleans. Talk about what it means to this city and all the Saints fans and players over the years after more than four decades to now go to a Super Bowl."

"Well, not only the seventy thousand that are here, but think of seven million that are in other parts of this world that are cheering for us tonight."

I quickly moved things along as I congratulated him and welcomed in Coach Sean Payton. The coach moved to the table and picked up the trophy, bringing it above his head to a roar from the crowd.

"That's yours and your team's, Sean," I said, chuckling. "The first coach to take the Saints to the Super Bowl, Sean. How did you do it?"

Payton looked joyful and exhausted and reflective all at the same time as he looked out to the stands, still full with screaming fans.

"This is for everybody in this city. This stadium used to have holes in it. It used to be wet. It's not wet anymore. This is for the city of New Orleans."

Once again he held up the trophy.

"I'm so proud," he continued, "to be able to coach these players. And there's really no one else I'd rather hand this to than Drew Brees."

As Payton gave the trophy to his quarterback, I stayed at the coach's side to try to get something more from him.

"Sean, can I get just a comment on—I mean, fans around the country were treated to a spectacular game. How do you survive a game like this?"

"Well, both teams were unbelievable. At the end of the game, I grabbed Brett Favre and said he was tremendous. Both teams played out of this world. And again, I'm just honored to be a part of this and to have these guys to coach."

I shifted over to Brees. "You and Sean Payton came to New Orleans under difficult circumstances. And I know you have one more win in you. Talk about the dream."

The question we all want to ask. The question all athletes *want* to be asked.

"There are so many words that could describe it, but I'm speechless right now. It's a moment that I've been waiting for a long time. And obviously, the job's not done yet, but we're going to enjoy this victory. And how about these fans?"

Once again, the Saints fans cheered him on.

"The best fans in the world. Best fans in the world. Who Dat Nation. Now we got to finish strong in Miami, baby."

The Saints had taken on the mighty Brett Favre and survived. Finishing strong meant they had to defeat the Indianapolis Colts and Peyton Manning. And Sean Payton and Drew Brees did just that when the Saints defeated the Colts 31–17. In Payton's memoir, *Home Team,* he spoke about the tradition of touching the Super Bowl trophy like it was some kind of lucky charm:

"From the stage I could see the players patting and rubbing the trophy. Everyone was acting like that trophy had the magic powers of some voo- doo charm. Who knows? Maybe it did."

If there had been some voodoo curse put on the Saints, it was surely gone. There would be no more unexplainable losses to come. No more hexes and mind-boggling ends to games.

Then again . . .

• • •

IT IS KNOWN AS "THE MINNEAPOLIS MIRACLE."

On January 14, 2018, the Saints played the Vikings once again in an NFC divisional playoff game in Minneapolis. Another dome, but instead of seeing people dressed up like Mardi Gras, you heard the constant blare of the Gjallarhorn. I was covering the Vikings sideline, and at halftime I thought this game might be a blowout with Minnesota up 17–0. Yet Drew Brees had proved many times before that the Saints were never out of a game. Sure enough, New Orleans came back with a thrilling drive and went ahead 24–23 with 25 seconds left.

Twenty-five seconds left for Case Keenum to pull off a miracle. Yes, Case Keenum. Not exactly a headliner like Joe Montana or Tom Brady or Drew Brees. After the Saints' field goal put them ahead by one point, the stadium suddenly became quiet. Vikings fans were stunned. They knew that their team never got miracles.

No game is over until it's officially over, yet I felt like so many others as I stood on the Vikings sideline waiting to see them lose the game. Erin Andrews was on the Saints' side and our producer told her to be ready to go live with Drew Brees when the game finished.

With 10 seconds remaining, the Vikings were on their own 39-yard line. Keenum stepped up for basically a long last-gasp throw. It looked too far for a Hail Mary, so the only hope for Minnesota was to get in field goal range. The play was aptly called "Seven Heaven." Three Vikings receivers lined up on the right side of the field. Keenum lofted a high ball to Stefon Diggs, who caught it inches away from our sideline.

Diggs launched in the air to catch it with two hands just as the Saints' safety went to tackle him. But the safety missed and somehow—in some incredible way—Diggs landed backward, then spun himself around, nearly fell, but balanced himself with one hand down on the ground all while sprinting and *staying in bounds.*

A 61-yard miracle touchdown. Happening right in front of me.

As Vikings coach Mike Zimmer told ESPN, "That didn't look like a curse out there to me. That looked like a Hail Mary."[2]

With the sound of pandemonium and insanity from the Vikings fans and the swirl of celebration and disbelief on the field, I ran out to interview Case Keenum. It's always best to get a winning athlete moments after the victory to hear what was going through their mind. Keenum was out of breath as I got to his side to talk to him. Vikings and Saints players all around us hugged each other and shook hands. They taped my interview with Keenum to play in just a few moments. Then my producer told me to hold on.

"Wait—it's not official yet," he said. "They're going to have to kick the extra point." In all the excitement, I forgot that they needed to make the conversion. But people were already celebrating on the field and Saints players were headed to the locker rooms. I had finished my immediate postgame interview with Keenum and was now attempting to talk to an energized Diggs while officials were telling everybody to get off the field for the extra point. I didn't want to do so without talking to Diggs, though, so I urgently waved for my crew to follow me, while above the roar of the crowd the stadium speakers blasted "Let's Go Crazy" by Prince.

Troy Aikman found this particularly amusing. He and Joe Buck were in the booth trying to make sense of everything happening down on the field.

"We heard [referee] Gene Steratore say by rule they have to kick this extra point."

"Well, they can't do it with Chris Myers out on the field," Joe Buck said.

"I—I don't know. We may be here for a while," Aikman said. "They gotta clear everybody off the field and at least snap it.

"Chris is still trying to get interviews," Aikman said, continuing to laugh.

As the field was finally cleared and both teams made it back out there, Case Keenum led the crowd in the Skull Chant. The Vikings ended it with the extra point. My producer told me to interview Keenum again, so I went back out there and we did it one more time, this time live. In a way it almost felt like a reenactment.

"The Vikings waited a long time for this," I said to Case. "They had to wait a little longer for that final snap. First of all, congratulations. The game of your life. The throw of your life. Tell me about the last play. Desperation time to Diggs for the win."

Case laughed in disbelief. "I can't even explain it. We were definitely in desperation mode. Just trying to give my guys a chance and Diggs made a heck of a play. Made a lot of plays. You've got to give our guys credit—man, we fought to the very end. And that's special."

With Case having time to catch his breath and put on a cap, he appeared to be soaking in this moment. He looked out to the crowd around him as he spoke to me.

"You had to be thinking just maybe—a penalty, a chance at a field goal here in that situation, right? I mean, you were down to your last down."

"Yeah, we missed a few there early. We knew we needed a chunk. Try to get in field goal range. But with the last play—I don't even know what just happened. It's crazy."

Once again the Vikings were piping in Prince's "Let's Go Crazy."

I asked him if this was the wildest game he'd ever been in.

"I don't even know right now. I can't—I have no words. If you ask me about this moment, what this moment means to me. It's probably going to go down as the third best moment of my life behind giving my life to Jesus Christ, marrying my wife. And this one's right there close."

Surely for Vikings fans this game would rank up there with the best games of their lives. The Minneapolis Miracle would go on to be one of the greatest plays in NFL history. Unless you happen to be a New Orleans fan. Saints fans might agree with this Billy Crystal quote from *The Princess Bride:*

"You rush a miracle, man, you get rotten miracles."

• • •

THE DOME IS A SPECIAL PLACE. THERE IS SOMETHING QUITE MAGICAL when teams come to New Orleans to play the Saints. It goes beyond the thunderous noise and the dedicated fans. There is always the vibe of a giant party, as if Mardi Gras has come to the NFL.

The season after the heartbreaking loss to the Vikings, I was covering the 2018 NFC Championship Game as the New Orleans Saints played my childhood team, the Los Angeles Rams. Could the Saints get back to the Super Bowl? Would there be any surprises or thrilling comebacks or epic finishes?

I had started the 2018 NFL season in the Dome, and it had been another stunner when the Tampa Bay Buccaneers led by quarterback Ryan

Fitzpatrick blew past the Saints 48–40. All of us had been shocked to see those kinds of points. That was what made this sport and my job so much fun—you never knew what was going to happen once the first quarter began.

The Saints-Rams game didn't disappoint. Except for the seventy-three thousand fans in the Superdome, and any Saints fan watching on television.

With 1:49 left, the game was tied 20–20. The Saints were at the Rams' 13-yard line and it was third and 10. Certainly enough time to run and execute a play, and certainly close enough to make a game-winning field goal. After a quick snap, Drew Brees threw a perfect ball to wide receiver Tommylee Lewis, but before he could catch it he was throttled by Rams cornerback Nickell Robey-Coleman. Anybody watching knew it was pass interference; Coleman never looked back but instead simply blasted headfirst into Lewis. Coach Payton went ballistic, but the Saints couldn't do anything about the no-call and had to settle for a field goal.

The Jared Goff–led Rams drove 45 yards and made a 48-yard field goal to send the game into overtime. Then, sure enough, after the controversial no-call that would be dubbed the "NOLA No-Call," the Rams would intercept Drew Brees and make a 57-yard field goal in overtime to win the game.

After the game, the NFL's senior VP of officiating would call Coach Payton and acknowledge that there should have been a call at the end of the play.

"He said not only was it interference, it was helmet-to-helmet," Payton said in a press conference. "They couldn't believe it."[3]

The day after the game, the massive headline in the *New Orleans Times-Picayune* summed up the game perfectly:

"Reffing Unbelievable."

• • •

IT'S JANUARY 5, 2020. THE VIKINGS HAVE COME TO THE MERCEDES-Benz Superdome to play the Saints in the Wild Card game.

This feels like a story I've already read.

But the New Orleans Saints are due. It's their destiny. They are 13-3. Sean Payton and Drew Brees deserve another Super Bowl victory. Plus, they are going against a Kirk Cousins–led Vikings. Cousins who can't win the big win, who is known for not being able to win a playoff game.

So it's the fourth quarter and—

Am I repeating myself?

The Saints are down 20–17 with seven seconds left.

How many times can this happen? I kept thinking as I watched.

New Orleans is going for a 49-yard field goal. Surely good news and positive vibes need to be coming the Saints' way.

Sure enough, they tie the game, and now we find ourselves in overtime. Another playoff game down to the wire in the Superdome.

Where was my buddy Bill Murray when you needed him? It felt like I was in *Groundhog Day*.

In overtime, Kirk Cousins comes out and ends up making two massive throws. First a 43-yard bomb to wide receiver Adam Thielen, then a four-yard shot to tight end Kyle Rudolph. As the air seems sucked out of the stadium and Who Dat Nation watches in horror, you can almost hear the echoes of Cousins in the distance.

"You like that?! You like that?!"

Soon enough I'm able to talk to the Vikings' quarterback, and I ask him the question everybody wants to know.

"Kirk, congratulations. I know it's about the team, but you got a lot off your shoulders with the throw to Thielen, then the game-winning touchdown in overtime to advance."

"Happy we won. It was a great game. Two good football teams. NFL's a great product, isn't it?"

Cousins speaks like the pro quarterback that he is, saying the right things, giving credit to New Orleans and the rest of his Vikings team. Before the interview ends, I can't help wanting to get to the thing that's been talked about so much: Cousins not being able to win "the big one." All the criticism and commentary thrown his way.

"I know you have a deep faith," I say to Kirk. "How heavy was this load you've been carrying? I know you try to handle it like a professional, but you can't block all the outside noise."

"No, I appreciate the question, Chris. You know, ultimately it's about team, and I'm just trying to do my part for this team. Help us win. And, you know, quarterback carries weight. It comes with the job. And like you said, my faith is important to me. It's the foundation of my life. And ultimately that's where I gain my peace and strength. Win or lose today, God's still on the throne and I take comfort in that."

"The first playoff overtime win in Viking history. Congratulations and good luck at San Francisco."

This is the third time in three consecutive seasons that New Orleans has lost a playoff game on the last play. The last two losses have come at home. In the Superdome.

The Boston Red Sox and the Chicago Cubs had overcome their legendary curses, and so had the New Orleans Saints in 2006. Yet a part of me can't help but wonder how these impossible things can happen again and again. How can they be so snakebit? An impossible catch . . . an impossible no-call. Time after time, the Saints have had a chance to win a big game and they've crumbled under the pressure. Sometimes it's felt like they've found a way to lose the game.

Sometimes I really can't help but wonder if that French Quarter voodoo sometimes finds its ways into the Superdome . . .

I kid because I care. I really do.

• • •

go back to that 1987 season when they first made the playoffs.

In Week 6, the Saints played the San Francisco 49ers, the Bill Walsh–led team of Joe Montana, Jerry Rice, Roger Craig, and Ronnie Lott. Remarkably, they kept the game close but were only able to get field goals, kicking five of them. The Saints' last-second field goal attempt that could have won the game for them was missed.

After the game, I was at the press conference where Mora launched into one of his memorable rants. He was visibly frustrated and as always spoke his mind.

"They're better than we are; we're not good enough. We shouldn't be thinking about beating these 49ers; we shouldn't be talking about it, 'cause the Saints ain't good enough. And you guys shouldn't write about us being a playoff team and all that bullstuff—that's malarkey. We ain't good enough to beat those guys and it was proven out there today. It's that simple. We're not good enough yet. We've got a long way to go; we've got a lot of work to do; we're close, and close don't mean shit. And you can put that on TV for me. I'm tired of coming close, and we're gonna work our asses off until we ain't close anymore, and it may take some time; we're gonna get it done; we aren't in there—we aren't good enough. They're better than us—black and white, simple fact!"

Jim Mora wasn't done.

"'Could've, would've, should've' is the difference in what I'm talking about! The good teams don't come in and say 'Could've.' They get it done! All right? It's that simple! I'm tired of saying, 'Could've, should've, would've.' That's why we ain't good enough yet! 'Cause we're saying, 'Could've,' and they ain't!"

Sometimes it doesn't take a voodoo priestess to break some mysterious, magical "curse." Sometimes it just takes a pissed-off head coach.

After losing that game to the San Francisco 49ers, the 1987 New Orleans Saints won the remaining nine games of their season and made it to the playoffs for the first time. And now we've come back to the start of this chapter. Or is it the end?

SIXTEEN

Bouncing Around with Barkley

When I first interviewed Charles Barkley, he was once again playing for the US men's Olympic basketball team in the 1996 Olympics in Atlanta. They were called the second Dream Team since they were stepping into the shoes of the 1992 team. Barkley's team featured greats such as Karl Malone, Scottie Pippen, and David Robinson. Barkley and I hit it off, and he invited me to join him for dinner and then to a party since it was the team's off night. Thus began a bond with Charles that has lasted to this day.

Barkley has the kind of personality that interviewers dream about. He's someone who people will tune in to and be entertained by no matter what the conversation is about. Some of his most notable quotes have come from the two Olympics he has played in. Like the time an interviewer asked if

America was going to love him as much as Michael Jordan by the end of the Olympics.

"Love me?" Barkley replied. "I'm their worst nightmare. A brother who won't be quiet."

One time Barkley was asked how he felt in 1972 when the Soviet Union beat the United States in an Olympic game.

"Well, I had just flunked my entrance exam into kindergarten . . ."

He once joked with reporters about noticing all the girls lying out topless at the swimming pool in Barcelona. "I'm gonna be in that pool so much the next two days they'll think I'm on the swimming team in Barcelona."

The always-honest Barkley never has hesitated about sharing his thoughts, with me or any other interviewer. He's always genuine, but I've also discovered he has a big heart, one that the world didn't always notice, especially back in those days. Barkley at times seemed more irritable with interviews at these Olympics. After one win during the '96 games, he responded to a question about the team's performance.

"We don't have to blow every team out," Barkley said. "We won a game by 30 points tonight. That's enough. I mean, when we win by 50, y'all will bitch and complain. And now we have a pretty decent, competitive game tonight and y'all are going to complain about that. I just told the guys, 'Listen, you can never please Americans.'"

Asked by another interviewer whether he was "guaranteeing a win," Barkley didn't hold back.

"You guys want controversies and bullsh—t. Obviously I think we're going to win the gold medal. If I say we guarantee it, that's irrelevant . . . If you want to write 'guarantee,' write it."

Talking about his second experience with the Olympics years later, he admitted that it wasn't as much fun as the first. In 1992, Barkley said everybody "got along like it was the greatest thing in the world." But there were some playing on the '96 team who began to complain about playing time. "I hated it."[1]

Barkley has always kept things real.

• • •

A SPORTS BROADCASTER WALKS INTO A ROOM WITH CHARLES BARKLEY, Michael Jordan, Wayne Gretzky, and Pete Sampras . . .

This isn't the start of a joke. It really did happen.

Years ago when I was in Lake Tahoe covering the American Century Championship, Barkley invited me to come to a room in the casino where he was playing blackjack. All he had told me was that he was playing cards with "his friends" and that I could join them.

"I don't really gamble much," I said.

"Come on and have a drink with us. Grab a bite to eat. Just hang out."

No big deal. Just hanging out with Barkley, Jordan, Gretzky, and Sampras.

As I sat down and watched the four men playing blackjack, the reporter in me wished I had a microphone and a camera.

They were just having fun being themselves. Laughing and trash-talking and taking each other's money. The last thing I wanted to do was interrupt them. This was an off night for them, and for me as well. When I'm not working, I always respect people's space, even if they happen to be some of the greatest athletes of all time.

As I've said before, I've always tried to treat famous people like the average guy and the average guy like famous people. Someone like Charles has always made that easy. Ever since I've known him, he's been real and authentic. I've always admired people who are honest and candid. There is something refreshing about that, especially in today's world.

"I'm going to come from the heart," Barkley once told me. "I'm always going to be fair and I'm always going to be honest. That's all I can do, Chris."

That's one thing I've always appreciated about Charles ever since getting to know him in the '90s. Not only is he a fun guy to be around, but he always speaks from the heart. Even if somebody disagrees with him, he is willing to listen and have a conversation.

It has been fun knowing Barkley over the years and to have our paths cross many times. A conversation with him has always been entertaining and enlightening. In so many ways he is the same man I met back in the '90s.

These days Barkley is as well known for his broadcasting abilities as he is for his time in the NBA. But when the All-American power forward from Auburn stormed into the league as the fifth pick of the 1984 draft, he made his presence known. He would go on to play eight years with the Philadelphia 76ers, four with the Phoenix Suns, and another four with the Houston Rockets. He would rack up many accomplishments and accolades, but winning an NBA championship would be the one thing that would elude him.

Whenever we talk about his time in the NBA, it's inevitable that Michael Jordan comes up. And when the endlessly debatable topic of "the greatest of all time" arrives, Barkley doesn't hesitate to speak his truth.

"The only player I ever played against that I thought was actually better than me was Michael Jordan. Really."

As the ever-confident Barkley told me, he believes that Jordan was the greatest player he has ever seen. This came from the hardest lesson he ever learned: losing the 1993 NBA Finals to the Chicago Bulls. After he was traded to the Phoenix Suns and they were going to play the Bulls in the Finals, Barkley had a conversation with Suns coach Cotton Fitzsimmons.

"Michael's a great, great player, but I think I'm just as good, to be honest with you," Barkley told Fitzsimmons. "I finally have a chance to prove it. I never had any help in Philly and now I got Dan and Kevin."

Barkley was referring to his Suns teammates Dan Majerle and Kevin Johnson.

"We're going to the Finals and I think I'm the best. And that was really painful because—honestly, for the first time in my life, I felt like that guy's better than me," Barkley said about Jordan. "Even when I was playing against Magic and Bird, I was like, 'Those guys ain't better than me. They just got more help.' Magic had Kareem and Worthy. Bird had McHale and Parish. But Michael Jordan was the only player I'm thinking who's on my level. And I got a chance to prove it and I came up short. That's on me."

. . .

BARKLEY AND JORDAN SHARE ONE DEVOTED PASSION: GAMBLING. Over the course of my friendship with the NBA player and broadcaster, I have not only seen Barkley gambling in person but have also spent a lot of time talking about it. Like every topic he discusses, Barkley has been blunt in his assessment of one of his favorite pastimes.

"Even though I can afford to do it, it's stupid to do it," he told me in 2013 during an interview.

Unlike most public personalities, Barkley was honest and forthcoming about his love of gambling. "It's a bad habit I've got. I'm not going to quit gambling. I got to gamble less."

I asked him if he had limits.

"No—that's the problem," Barkley said, talking about the story I had brought up about his gambling with the golfer John Daly. "See, that's a problem with John and myself. We don't have limits, but we can afford to gamble. Most people get to the point where they're broke and then they get in trouble, start stealing and doing crazy stuff. When we get as much money as we've been blessed to have in our life, we just keep gambling."

"What's the thrill for you?" I asked.

"When you walk out of there with their money," Barkley told me with a grin.

He said that the most money he had lost in one sitting was $2 million one evening, while the most he had ever won was a million and a half.

"It's stupid to lose that much," Barkley admitted, then added about gambling that "people only say it's a problem when you're losing."

"Do you have it under control in your mind, or do you think it's a little bit—"

"Do I have it under control?" Barkley asked, interrupting me. "If you lose $10, $15 million, you don't have control. That's a lot of money. That's your type of money."

I laughed at his joke. "That's why I don't gamble. I couldn't afford to lose. It would bother me to lose that."

I asked him if gambling replaced the rush of playing in an NBA game or championship.

"No. Nothing can replace it. Gambling is fun . . . a lot of people gamble, and that's why even some of the casinos make some big money. It's fun, it's exciting."

There was another side of Barkley that I got to see while he was gambling. Once, back in 2000, I was on vacation in New Orleans, and Barkley happened to be in town as well. They'd recently opened the Harrah's Casino in New Orleans, so Barkley invited me to come over. It was later at night and the kids were asleep.

"Okay, I'll come over," I told him. "But I don't gamble."

I walked over to Harrah's and watched him gambling for the first time. It was an interesting thing to see. He might be up by $25,000 one moment and then down $50,000 the next. But by the end of the night, he ended up with close to $20,000. As we were leaving the casino floor to exchange his chips, we passed by an older African American security guard who was off to the side. It was two or three in the morning, so nobody was around, and at the time I was barely paying attention. But I noticed

Barkley go over to the woman and say something to her. The next moment he gave her his chips.

"You go and take care of your family," Barkley told her.

At first the woman didn't think the chips were real, but when she realized they were, she couldn't believe it.

"This is thousands of dollars!"

Barkley just nodded and smiled as he walked out of the casino.

This and other experiences like it made me really respect the outspoken and hilarious Barkley. He would be the guy picking up the check for everybody in the bar. The guy with the big heart asking how things were going with your family. He could also just as easily say you were full of it if he thought you were.

"That was the hardest thing for me when I first started," Barkley once told me. "I would say something very simple and people would start writing letters and calling in to the team saying stuff. I'm like, 'Huh?' I think after my third year I said, 'Oh, I can't please everybody. I'm just going to please me. I'm going to say what I think and what I feel and I'm not going to worry about the negativity.' And after that third year, I've been the same since. I'm going to give my honest, fair, balanced opinion. Some people gonna like and some people won't."

This attitude not only followed him throughout his professional career with the Philadelphia 76ers, the Phoenix Suns, and the Houston Rockets, but it also has been his mantra as an NBA sports broadcaster.

The risk-reward in gambling has never been worth it for me; I'd rather watch other people play. Barkley was always amusing whenever I saw him playing blackjack or roulette. He was superstitious like so many others. Sometimes he would start winning and then not want me to leave.

"It's two in the morning and I have to work tomorrow," I would tell him.

"No, no. You have to stay. I'm on a hot streak."

The same went when he would start to lose.

"Anytime you want to leave, Myers, you can beat it," he once told me.

"I just got my drink . . ."

For Barkley, he was always trying to have fun with it. He admitted that he got to a point where it really did become a problem, something he talked about in an interview in 2021. I asked him if he had any advice for others about gambling, and his reply surprised me.

"If I had advice for anybody, I'd tell them not to gamble."

I couldn't help but burst out laughing.

"I love to gamble," he continued to tell me. "I love the juice. I love excitement. Losing always sucks. But, you know, for me, I kind of went off the deep rails probably. I went off the deep rails for a minute."

When I asked him to specify how, he went into more detail.

"No—I was trying to beat the casino. You can't beat the casino."

Barkley explained how his friends helped him to see what his gambling problem really was.

"Charles, gambling's not your problem," Barkley's friends said. "Being a f—ing idiot is your problem."

"Explain to me why you say that," Barkley said.

"Charles, we've been to Vegas a thousand times. You've been up $200,000, $300,000, $400,000, $500,000. And instead of quitting while you're ahead, you're always trying to get back to that mythical million dollars that you won two out of twenty-five times. But you lost the million the other twenty-eight out of thirty times."

If you quit while you were ahead, they told him, you could actually have fun.

"You can't break the casino," they said again and again.

Now whenever Barkley decides to gamble, he decides on a figure before he goes.

"Let's say $300,000. If I win $300,000, I quit. If I lose $300,000, I quit. And I have a lot more fun gambling. Obviously, it's fun to win a million, but the pain of losing a million is worse. So I just take my advice.

You just got to learn to gamble in moderation is what I was really trying to end my story with. Because you can't break the casino. The casino can break you."

• • •

LIKE SO MANY PROFESSIONAL ATHLETES, BARKLEY DISCOVERED A love of golf. But it took him a while to even figure out how to play.

"I could not hit that little ball. A little ball that was just standing there. I'm like, 'This is impossible.' I'm one of the best athletes in the world, and I can't hit this ball that's just sitting there."

It was 1986 when Charles Barkley first tried to play golf. As he told me during an interview, he had seen his fellow Philadelphia 76ers teammate Andrew Toney hitting his golf clubs one day. Barkley asked him what he was doing.

"Golf," Toney replied.

"I've seen that on TV before," Barkley said. "It looks interesting."

Toney asked if Barkley wanted to play, so the two of them went to a golf course. But he quickly discovered he couldn't even hit the little ball. So he decided, "No, I've got to get better at this." Once Barkley began to play and become better, he started to really like it. And as he did, he made a wonderful discovery.

"I realized golf is one of the few places you can get peace and quiet," Barkley told me. "You know, I tell people, when you go to the grocery store, people want to talk to you. You go to a dry cleaner, people want to talk to you. Golf for me—being out there with three of my friends for four or five hours, smoking a couple of cigars, having a couple beers. You're not autographing or people aren't taking pictures. It is one of the coolest, most relaxing things you can do."

For someone like Barkley whom everyone knows, anytime he went anywhere in public, people would be all over him. So what could he do?

He got tired of being at home all the time. But on a golf course, he could have his privacy.

"These people out here, they ain't gonna bother you. There's no big crowds out here. So to me, golf is just such a pleasure to be out there with nobody around. Especially since I'm on the East Coast during the summer, walking around these big-ass trees because I like to walk when I play. Just out there in nature. And it's just such a calming effect. You look at these trees; they've been there now for a hundred years. They're massive . . . It's pretty amazing and awesome."

• • •

BARKLEY'S "CAN'T PLEASE EVERYBODY SO I'M GOING TO PLEASE ME" attitude and his outspokenness have gotten him in trouble many times. As he once said in the 1993 book *Outrageous,* "I don't create controversies. They're there long before I open my mouth. I just bring them to your attention."

We talked recently about being outspoken in our day of cancel culture. Barkley was adamant about one point:

"Context matters."

He believes people should be able to crack jokes these days and shouldn't be canceled unless somebody crosses the line.

"One thing I try to do is I try to never make it personal. I think that's really important. But I do think context matters. If somebody feels like I've said something where I crossed the line, I think I'll dial it back and listen to it."

Then again, some people are just jerks who try to provoke others, Barkley told me. With so much junk out there, he tries to be very selective in what he says. But when he decides he's going to say something, he will get your attention.

"This thing has gotten so out of hand now where now they're going after comedians who are telling jokes. I mean, like, we've had a couple of meetings at Turner and the lawyers and HR keep telling me this bullsh—t about context doesn't matter. And I say, that's the reason we're in this sh—tty place we're in as a country right now. Context *does* matter."

Barkley has known ever since coming to the NBA that you can't overreact when people criticize you. He also told me years ago how he made the decision not to do social media.

"There's so much negativity out there," Barkley said. "It's hard on these people today with the scrutiny, the cell phones, you got all these talking heads on television, everybody's got a blog and they can say whatever they want about you."

• • •

AFTER WE LOST CHRISTOPHER, BARKLEY OPENED UP AND SHARED with me about his younger brother, who passed away in 2009. Darryl Barkley had struggled for many years, experiencing a paralyzing stroke caused by drugs when he was only twenty-one years old. Even after conquering his drug problem, Darryl continued to have health issues, and he died of a heart attack.

"One thing to make sure you do," Barkley told me. "Make sure you don't forget about the other sibling. Even after losing Darryl, I still have my brother John. The world doesn't end for everybody."

It was a reminder that losing someone is painful, but you still have to be thankful for the people who are there in your life. You can't let your grief overshadow the good things you still have.

I've appreciated over the years the sense of gratitude Charles carries in his life. In 2006, he shared some of this with me.

"I'm forty-three years old and I've had more money beyond my wildest expectations. I've been all over the world. I met presidents. I met kings. It is only because of basketball. That's the only time I get emotional about basketball, because it has given me every single thing in my life. That's when I get emotional. I mean, I'm forty-three years old. I've never had a real job. And hopefully, knock on wood, I'll never have a real job because I've saved my money wisely. I've invested very well, but it's only because of basketball. I get emotional when I see things that guys don't appreciate. Because no matter what sport you play for a living, it's the best job in the world."

Barkley once shared how after Hurricane Katrina in 2005, he bought $1 million worth of housing for the people in New Orleans. Up to that point in his life, he felt it was the greatest thing he had ever done.

"All the stuff I've done—I always used my fame and my money to do great things. And I've always said that. Like I use basketball. Basketball's never going to use me . . . We're not famous and rich just to make money and be on television. We're supposed to do great things. That's what we're supposed to do."

As he reflected on his life while we spoke, Barkley told me about meeting one of his heroes.

"The first time I met Muhammad Ali was the greatest day of my life. Ali's my personal hero. He's amazing. And, you know, I've just met some—it's been an amazing life. Like every now and then I'll sit around and think, 'Wow—little fat kid from Leeds, Alabama, did pretty good.' You know, because I've exceeded all my expectations.

"You know, when you're growing up in the projects and your mom is a maid and your grandmother's cutting meat in a meat factory, you're not thinking, 'Wow, I'm going to play in the NBA.' You don't think you're going to go to the Olympics twice. You don't think you're going to go into television. . . . It's been a crazy, amazing ride."

SEVENTEEN

The Comeback

It's almost the middle of the third quarter in Super Bowl LI and the New England Patriots are getting their butts kicked. It's easy for people to assume this game is over. The Atlanta Falcons added to their lead to make it 28–3. No team has ever come back from this massive of a margin. Even when I talked to Bill Belichick at halftime and asked how his offense could get him back into the game, the coach gave me a blank stare. Right now it's looking like I'm going to have to go through another grueling ordeal of interviewing Belichick after a Super Bowl loss.

Yet as I look at the players on the sideline, I don't see any signs of giving up. In fact, what I see is a quiet confidence. There are some Patriot players who are fired up and some who are angry, but it seems as if they still all believe they can win. I can't read their minds but I can see their expressions and watch their reactions. I can almost hear what they're thinking.

As long as there's still time on the clock, we're not worried about the score.
We have a plan and we're going to get these guys.

And if anybody is thinking this right now, it's Tom Brady. He's fiery, but he's also in command and in control. There is no panic. "Let's see what we got." There is a *we got this—we can rally* attitude.

As a sideline reporter, I can never quote during the game what's going on around me, but I'm truly astounded at the non-panic I'm seeing. That's the start. I don't see faces of doom that realize they're running out of time and that things are slipping away from them.

As Brady and the Patriots offense take the field, it feels like the seventy thousand-plus people in the stadium around us are all Atlanta fans. They won't stop cheering for their Falcons. Patriots fans seem in a muted state of disbelief.

I'm thinking what everybody else is thinking.

Is there a chance that Brady can pull this off?

Brady's whole career has been about coming back. About never giving up. About going the distance.

Can he pull off the impossible?

• • •

"I WAS THE BACKUP QUARTERBACK ON OUR 0-8 FRESHMAN HIGH school team. I didn't even play. You know. We didn't win a game and I couldn't even get on a field."[1]

Tom Brady shared this with former teammate Rodney Harrison in an interview for *Sunday Night Football* in 2019.

"I was kind of a late bloomer. Recruited to Michigan late, start as the seventh quarterback, you know, had to work really hard to even play. Thought, 'Oh, man, I'll make it in pro football.' Got drafted in the sixth round. No one thought I'd make the team."

This underdog mentality has helped shape Brady's entire career.

"I always had a lot of belief in myself, and I always tell a lot of young quarterbacks, if you don't believe in yourself, why do you think those guys looking at you are going to believe in you? When you step in the huddle, they have to look at you and go, 'Man, that guy's ready to get the job done.' Because if they don't see that, they're going to start questioning, 'Oh my God, I don't think that guy can get the job done.' So you got to believe in what you know—who you are—what you do—what you bring to the team. And then if you do that, they're going to feed off that as well."

• • •

JUST SCORE ONE. THAT'S THEIR MENTALITY.

With 2:06 left in the third quarter, the Patriots manage a touchdown when Brady connects with James White for a five-yard score. Yet even there things go wrong when Stephen Gostkowski misses the extra point, leaving it 28–9.

Brady shared what he was thinking in the 2023 documentary *Man in the Arena*:

"We know it's a long shot, but f—it. We have nothing to lose. We're already down."

The quarterback has always played with a long-shot mentality, especially when he first got drafted by the Patriots in 2000.

• • •

"TOM, YOU'RE COMING INTO A SYSTEM WHERE THEY HAVE A QUARTER-back everybody knows. What's your feeling about backing up Drew Bledsoe?"[2]

The story is part of the legend. Tom Brady is chosen as the 199th pick in the 2000 NFL Draft. Years later the Patriots shared their first phone call to the young quarterback from Michigan.

"All I was looking for was a place to get my foot in the door and try to be great for the team that picked me," Brady said on the call. "Drew Bledsoe is certainly one of the best quarterbacks in the NFL, and it's gonna be great to learn under him and compete for a job with the Patriots."

Right away we can hear Brady's attitude. He wasn't just going to learn under Bledsoe—he was going to compete for Bledsoe's job. The Patriots also had another quarterback, Michael Bishop, whom they had drafted the previous year.

"I know Mike, seen him play last year and I know he's a heck of a player," Brady acknowledged. "You know, it's just up to me. I think that the team picked me to come in there and go out there and be a team player and fight every day, and that's really what I plan to do. I've always really concerned myself with the things I can do and I don't put a whole lot of thinking into the other guys because I know that I'm not really at my best when I'm not controlling and playing as well as I possibly can."

After talking to the twenty-two-year-old Brady, the Patriots brought up their star quarterback again.

"And the fact that you were—at least according to the scouting report—so much like Drew, is it a plus for you to be working under him?"

"Oh, definitely, definitely," Brady replied. "I can remember seeing him in the Super Bowl, and I mean—the poise and composure, and the way he plays the game. It's great to see and I'm just extremely excited to get an opportunity to go and learn under him and be ready to play when the team calls on me."

Those were remarkable words when they played out in 2001. In the second game of the season, a scrambling Drew Bledsoe was blasted on the sideline by New York Jets linebacker Mo Lewis. Bledsoe had already led the Patriots to one Super Bowl and was poised to do it in the future, but this tackle nearly killed him. Bledsoe suffered a collapsed lung and heavy internal bleeding.

The rest is history. Brady came in for Bledsoe and the Patriots finished with an 11-5 record. They went on to defeat the St. Louis Rams and their "Greatest Show on Turf" team in Super Bowl XXXVI, completing the first phase of Brady's saga with this Cinderella story.

When I interviewed Drew Bledsoe years later and brought up Brady, the quarterback was nothing but classy.

"It was an extremely difficult situation, but I was still, through all of it, was able to help Tom, help the team, be a team guy . . ."

Even after Bledsoe healed and became healthy enough to be the starting quarterback, the Patriots continued with Brady. I mentioned Bledsoe taking the high road through all of that.

"I'm very proud of Tom and what he's accomplished. You know—he was this young kid—this young skinny kid that came in and didn't have a real strong arm. Was kind of real slow. Didn't move around real well. But he worked so hard and learned so much over that first year. And then when he had his chance the next year he steps in to get it done. So I'm very proud of him, what he's accomplished, and there's a part of me that feels like I was part of helping him develop some."

I can only wonder what Bledsoe was thinking while he was watching Brady in the Super Bowl against Atlanta.

• • •

PATRIOTS KICKER STEPHEN GOSTKOWSKI HAS A CHANCE TO MAKE UP for the missed extra point when the Patriots force the Falcons to punt and then make a field goal with 9:44 left to play in the game.

Twenty-eight to twelve. Sixteen points. A two-score game.

Suddenly the unthinkable could actually happen.

This is one of the reasons we watch this game. To feel this whiff of possibility. This echo of excitement. This glint of hope.

Hope, as it turns out, is the reason Tom Brady is playing. Perhaps no other game has meant as much to him as this one.

There are always reminders that there are things that are bigger than this game, bigger than winning and losing. When I did my first Super Bowl in 2005, one of the storylines coming into the game was the passing of Brady's grandmother just a few days before. The Patriot quarterback always spoke so highly and proudly of his close-knit family. He felt badly that he was the only member of the family who was not able to attend the vigil for his grandmother's passing due to his preparation for this game.

Brady used that extra bit of motivation to beat the Eagles that day.

Tonight Tom is playing for his mother.

For most of the Patriots season, Galynn Brady had been unable to attend her son's games due to her battle with breast cancer. Yet despite having gone through chemotherapy and radiation, Galynn was able to make it to the Super Bowl to support Tom. In the locker room before the game, Patriots owner Robert Kraft told Brady that they had to win this one for his mom.[3] Everybody wants to win it for her.

If there is any symbol of strength and perseverance, it is Galynn Brady.

But will it be enough?

• • •

CALM UNDER PRESSURE. THAT'S ONE OF BRADY'S GREATEST STRENGTHS. All the great quarterbacks have had this trait.

I once asked Joe Montana, the quarterback that Brady liked to emulate as a kid, how he could manage this in a game.

"What is your definition of calm under pressure, whether it's in a game or anything that you do?"

"It's really more concentration than cool under pressure when things get tight," Joe told me. "You still have to be able to concentrate. And I think a lot of guys get caught up in the fact that you got to hurry right now as opposed to guys who are thinking—like you watch a guy like Brady in the pocket at the end of the game. He's in no hurry. Doesn't look any different than he did in the first part of the game. And you can tell he's concentrating on what's going on down the field and that's where it has to be. You can't be thinking about the clock because you work the clock every week, every day in practice. And you know what you can do, what you can't do, how long it takes to do certain things and when things need to hurry up more. But I think you just have to have a pocket presence at that point in time."

• • •

EIGHT MINUTES AND THIRTY-ONE SECONDS LEFT IN THE GAME. AT-lanta has a seemingly easy third and one from their own 36-yard line. Matt Ryan takes the snapped ball and—

Linebacker Dont'a Hightower mows into him, knocking the ball loose, and Alan Branch jumps on it.

The Patriots have the ball.

It's happening. Everybody feels it.

Just as Joe Montana told me, Brady is doing what he knows he can do. Throwing a bullet. Then another. Then another. He's moving them along but not rushing things.

Even after a touchdown throw to Danny Amendola, there doesn't seem to be any pressure as Brady makes it clear that they're going for two. A direct snap to James White, who runs it in to make it an eight-point game.

• • •

THERE'S SOMETHING ELSE HANGING OVER BRADY AND THIS PATRIOTS team:

Deflategate.

The scandal involved Brady supposedly ordering balls to be deflated in the 2014 AFC Championship Game victory against the Indianapolis Colts. The long saga ended with Brady being suspended for four games and the team being fined and forfeiting draft selections. The quarterback would appeal and win the suspension, yet a court would later reinstate this and Brady would miss the first four games of the 2016 season.

When everything was over and Brady spoke about Deflategate, he refused to let his emotions interfere with his playing.

"What I've learned from myself is, I don't want to give my power away to other people by letting my own emotions be subjected to what their thoughts or opinions are. So if someone calls me something, that's their problem. It's not my problem. I'm not going to give away my power."

The Deflategate saga has followed Brady ever since. This is the first Super Bowl he is playing in after everything happened. When asked during a press conference whether the Deflategate experience gave him extra motivation, Brady gave the diplomatic answer:

"I'm motivated for my teammates. They are all the motivation I need. It takes a lot of work to get to this point. Nothing that has happened in the past is going to help us win this game. What's going to help us win this game is going through that process that we talked about and being ready to go, and that's enough motivation for me."[4]

Yet one has to imagine that there's some part of Brady that wants to prove all the doubters and naysayers wrong. There has to be some chip on his shoulder tonight, even if it's a small one.

We all love to prove our doubters wrong. Even people like me.

When I was attending Miami Dade Community College, one of my professors brought up something from my childhood that I've always been a little self-conscious about. We were doing production pieces and he noticed something on my forehead. It was a scar I got during my childhood when I had a skin infection known as impetigo. Maybe on this day it was more noticeable under the bright lights we were using.

"You know, Chris. With that scar—I don't think you should count on ever getting on the air."

The professor wasn't trying to be a jerk or scare me; he was probably just giving me his honest career advice.

"You'll never get on TV with that," he told me. "You'd have to have some kind surgery. It would be better if you planned on radio."

Back then plastic surgery wasn't as advanced, and obviously I didn't have a lot of money to even think of that. So for someone in college wanting to be on television, this sort of statement could have really stopped me in my tracks.

It also could have done something else. Fuel me.

You're wrong, I would think. *I can get on the air. In fact, I will make a career of being on the air.*

A chip on the shoulder can be a useful tool if you use it to your advantage.

• • •

ATLANTA DRIVES AND GETS WITHIN FIELD GOAL RANGE, BUT A SACK and holding penalty drive them back, forcing them to punt.

With two and a half minutes remaining, Brady begins the drive. But after a hit leaves him reeling, the quarterback blocks out everything else and is clearly laser focused.

The great wide receiver Jerry Rice once spoke to me about playing with blinders on and blocking out everything else in the Super Bowl.

"I was so focused in and I knew exactly what I wanted to do after I broke the huddle . . . Once that huddle broke—man, it was like complete quietness. That is almost like—you talk about Michael Jordan, Larry

Bird, all these great players talk about going into the zone. Tiger Woods. I couldn't hear anything. It was just like I was just so focused on my route running, catching the ball and just moving the tape."

That's the place in which Brady finds himself. A 20-yard pass. A 13-yard pass. A seven-yarder.

With 57 seconds left, James White runs it in. Amendola makes the two-point conversion.

On the sideline, players are telling Brady to win this thing for his mom. There is no longer quiet confidence. Now it's a triumphant roar.

Surely I don't need to tell you how this game ends, but I will. As the game goes to overtime, the Patriots win the toss and begin their drive at the 25. A touchdown and the game is over.

The Falcons defense is reeling. As Brady and the Patriots get closer and closer to a victory, I get in position to hit the field immediately after they win.

Brady finds White for six yards, then Amendola for another 14. It doesn't appear like they're interested in running as Brady steps back behind his incredible offensive line and throws again, this time to Chris Hogan for 18. A dangerous pass to White pushes them backward, but he sends another dart to Julian Edelman for 15. A throw to White brings the Patriots down to the 15-yard line. Brady's next pass is dropped, but the Falcons are charged with pass interference. Two plays later, White plows across the goal line for the winning touchdown.

Right after the touchdown is verified, everybody rushes the field. The massive celebration starts, but I can't party just yet. I have a job to do.

• • •

SINCE I'M THE PATRIOTS SIDELINE REPORTER, I'M INTERVIEWING Brady. And normally there is chaos on the field, but since the game went into overtime, things are different. *Everybody* is down here on the field.

All the media—local and international—are here ready to go. There's also many more people. Normally I have an NFL representative who is there to support me, but I don't have one tonight. My field producer is helping me around.

The greatest Super Bowl comeback ever. I want to get there as quickly as possible to get Brady's raw emotions.

As we go live, I'm on the sideline rushing with so many other people. It's literally a stampede. Physically it's a little dangerous; the security guy with me ends up getting trampled and knocked over. The cameraman beside me is lost as I get hit and bumped in this herd of humanity.

My producer, Richie Zyontz, is in my ear telling me to get Brady.

"Should we take a break?" Zyontz asks.

"No," I say. "I don't want to do a commercial."

"Okay. Let me know when you're there. We can use whatever camera we have."

Getting to Brady isn't easy. There really is an art in this. It helps to have a cameraman at your side, but I've lost mine. I feel like a salmon swimming upstream, fighting through this sea of people. It's only for a few moments, but when I finally get close to Brady, I feel like I played the last few snaps in the game.

The crowd is smothering as Brady hugs teammates. Even though the cameraman isn't in position, I know we have the overhead camera and I'm still holding a microphone. As I get to Brady, I ask him about doing an interview.

"Really?" he asks. "We're going to do it right now?"

I know he's in the middle of this moment—these emotions and congratulations and celebrations—so I can understand why he's hesitant.

"Let's go," I tell Zyontz.

So they come down to me and Brady is smart and savvy enough to go through with the interview. He knows we're live in front of a hundred million people and he doesn't want to disappoint them or blow them off.

"We're live, Tom, on Fox. We're live. Americans saw the greatest comeback in Super Bowl history."

With ticker tape floating over us and cameras nudging behind my back, I wait for a second as I place the microphone in front of Brady.

"Tom, can you just talk about what you were thinking and how you brought the team back when you were down 25?"

"You know, we all brought each other back. We never felt out of it. It was a tough battle, but, you know. They have a great team. I give them a lot of credit. We just made a few more plays than them."

Tom looks exhausted and elated as he speaks.

"Your fifth—they're all sweet, but this is incredible," I say. "First overtime, the way you came back. Is the most recent one the best?"

"They're all great. You know, I think this team resembled a lot of teams from the past that had a lot of mental toughness, great defense. Everyone rose to the occasion in the second half and overtime."

I have to ask the next question.

"And you said you're not motivated by the past, but a little redemption maybe in this moment?"

"Nah—this is all positive, man. This is unbelievable. I'm going to go see my family."

I nod, knowing that's a clue to wrap things up.

"I know it's emotional. Thanks, Tom. Congratulations."

"Thanks."

"All right. Super Bowl history with Tom Brady."

EIGHTEEN

Smell the Roses

Everybody loves a happy ending. Especially when it happens to a guy who has worked so hard to achieve it.

Moments after the dramatic conclusion to Super Bowl LIV, I work my way through a swarm of celebration to interview one of those guys. Andy Reid has been so close so many times, but he's never won the big game. As the head coach of the Philadelphia Eagles for fourteen seasons, he reached the playoffs nine times and the conference championship five times. Only once did the Eagles get to the Super Bowl; the result was a crushing loss to the New England Patriots in Super Bowl XXXIX. After being fired from Philly in 2012, Reid was hired as the head coach for the Kansas City Chiefs. Since then he's once again been close so many times—a loss in a Wild Card game in 2013, consecutive divisional round losses in 2015 and 2016, and another loss in a 2017 Wild Card game.

Then came the 2018 AFC Championship loss in overtime against Brady and the Patriots.

So many times . . . So close.

I am here once again at the big game in 2019 with a triumphant Andy Reid. The Chiefs have been a comeback team the entire postseason, and this game is no different, with the Chiefs putting up 21 points in the final six minutes to come back and win. Patrick Mahomes was amazing and Reid made adjustments at halftime to get receivers open in the second half.

Under a blizzard of confetti, I put my arm around Reid to interview him. It's mayhem around us.

"First, congratulations," I tell the coach. "An emotional moment—"

I feel someone tugging my shoulder behind us, so I turn to see an exuberant Patrick Mahomes, who chants a "Let's go! Let's go!" and then turns to start to walk away. I pull him back toward us.

"Stay here for a second. You're twenty-four. You're a Super Bowl champ." My attention moves back on Reid. "Kansas City's waited fifty years. Must've felt like a hundred for you."

As Andy grins and looks out to the stands, his wife slides in beside him to add to the free-for-all on the field.

"It was great—it was great, man."

"Worth the wait?" I ask.

"Absolutely. Absolutely. Love this guy right here, man. And all those guys who came before. Love you too, man. That's all. This is what it's all about. What a great team. Great coaches. Appreciate every bit of it."

You can see the utter joy on Reid's face. I quickly go back to the quarterback.

"And let me just ask you. At age twenty-four, to be a Super Bowl champ. You two have a unique relationship when you're—when you're down with nine minutes to go, down 10. Double-digit comeback. What's magical about you guys working together?"

"I mean, we never lost faith," Mahomes says. "I think that's the biggest thing. Everybody on this team, no one had their head down and we believed in each other. And that's what we preached all year long. And we got this guy right here to get us here. And then we found a way to get it in the end."

"And the hurry-up offense," I bring up to Reid. "Was that your idea or his to go to that at that point? I know the score was one thing, but boy—"

"Down by a couple scores, you gotta jump in it," Reid replies.

"Yeah, we had to jump in it, like you said," Patrick adds right on cue. "And our defense got some big stops for us and we found a way to win it in the end."

"Patrick, you had to overcome after not having any interceptions in your postseason. I mean, you took over and bounced back from that."

"Yeah. I mean, Coach Reid told me after both of them to keep firing, keep believing in your eyes, keep throwing it. And he gives me the confidence to go out there no matter what I do. And it worked out well in the end."

Keep firing.

Keep believing.

Keep throwing.

Talk about believing in your quarterback.

I shift gears from asking about the game to seeing how they're feeling.

"We saw a lot of emotion from you throughout the game," I say to Patrick, then once again move to Reid. "And you were very calm, but now you can afford to be emotional."

"I'm good, man. I'm good. My heart is racing. I'm getting older, man. I can't let it race too fast."

A classic statement from Coach Reid. He's always been good with his quick wit.

I know we're almost out of time, but I want to bring Reid's wife into the conversation.

"All right. And your better half, Tammy. Forgive me, Mrs. Reid. He's been okay through this?"

"He has been calm as a cucumber," Tammy says. "He's just like it's another game."

There's nothing calm down here around us as people are pulling Mahomes and Reid away while other reporters wait impatiently. I thank them and let them go.

I wasn't as smooth as I would have wanted to be with this interview, but it's less about the questions and more about their emotions and reactions as other people slide in to get their chance for the next interview.

To see these two superstars' immediate live reactions to their special moments is tough to beat. To see a pair come together like this—a battle-hardened veteran who never gave up and a wide-eyed wunderkind at the start of his journey—is another reason to love the game.

In his postgame press conference, Reid is repeatedly asked about his place in NFL history and what this sort of achievement means.

"You've mentioned about how your mentors belong in the Pro Football Hall of Fame," one interviewer says. "Why is that honor so important for you? What's so special about achieving that?"

Reid isn't interested in this sort of discussion.

"My mind doesn't go there. I'm humbled by all of that stuff, but that's not where I go. Whether we win or lose, I don't think of it that way. I always tell you that each team has its own personality and you work with that—that's the part that I enjoy, watching teams grow and the relationships that you develop. I don't think much past that about what goes in the future. That's out of my hands. I try to control what I can control, and that's trying to get us to be better as a team."

The subject comes up once again moments later.

"You don't make things about yourself, but now that you have won a Super Bowl, is it freeing to accomplish what so many people around the league have said about you?"

"I mean, I really don't worry about those things," Reid says. "I didn't before Sunday and I probably won't after Sunday. I think we all try to do our best; I'm no different. I try to do the best I possibly can at the job I'm presented. You can't do anything more than that if you exhaust that part of that. That part doesn't change, and I'll keep doing that. With that, I also respect that it's a team sport and it's not about one guy at all. I learned that when I played offensive line, as you know. It takes five guys to dance the dance and you have to be doing it the right way. It's not about one guy there and you learn real quick that it's about a team."

Reid constantly and consistently places the emphasis back onto the team and the players and this season. He doesn't want to talk about his former losses, nor does he want to think about the Hall of Fame. But an interviewer can't resist asking him what finally winning a Super Bowl means for his legacy.

"I don't care about that," Reid says. "I mean, I really don't. This is a pure team sport. I love that part of it. I mean, that's why I got into it. And I didn't get into it for any other reason other than to win games and win them with great people. And so we bust our tails to do that as coaches and players. That's the part that I think needs the respect. And so the other stuff—you take care of that, everything else happens. And that's not really where my mind goes. It's really the last thing on my mind."

We can't help but ask thoughts about one's place in history, about the legacy someone has built. Those are the questions we want to ask winners.

Some of the most interesting answers, I've discovered, are from coaches and players who have never gotten to this place in their career.

• • •

"PEOPLE USE YOUR NAME IN AN EXPRESSION WHEN GREAT PLAYERS don't get that ring. 'This is how you go on to become another Ernie Banks.' Have you heard that? Are you bothered by that?"

I asked the greatest player in Chicago Cubs history who never played in a single postseason game this question back in 1997 on *Up Close*. Ernie

Banks was known as "Mr. Cub." As a shortstop and first baseman for the Cubs, he still holds the MLB record for most games played without making the playoffs.

Two thousand five hundred and twenty-eight games, to be exact.

"I've heard it a lot," Banks said. In his cap and a colorful shirt, the sixty-five-year-old grinned as if he enjoyed being asked the question. "I've heard it with Dale Earnhardt and Don Mattingly. I've heard it with Gale Sayers, Walter Payton, because Walter got into the Super Bowl."

"Well, it's nice to hear your name anyway, right?" I asked with an affirming chuckle. "People remember."

"It's really nice. Like with Cal [Ripken Jr.]. To mention my name as a shortstop. It's just wonderful. And that's the real beauty of sports to me, Chris, is that those of us who've gone ahead of the generation today—they bring us back by either breaking our records or bring us back to talk about what we did or did not do. And it's a good feeling to be remembered."

There was a genuine sense of gratitude on Ernie Banks's face.

"But how about the association with not winning the big win, though?" I had to ask. "Or not getting the chance really in the postseason? Does that haunt you still that you didn't? Do you feel cheated?"

"Yes, it does. I feel cheated. I feel it has haunted me for years to date right now thinking about playing in the World Series. I used to dream about it all the time. And my dreams are always about what Reggie [Jackson] did in 1977 in New York. Hit three home runs in the final game, unfortunately the Dodgers, they won and all that. That was my thinking—'Boy, I'd like to have done that.' But it does haunt me. I think about that a lot."

When I asked Charles Barkley the same sort of question, he had a more practical view of it.

"Does the Hall of Fame change the way you view not having won a championship in your career?"

"Not at all," Barkley told me. "I think it's more important to be in the

Hall of Fame, obviously, as an individual, but it's a team thing also. But I mean, I did, I had a great impact on the game. There's a lot of guys who can't play who win championships. I don't begrudge y'all now, but some of you guys just—you know, you're just on the team. But I say this simple—it means I did good."

George Karl, one of nine coaches to have won a thousand NBA games, gave me an interesting answer to the question of never winning a championship. He went to the postseason twenty-two times with five different teams, yet he never won "the big one." I asked him what was more important: championships versus winning.

"As a coach, if I said to you, thirty years of coaching. If you had twenty-nine winning records and one losing record and no championships, would you take that? Or would you take fifteen winning seasons and fifteen losing seasons, but win a championship? What's the better career? I think the better career is twenty-nine years of excellence. I really do. I mean, and I look at a lot of great coaches who have not won championships as better coaches than coaches that have won championships. But in our society, it's the championship. And I might be rationalizing now because I've never won the championship. I've been in a lot of finals but have not won the championship. And there is a drive in me to win that championship. But I also have a drive in me to do what I do well and that's develop winning programs and hopefully develop a program of excellence."

We all want to understand what it's like to get there. What does it *truly* take? What is the mentality of those who finally achieve greatness?

It's a whole other thing to bring up the subject of winning a championship to those who have already won one.

"You think you'll ultimately be measured by championships?"

I asked Kobe Bryant this in 2006. The Los Angeles Lakers guard had already won three of them; he would win two more with the team in 2009 and 2010.

"Oh, definitely. You know, that's why I play the game. Winning is the ultimate goal. What we all aspire to be is champions."

When I asked Kobe what drives him to continue to push himself further, even after having won three NBA Finals, he gave an honest answer.

"The thing that I'm afraid of is not winning another championship. That's the thing that really drives me."

His words have echoed those of many other champions I've interviewed. The drive to succeed and the desire to win more titles. Success, as I've discovered over so many years, is measured in different ways by athletes.

• • •

IF I HAD TO PICK ONE PERSON THAT I WOULD HAVE TO QUOTE TO TALK about success, it would have to be John Wooden, one of basketball's greatest coaches. I interviewed "the Wizard of Westwood" a number of times to talk about how he held college basketball spellbound during his run of ten national titles at UCLA. I even had the great honor to do Wooden's last interview before he passed away in 2010. When I sat down with the Hall of Famer in 2006, he was ninety-six years old and ready to reveal the magic formula to a long and happy life.

"You look great," I told Wooden after welcoming him. "And when you hear people say that at ninety-six years of age, what's your response usually?"

He gave a sly grin. "I'm just happy to be here. Every day is a good day."

After talking about the state of college basketball at the time, I brought up the subject of his achievements.

"For a generation of fans who have read and heard about you. The accomplishments. Four undefeated seasons of 30-0. The seven straight NCAA titles. I mean, we could go on and on, but your coaching style. How would you describe that in a sentence or two?"

"Well, I wanted it more to be the emphasis completely on my players," Wooden said. "At game time, I didn't want people to see me, I wanted them to see my players. My job, as I used to tell my players, is during the week. Now on the game time, it's your job now. Now you do your job. I'll find out whether I've done my job by the way you play during the week."

Our conversation went into the three-point shot and then into the subject of education. Then we went on to some of the players he had coached and back onto him. I asked him how he had either counseled or advised coaches who came to him for advice. What should they do to find the same sort of success he had?

"Be themselves. Don't try to emulate somebody else. That goes back to the comparing. Learn from others but don't try to be better than somebody else. Just make every effort to do the best of what you're capable and be yourself."

I eventually asked him if there was a secret to his longevity or a formula for his success.

"I would say just having peace with yourself, and I think I have peace with myself. I'm not afraid. When the time comes—I know it comes to all of us. And I think maybe having peace with myself enables me to accept things as they happen and without any extra stress."

I brought up the loss of his wife, Nellie, who passed away in 1985. Wooden never remarried.

"She's the only girl I ever went with," he said. "And we had fifty-three wonderful years together and she put up with me and no one else could put up with me like she did."

This shifted us into the subject of mortality, a subject Wooden seemed eager to talk about.

"Someone said, 'Coach, are you afraid of death?' But I said, 'No, I'm not afraid of it. I'm not going to intentionally hurry it up.'"

John Wooden shared with me a poem someone had written to him entitled "Yonder." It had been inspired by a comment from the coach when he said he would be with his wife, Nellie, again "out yonder." He quoted from the poem:

Once I was afraid of dying. Terrified at ever lying.
Petrified of leaving family, home and friends.
Thoughts of Absence from my Dear Ones,
Brought a melancholy tear once
And a dreadful dreadful fear of when life ends.

But those days are long behind me,
Fear really does not bind me.
And departure does not hold a single care.

Peace has comfort as I ponder
A reunion in Thy yonder,
With my dearest one who is waiting for me there.

"That was a very touching moment," Wooden said when he read the poem. "Maybe that's one of the reasons that I have some peace with myself."

The poem was written by Swen Nater, a Dutch basketball player who played for the UCLA Bruins under Coach Wooden.

I had to bring up the ideas behind Wooden's "Pyramid of Success," the set of principles that have resulted in teaching tools and books on success. He explained that he had wanted to help students achieve success and he got the idea of a pyramid. The idea took many years to come together. As he talked about this, Wooden shared his definition of success.

"Peace of mind attained only through self-satisfaction in knowing you made the effort to do the best of which you're capable."

"How have you handled setback or regret?" I asked. "Do you have regrets in your life or what? What would be the greatest?"

"My regrets are not what I've done, but what I should have done. Many things. I believe I should have done more for Nellie and instead of her wanting to do the things that I would want to do and that's a regret.

And as far as my teaching is concerned, the decisions I made, I thought they were right. And even if they didn't work out properly, it was proper for me to do what I thought was right and learn from the mistakes that I would make. But that wouldn't be regrets. It would be disappointments. Don't look back."

• • •

LOOKING BACK IS SOMETHING ALL PROFESSIONAL ATHLETES AND coaches eventually have to do. It's never easy to say goodbye to the sport they have grown up with and loved and found success in.

In 2006, I interviewed Pete Sampras, one of the greatest tennis players ever to play. After winning fourteen majors, he officially retired in 2003. Three years later he spoke openly about the decision to finally leave tennis and what retirement has been like.

"I knew it was time for me to move on. I was really content with what I did in my career. But I have my moments where I look back at Wimbledon and I'm like—I miss those days."

"But what else is there for Pete Sampras? Have you thought about this? Have you wrestled with this?"

"I wrestled with it," Sampras said. "It's a tough transition. You go from being focused and working hard and goal oriented to really stopping. And that's tough. I mean, it is tough. I have my moments. I have my moments where the walls start closing in on me. I can see why players come back. I really do."

Sampras said that while being a father and a husband was important, it was hard to make the adjustment of not going out every day to work on tennis. He had been passionate about one thing: playing tennis and winning.

"It's just kind of rebuilding your life a little bit and kind of reinventing yourself. And it's just a tough transition."

Sampras mentioned comparing notes on retirement with Charles Barkley.

"Barkley and I talked about stopping and how it's just a tough transition. You know, he keeps himself busy by doing some commentary and staying in shape and playing golf and all that. And I'm doing a few things here and there. We were kind of in the same boat where it's such a tough transition."

I will never forget talking to Joe Montana years after he had retired. I spent some time with him, and what stood out to me was that he was trying to replace the rush of an NFL game but couldn't. He tried flying planes and breaking horses, but nothing felt the same. Montana had to accept that there is nothing like playing football in the NFL. He had to accept that he wasn't a football player anymore, to be happy because he'd had a nice career and he was healthy. Yet accepting this was difficult.

When I interviewed Montana's teammate Jerry Rice in 2022, the subject of staying busy and no longer playing football came up. It started when I asked him about his motivation and how he stayed at such a consistently high level of play during his career.

"I just felt like I never had arrived," Rice told me. "I was putting up outstanding numbers. I was winning Super Bowls. I was doing everything. But I still felt like I still had more inside of me where I could go work harder and become a better receiver. So I never got complacent or anything like that. And one of my coaches told me—Larry Kersey—way back in the day, 'Jerry, one day you got to sit back and you got to smell the roses. You got to think about everything that you have accomplished.' And for some reason, I would never let that in my head. I just kept pushing myself. And I think that was that drive that continued to make me work out during the offseason to be in the best shape that I could possibly be in and to go out and perform at a very high level."

"Are you smelling the roses now?" I asked Jerry.

"No, I still can't smell the roses."

I knew Jerry was staying busy doing a lot of different things. He was on *Dancing with the Stars*. He had businesses and did motivational speaking and authored books and on and on.

"So you're still working," I said. "Do you ever think that it's too much? I mean, what's a relaxing day for Jerry? Obviously, you know, when you were playing, it was one thing, 'cause when you were all going to tape or physically doing it. But what's a relaxing day for you? You ever just kind of sit and watch a sunset or something?"

"Are you asking me that?" he said, laughing and mockingly scolding me. "What is a relaxing day for you? You know, we don't have days like that. We don't have days."

Point well taken, Jerry.

"You're right," I told him. "We don't. We're afraid those days will be taken away. So you keep chasing the work."

• • •

I INTERVIEWED LOS ANGELES DODGERS MANAGER TOMMY LASORDA right after he was inducted into the Hall of Fame. He spoke to me about what this was like compared to winning a World Series and all of his other milestones and victories.

"Well, let me just say about the World Series and world champions, All-Star victories. Manager of the year. I've managed Most Valuable Players, Cy Young Award winners, nine rookies of the year. All of that comes and goes. But the Hall of Fame is for eternity."

He told me there were tears of joy and appreciation and happiness when he heard the words, "You are to be inducted into the Baseball Hall of Fame."

"I know a lot of people who are in the Hall of Fame," Lasorda told me. "Whenever I see them, there's something special for me. I've put them on a pedestal. I look at them with appreciation and gratitude for what they have done for our game. They were special. They made it possible for me to be in the Hall of Fame with those guys. I can't—I just can't believe it."

• • •

UNDER A BLAST OF SNOW ON JANUARY 7, 2024, AT GILLETTE STADIUM, I called Bill Belichick's last game as the coach of the New England Patriots. It was cold and miserable as the Patriots lost to the New York Jets 17–3. Yet despite the awkward way of going out, Belichick was the warmest I had ever found him. A lot warmer than that chilly interview he did after the loss in Super Bowl XLII.

For the Super Bowl versus the Philadelphia Eagles, I remembered that Belichick's father had been there on the field. Steve Belichick had served in the Navy and also coached football. When Bill introduced me to his father, I mentioned that my dad proudly served in the Navy in World War II, so we talked about that for a short while before the game. Bill's father was a nice older gentleman.

On the Friday before Belichick's last game for New England, I was able to let him know what a pleasure it had been to cover him through the years, especially being on the sideline for some of those Super Bowls. I mentioned the pleasure it was to meet his father and talk with him about my own father. Then I asked him about his future.

"Can we assume you're going to be back in New England?"

In typical Belichick fashion, he said bluntly, "You can assume whatever you want."

Then Belichick told me that he had a commitment to coaching, and that's what he was going to do.

"It's the same kind of commitment, Chris, that your dad and my dad had when they committed to things."

It was one of the most enjoyable conversations I can ever remember having with Belichick. He spoke about players who stood out over the years, not the big names and high draft picks but the guys nobody had ever counted on that he saw an ability in. Guys who responded to his work ethic and who desired to get better.

Even after so many games and victories, Belichick still loved being a coach. He probably always will.

• • •

HAPPINESS. CONTENTMENT. MAYBE THIS IS AT THE HEART OF WHAT ALL my questions ultimately come back to.

How are you feeling now that you're a champion?

How can you find joy in losing the big one?

How can you be at peace after stepping away from the game?

How can you fill that competitive drive inside when you no longer have the ability to perform?

Back on *Up Close,* Jim Brown seemed to have a good perspective on leaving his sport. I asked him why he left the NFL while still at the top of his game.

"I understood the nature of the profession. I was a gladiator. Art Modell was the owner. He invested the money, he had the power, and he called the shots. I utilized it. I loved it. I had fun and I left because I understood *timing.* I left at the age of twenty-nine years old. MVP. Conversation over. I don't have to get into that conversation anymore. So that was it. I was going into the movies. I was going to make more money. I was going to deal with pretty women. I was going to travel all over the world. And that also made sense. And I prepared myself for the movies while I played. It wasn't a big question. A lot of people who love the game say you should have stayed. But no, there was no reason to stay."

"Did you accomplish all that you wanted to do?" I asked Brown. "When you look back now, some of your records, you could have tacked on a lot more."

He laughed at my statement. "Well, you see, that's a very strange kind of conversation. You know, I played nine years. About four of those years were twelve games. Five were fourteen games. I never missed a game. Obviously, I didn't play for records. And I naturally wouldn't look back and figure I had to stay for records. So I don't want to, you know, make you feel strange by asking the question, but there's no thought of that kind of thing in my mind."

This sounds a lot like John Wooden's definition of success—being satisfied knowing you gave the best effort you could.

I've always believed that with hard work, dreams can come true. If you can imagine something and if you want it badly enough and you sacrifice and you work through it and you get some breaks, it can happen. It's just like the kid throwing the ball in the backyard. I grasped this in third grade with my sportscasting dreams. Your dreams can go further beyond anything you might imagine.

Dreams of wanting to get on the radio can turn into getting on TV and being a sportscaster in L.A. and landing on a network and treating each night like a Super Bowl and then finding myself in the middle of the Super Bowl.

The dream can happen. Maybe not in the way you imagined. Maybe there's going to be a lot of disappointment and heartbreak along the way. But if you really believe in something like the thousands of athletes I've encountered have believed, then you have to get up every day and work toward that dream.

It reminds me of Andy Reid finally finding success. After all the years spent working so hard and coming so close, it finally happened in 2019. Then he found success again in 2022 and 2023, cementing his legacy. And chances look good that Reid and Mahomes might win another one.

For me, working toward that dream has always been the passion. I can admit that Jerry Rice was right when he said we don't have relaxing days. I'm still trying to figure out why I'm so driven. After being in so many different exciting roles, I still love the profession I'm in. I like to watch and meet these athletes. For me, it's always been about blending a hobby with a job. Sometimes I've overdone it with the amount of time I've spent working. Over the years I've gotten better at that, but I still love the work.

"How do you stay relevant?" I once asked Bill Murray.

"I like doing what I do," Bill said. "As long as people keep asking me to do the work. That's what relevance is to me. I don't care to have streets named after me."

That's the joy and contentment that I've found. I once heard Johnny Carson say, "In America, a man is his job." I think this statement has always stuck out to me because I think you really do take on a lot of the identity of your job, regardless of what profession you might be in.

"If you're happy in what you're doing, you'll like yourself," Carson said. "And if you like yourself, you'll have inner peace. And if you have that, along with physical health, you will have had more success than you could possibly have imagined."[1]

Epilogue

Dale Earnhardt once said in 1980, "I never wanted to do anything else." I understand what he meant. It's a wonderful thing to discover a calling—an unstoppable passion—that drives the rest of your life. Especially when you discover it in your childhood.

When I first saw the Cameron Crowe movie *Almost Famous,* I thought it resembled my life in a lot of ways. That film is about a fifteen-year-old named William Miller who dreams of being a rock journalist. Not knowing his age, *Rolling Stone* sends him out on the road to cover a rock band named Stillwater. Suddenly Miller finds himself surrounded by his heroes and doing the one thing he loves—interviewing them for a front-page story. The film was a semiautobiographical depiction of director Cameron Crowe's real life.

My journey began like that teenager—getting on the radio without them knowing my real age, then suddenly finding myself interviewing people like Muhammad Ali and Don Shula. My story continued, however, going through local TV and ESPN and Fox. It's been a wild bus ride full of unexpected moments.

At the end of *Almost Famous,* William Miller finally interviews the lead singer of Stillwater.

"So, Russell . . . what do you love about music?" Miller asks the rock star.

I love the response.

"To begin with, everything."

That is how I've always felt about sports, going all the way back to my first love.

• • •

THERE'S REALLY NOTHING LIKE THE NFL.

I love those moments when I'm working a game on Sunday. I always arrive at the stadium early and I take everything in for a moment. I still appreciate the chance to be there. There's an excitement stepping onto the field and a rush calling the game. Despite how much you might prepare, every game is so unpredictable. With the players and the fans and the viewing audience, it's amazing to be in the center of it all. I've been lucky to have been able to fill a variety of roles as well. That was one of the reasons I went to Fox. I knew there would be lots of opportunities to do different things.

I recently had a jolt of memory walking into a stadium one chilly morning. Perhaps it was because I've been spending time on this book looking back on my life, something I've never really done. Something I've been too busy to really ever do. But on this early morning, I suddenly was reminded of a road trip I took with Christopher to cover the Baltimore Ravens.

The fond memory seemed to come out of the blue. But then again, it never leaves me. It's one of those gifts that our son left behind.

As I recently stood in the football stadium remembering those trips with our son, I found myself thankful. I've learned that you can either be angry or be thankful for the time you had. At least we had nineteen years with Christopher. We also have this faith that we will reconnect with him one day. You have to live that way or else life won't matter. This belief helps you go forward, even if it seems a little bit Pollyanna-ish in its thinking.

• • •

SOME DAYS ARE BETTER THAN OTHERS. JUST LIKE SPORTS WILL SHOW us, there are days when you simply collapse. Where everything goes wrong and you're blown out. Sometimes it doesn't matter if you're the better athlete or better team. If you're undefeated or if you're a legend. Sometimes your opponent will beat you.

Life can be like that.

This past Father's Day for me turned out to be tougher than usual, and I wasn't sure why. Maybe it's for the reason I just mentioned—because I've spent the past year going down memory lane. You'd think that after eleven years, the grief might be gone and the regrets can remain at bay. It had been an enjoyable day hanging around with our son, having a nice dinner at home and relaxing. There were some Father's Days in the past where I was traveling, so I was happy to be with Alex. Yet I felt sad at the same time. And a little angry. Angry that Christopher wasn't there. And angry for the times I wasn't there either.

I don't live my life with regrets. I've tried to move forward and learn from my mistakes. But I know I've been guilty of enjoying my career so much that at times I didn't spend enough time with my family because of the kind of job I had. Men and women these days have careers that keep them busy. You want to make sure you're doing the best job you can so that you can give your kids the kinds of opportunities that maybe you didn't have when you were younger. So you're building a career and you're thinking you have all this time, but you can't go back.

This is the sort of guilt trip that no parent should put themselves through.

We didn't know we were only going to get nineteen years.

These are the things you deal with. I've talked to other dads who've gone through this kind of thing, who have been successful in their careers, and they've encouraged me. There are things we could all do better, they have told me. Don't blame yourself. Don't blame other people. Be thankful for the time you had.

I thought of all the times I was thankful for. ESPN and Fox had always been good if I needed time for my family. I have many memories to be proud of. Organizing trips to Disneyland and Legoland and the beach. Times when I volunteered during the week in their school when the boys were young.

Rick Hendrick texted me like he does many holidays, just to tell me he was thinking about me and knew what I was going through on this day. He hoped I was having a good day. I wasn't at a point where I needed to call him—a point I've been at in the past—but it was just good to hear from him. For so many years, he's been this way. Always getting back to me when I reach out to him and always being willing to talk me through things. He's a very busy man, so it's incredible for him to do this. I feel really blessed. I admire Rick for the way he helps and encourages people like me. He knows some days are going to be tougher than others because he's been there.

I know I still have to take things day by day.

Kobe Bryant once told me this. I remember when I interviewed him in 2006, he was reflective as he looked at his life and his career.

"I just want to take it day by day," Kobe told me. "I remember we had Michael Jordan's last All-Star game and they had this beautiful ceremony for him at halftime. And I had the honor to sit next to him during that process. They were showing all the highlights from when he first came into the NBA and I was just kind of looking at him. Just kind of sitting back and thinking, 'Wow.' Did it go by that fast for him? Like, 'What is he thinking about right now? Does it all seem like a blur?' So from that point on, I wanted to make sure that I appreciate every day. Or try to as much as possible."

Those words are more poignant and haunting now that Kobe is no longer with us.

Appreciate every day.

I'm trying to as much as possible.

• • •

SPORTS HAS A MEMORY OF ITS OWN. SOMETIMES IT REMINDS YOU OF the past with the simple crack of a bat or the swell of the stadium. I'm watching the World Series—not from the field but from my home. And in this reflective season I've been in, I can't help but think about the 2009 American League Championship Series between the New York Yankees and the Los Angeles Angels. I was a reporter for the American League playoffs, so since the Angels were playing the Yankees out in my hometown, I was assigned to do the game.

This is one of the proudest moments in my life, and it's because I didn't attend the game. Instead, I was at the opening night of a high school play that Christopher had a starring role in.

Drama was something Christopher decided to try out, so he took some drama classes and had some small roles in other plays like *The Wizard of Oz*. I volunteered my time to help out when I was able to. But this time he had gotten the main role in the Shakespeare play *The Merry Wives of Windsor*. In his previous plays I had been able to catch a rehearsal, but I had never been to an opening night before. But this was important, so I asked the guys at Fox. They said it was fine for me to go. Instead of having a front-row seat to watch Derek Jeter, Jorge Posada, Mariano Rivera, and

Andy Pettitte, I sat in the front row with our family to watch Christopher. He did an incredible job.

It was funny to see all the dads at the play, looking at their phones to check the score and watch the plays. I tried to ignore them, but I knew the game was happening. But I deliberately forced myself to be there, to be present for Christopher, to ignore anything else. I had been at those big events before, and I would be at them in the future. But this was bigger than sports.

Afterward it was fun to talk to everybody and see the excitement on Christopher's face around all his castmates. I was able to hang out with him that night and talk. It was a bonding experience that I will always cherish.

• • •

LOOKING BACK OVER MY LIFE, THERE HAVE BEEN TIMES WHEN I'VE thought the same thing. In a lot of ways, dreams have been a constant theme in my life. Dreams of mine and dreams of others. So many others.

I once asked San Francisco 49ers wide receiver Jerry Rice what he felt was his greatest career achievement. With three Super Bowl victories, including one where he earned Super Bowl MVP, Rice had a lot of achievements to pick from.

"I think I'm more proud that I got the opportunity to live a dream," Rice told me. "Because as a kid, I remember growing up and I would always just ask my parents for a football, not knowing that I was destined to play professional football. But I would just get that football and I would go out there on that Christmas Day. I would kick that ball around. I would throw it around with my brothers and stuff like that. I asked for a football every year. And then I get the opportunity to live the dream of so many individuals to play professional football."

That's how I have felt ever since I found myself interviewing the greatest boxer of all time. What an opportunity it's been to live the dream in the world of sports and to witness so many incredible moments. So many experiences that have risen above the games themselves.

A legendary pro beyond his prime surprising everybody and winning another.

A city finally making it after years of failure and feeling a sense of hope.

A country coming together after a natural disaster.

A society spellbound after a national tragedy.

A team breaking the curse.

A legend making a comeback.

An icon changing the sport and leaving a great legacy.

All of these began as simple dreams inspired in the backyard while throwing a football or in the driveway shooting hoops or on a Little League baseball field or on a dirt track driving cars. Interspersed with those dreams come disappointments and defeats. There can only be one champion. With every win there's also a matching loss. So maybe that's not the point. Maybe the point is deciding to play in the first place. Maybe it's about the pursuit of that dream. And sure—maybe a victory is part of that pursuit, but in the end it's not about that W.

It's about going the distance.

I've spent a lifetime built around those who went the distance.

Maybe there is a field of dreams that waits for us one day. A place full of answers. A place without regrets. But until then, I'm going to keep asking questions.

Curiosity has been good to me.

Notes

Epigraph

1. Ed McMahon, *Here's Johnny!: My Memories of Johnny Carson, the Tonight Show, and 46 Years of Friendship* (Nashville: Rutledge Hill Press, 2005).

Chapter Two: A Rising Star

1. Thomas Stinson, "The Master: Thirty Years Ago in Augusta, Jack Nicklaus, 'the Golden Bear,' Prowled One Last Time," *Atlanta Journal-Constitution*, April 1, 2016, http://specials.myajc.com/jack-nicklaus-the -master/.

2. Bob Ehalt, "Risen Star: The Pride of Louisiana," America's Best Racing, February 15, 2023, www.americasbestracing.net/the-sport/2023-risen -star-pride-louisiana.

3. "Remembering New Orleans' Risen Star, 1988 Champion 3-Year-Old Male," Turf History Times, February 8, 2022, www.turfhistorytimes .com/february-news-remembering-risen-star-and-fair-grounds-turf-writer -bob-fortus/.

4. George Gurtner, "Stories Still Told of Legendary Racetrack Figure," Nola.com, November 30, 2014, www.nola.com/entertainment_life /stories-still-told-of-legendary-racetrack-figure/article_82752141-5650 -5d74-838b-fb4e929658df.html.

Chapter Three: Don't Let Them Rattle You

1. Alex Pavlovic, "1989 Bay Bridge World Series Earthquake: Oral History of the Moment, Aftermath," NBC Sports Bay Area, June 22, 2020, www .nbcsportsbayarea.com/mlb/1989-bay-bridge-world-series-earthquake-oral -history-of-the-moment-aftermath/1286611/.

Chapter Four: Life and Death

1. Jackie Robinson, as told to Alfred Duckett, *I Never Had It Made: An Autography* (New York: G. P. Putnam's Sons, 1972).

2. George Vecsey, "For Tim Burke, a Different Kind of Save," *New York Times,* August 6, 1989, www.nytimes.com/1989/08/06/sports/sports-of -the-times-for-tim-burke-a-different-kind-of-save.html.

3. Richard Demak, "An All-Star Father," Vault (*Sports Illustrated*), July 24, 1989, https://vault.si.com/vault/1989/07/24/an-allstar-father.

4. Cydney Henderson, "Kobe Bryant Quotes: NBA Hall of Famer's Most Motivational, Inspirational Words," *USA Today,* December 16, 2021, www.usatoday.com/story/sports/nba/2021/12/16/kobe-bryant -motivational-quotes-nba-lakers/8667478002/.

Chapter Five: Licensed to Kill Gophers

1. Vivian Brown, "Laughter Cures Ills," *News and Courier* (Charleston, SC), July 13, 1972, p. C10.

2. Michael Clair, "Fun Fact: Bill Murray Once Played Baseball and Got a Hit," Cut4, MLB.com, February 17, 2015, www.mlb.com/cut4/fun-fact -bill-murray-once-played-pro-baseball-got-a-hit/c-109556570.

3. Joseph Hulscher, "Bill Murray Grays Harbor Loggers," YouTube, www .youtube.com/watch?v=cdYvPNITDbg.

Chapter Six: A Jacket, Tie, and Bermuda Shorts

1. Nancy Coleman, "How the Investigation into Richard Jewell Unfolded," *New York Times,* December 13, 2019, www.nytime.s.com/2019/12/13 /movies/richard-jewell-bombing-atlanta.html.

Chapter Eight: This Is Not *60 Minutes*

1. Josh Meyer and Eric Malnic, "O. J. Simpson's Ex-wife, Man Found Slain," *Los Angeles Times,* June 13, 1994.

2. *O.J.: Made in America,* directed by Ezra Edelman, ESPN Films, 2016.

3. Vincent Bugliosi, *Outrage: The Five Reasons Why O. J. Simpson Got Away with Murder* (New York: Norton, 1996).

Chapter Nine: Are You Capable of Killing?

1. Alan Abrahamson, "Simpson Expands on Slaying Remark Made to Magazine," *Los Angeles Times,* January 17, 1998.

2. Tim Goodman, "Must-See TV: O.J. Talks on ESPN," *San Francisco Examiner,* January 16, 1998, www.sfgate.com/news/article/must-see-tv -o-j-talks-on-espn-3108871.php.

3. Milton Kent, "Usually Easygoing Myers Puts Simpson Under Careful Scrutiny," *Baltimore Sun,* January 16, 1998.

4. David Margolick, "Jury Takes Close Look at Simpson's Hand," *New York Times,* March 21, 1995.

Chapter Ten: Where Are the Tigers?

1. Tim Kawakami, "There's Also Chaos Outside the Ring," *Los Angeles Times,* June 30, 1997.

2. "Tyson Jailed over Road Rage," BBC News, February 6, 1999.

3. The Associated Press, "Tyson Buying Luxury Home in Las Vegas," *Los Angeles Times* archives, April 12, 1995, https://www.latimes.com /archives/la-xpm-1995-04-12-sp-53783-story.html.

Chapter Eleven: The Intimidator

1. Ken Willis, "Dale Earnhardt: On the 71st Anniversary of His Birth, 71 Memories of the Intimidator," *Daytona Beach News-Journal,* April 29, 2022.

2. "Earnhardt Has Back Surgery," CBS News, December 17, 1999, www.cbsnews.com/news/earnhardt-has-back-surgery/.

3. Ryan McGee, "Dale Earnhardt's Death at the Daytona 500: The NASCAR Safety Culture Before the Crash," ESPN, February 10, 2012, www.espn.com/racing/nascar/story/_/id/30861999/dale-earnhardt-death-daytona-500-nascar-safety-culture-crash.

Chapter Twelve: Why Not Us?

1. The Associated Press, "Bosox acknowledge being idiots," https://www.recordonline.com/story/sports/2004/10/07/bosox-acknowledge-being-idiots/51131336007/.

2. "Yankees' Bullpen Comes Apart in 14th," ESPN, October 19, 2004, www.espn.com/mlb/recap/_/gameId/241018102.

Chapter Fourteen: Dreams Brushing by You

1. Marty Smith, "Hendrick Stronger 10 Years Later," ESPN, October 23, 2014, www.espn.com/racing/nascar/cup/story/_/id/11747941/nascar-reminders-plane-crash-tragedy-always-present-rick-hendrick.

Chapter Fifteen: The Faith of a Saint

1. Mike Scott, "The Superdome Curse," Nola.com, October 22, 2018, www.nola.com/multimedia/photos/the-superdome-curse/collection_7b10bc9b-7de3-55b0-b92b-f677cfa1bb3c.html#17.

2. Kevin Seifert, "Inside the 'Minneapolis Miracle'—the Play That Saved the Vikings' Season," ESPN, www.espn.com/nfl/story/_/id/22102295/inside-play-saved-minnesota-vikings-season-crushed-new-orleans-saints.

3. "Quotes from Sean Payton Following the NFC Championship Game Against the Los Angeles Rams," New Orleans Saints, January 20, 2019, www.neworleanssaints.com/news/quotes-from-sean-payton-following-the-nfc-championship-game-against-the-los-ange.

Chapter Sixteen: Bouncing Around with Barkley

1. Dana Scott, "Charles Barkley Calls 1996 Olympic Dream Team a 'Nightmare,'" Complex, July 26, 2018, www.complex.com/sports/a/dana -scott-bio/charles-barkley-calls-1996-usa-olympic-dream-team-nightmare -jason-williams.

Chapter Seventeen: The Comeback

1. NBC Sports, "Tom Brady on Being Labeled the GOAT, Aaron Rodgers," YouTube, www.youtube.com/watch?v=o8CrKP_3YPw&t=416s.

2. New England Patriots, "Exclusive: Tom Brady's First Phone Call as the 199th Pick in the 2000 NFL Draft," YouTube, www.youtube.com /watch?v=8hlB24Cy-zM.

3. Devika Pawar, "Tom Brady's Cancer-Surviving Mom Fueled His Super Bowl LI Win—'She's My Everything,'" Sportskeeda, February 21, 2023, www.sportskeeda.com/nfl/tom-brady-s-cancer-surviving-mom-fueled -super-bowl-li-win-she-s-everything#.

4. Lorenzo Reyes, "Patriots' Tom Brady Maintains Deflategate Provides No Extra Super Bowl Motivation," *USA Today,* January 27, 2017, www .usatoday.com/story/sports/nfl/patriots/2017/01/27/tom-brady-deflategate -roger-goodell-super-bowl-2017/97151666/.

Chapter Eighteen: Smell the Roses

1. Kenneth Tynan, "Fifteen Years of the Salto Mortale: The World of Johnny Carson," *The New Yorker,* February 20, 1978, www.newyorker .com/magazine/1978/02/20/fifteen-years-salto-mortale.

Photo Credits

All photos in the insert are courtesy of the author except
for those listed below.

Page 2, middle and bottom: ESPN Enterprises, Inc.
Page 3, middle: ESPN Enterprises, Inc.
Page 4, top and middle: Major League Baseball trademarks and
copyrights are used with permission of Major League Baseball.
Visit MLB.com.
Page 4, bottom: Tom Pennington/Getty Images

About the Author

CHRIS MYERS is an Emmy Award–winning play-by-play announcer, reporter, and studio host, whose career spans more than four decades, including thirty years at major networks. One of the industry's most versatile broadcasters, Chris has contributed to the coverage of a variety of sports, including the NFL, MLB, NASCAR, and basketball at both the NCAA and NBA levels, and has been the network reporter for multiple Super Bowls and World Series.